PLANNING DEVELOPMENT PROJECTS

A Practical Guide to the Choice
and Appraisal of Public Sector Investments

PLANNING DEVELOPMENT PROJECTS

**A Practical Guide to the Choice
and Appraisal of Public Sector Investments**

G. A. Bridger and J. T. Winpenny

Overseas Development Administration, London
1983

ISBN 0 11 580242 8

Printed in the UK for HMSO Dd 716927 C60 8/83

The Overseas Development Administration (ODA), London, has undertaken publication of this book by two development economists because it believes it to be a potentially valuable aid for those personally involved in the development process. It is hoped that it will also give the lay reader a greater awareness of the complexities, considerations and skills involved.

The views expressed in this publication are those of the authors and do not necessarily reflect the official policies of the ODA.

Gordon Bridger, BSc(Econ), MA(Econ), is an Economic Consultant and Director of Economic Services for the Crown Agents. He was for fifteen years first Senior Economic Adviser, then a Director of Economics in the ODA where he was responsible mainly for advice on the UK's bilateral aid programme. He has also been Specialist Adviser to the Select Committee of the House of Commons on Overseas Aid, Regional Marketing Officer for Latin America for the FAO, and Economic Research Officer for the UN Economic Commission for Latin America and the UN Economic Commission for Africa. He has lived and worked in several developing countries and visited most of them in the course of his duties.

James Winpenny, MA, MPhil, is an economics graduate of Cambridge University and worked as a university lecturer before joining the ODA. In fifteen years with the ODA he has worked on most facets of the aid programme, including a spell in the Development Division in Beirut. He has first-hand experience of aid projects in Latin America, the Caribbean, Africa, the Middle East and South Asia. He has been a consultant to the UN Industrial Development Organisation and the International Labour Office. His current position is Senior Economic Adviser, with particular responsibility for South Asia, Caribbean and Pacific countries.

Contents

Financial institutions

Postscript on projects   205

Glossary   207

PREFACE

The best way of introducing the contents of this book is to describe the kind of people for whom it is written. Its potential readership consists of those concerned with all aspects of public sector investment – the selection, design, appraisal, finance and implementation of those projects. It should be of interest to readers in many different countries especially those in the developing world. It is concerned mainly with projects in the public sector, although it should also be relevant to private sector ventures over which the government has important powers (of approval, finance, and regulation), since many similar considerations apply.

The scope of the book goes beyond that of most books that are concerned with **appraisal**. Appraisal comes near the end of a series of stages in the birth of a project; the perspective here is wider, and starts with all those aspects involved in the **choice** of projects. Although the book has little directly to say about project management once it gets under way (since this is a very large topic) it does deal with some common difficulties encountered at the implementation stage, and stresses problems of maintenance and staffing.

Three main parties are involved in the development process. First there are all those in the country itself who have an interest in creating projects and bringing them into being. We could apply the stereotype **'promoter'** to this group, even though it brings together people with such varied backgrounds and interests as politicians, officials, professionals, and members of the public (including consumers) likely to be affected. The promoters need to be able to tell good projects from bad. Although one might imagine that the beneficiaries of the project would know where their best interests lay, this is not to say that their views alone would result in a project that was always technically and financially sensible. Politicians and officials need to be able to detect projects that could turn into political, financial and administrative liabilities, or which would not be able to attract suitable funding.

The second group can be called the **'professionals'**. Their distinguishing feature is that they should provide an independent and objective view on the project. Promoters and financiers appeal to their experience and professional integrity for an impartial and informed opinion on the project, or they are asked to design a sound project to meet the intended purpose. Such technicians and consultants should be well grounded in their respective fields and should be conversant with criteria for the selection and appraisal of projects. Nevertheless, if commissioned, they need to get quickly to the nub of the issue and to develop an instinct for good and bad points in the projects they are considering. The practitioners of a particular discipline (economics, engineering) may lack a broad background knowledge of the sector they are asked to operate in. They may have to work with specialists who need to be set the right questions in order to produce a satisfactory total project. For some sectors practical guides or manuals exist as an aid to planning (some are quoted in this book).

'Financiers' make up the third target group for this book. This is a shorthand for those people and agencies, both inside and outside the country concerned, who may be called upon to finance the project. The need for them to quickly grasp the essential features of the project is obvious, even though they may wish to go on to carry out their own detailed analyses. Private bankers and investors need to form a view on the likelihood of the project generating enough surplus to repay their involvement. The same is true of development banks, even though they may take a broader and longer view of the national interest. External aid agencies are often faced with the need to make rapid decisions about project requests before fully detailed appraisals can be carried out. Decisions taken quickly 'in principle' to consider a government project request tend to commit such agencies far more than they imagine at the time, as the project soon becomes very 'political'. A bad 'seat of the pants' judgement (e.g. one made during a mission) can commit an agency to a lengthy process of appraisal from which not even the most thorough subsequent appraisal report can extricate it. (Such implied commitments are therefore to be avoided.) This is another case where project choice precedes appraisal, and cannot easily be countermanded by it.

The book starts by enlarging on the circumstances in which the choice of projects comes to be made, dwelling on the three main groups identified above. It continues with an outline of the essentials of project appraisal methods. The heart of the book is, however, the series of chapters which serve as guides to project preparation in specific sectors. The book ends with a final postscript on projects.

The book should be regarded as a practical guide – one which the authors themselves would have found useful. It represents guidance which workers in this field have to discover for themselves, often at some cost, since it is not readily available in published form.

The book has been kept short. The authors have avoided entering the controversial area of different appraisal methods on the grounds that this has been well treated at great length in numerous other texts. Potential readers of this book would probably not have time to read anything much longer. Brevity is a salutary discipline with which to approach this subject.

The views expressed in the book germinated and grew while both authors worked at the Overseas Development Administration (ODA). They cannot speak too highly of their colleagues at ODA and the Special Units whose collective wisdom and experience shaped the book. Apart from recording this general debt, the authors remember the more direct help given by a number of colleagues who read and commented on earlier drafts of some of the chapters. Some others made valuable comments on the later versions. It would be a lengthy and invidious task to compile a list of all those who helped directly and indirectly, but the authors acknowledge with gratitude the encouragement and advice they received. Without them the book would have been stillborn.

Martin Surr wrote an early draft of the chapter on railways that proved useful in writing the final version.

The authors recall the various individuals outside ODA to whom they have had recourse for specialist advice on particular chapters. The list includes: Tom Berrie, Patrick Crooke, Anthony King, Allan Maskell, Ray Millard, Don Pickering, Peter Prynn, Rolf Schicht, Ian Varney, David White and William

Wyllie. These people helped to rescue the book from possible technical errors, for which the authors are grateful.

Miss Diana Braint gave vital help at all stages.

This should not be construed as the authors' attempt to spread responsibility for remaining errors of fact, analysis and judgement. The book is their own, and any failings it has cannot be laid at the door of their many helpers.

G. A. B.
J. T. W.
June 1983

CHOICE AND APPROVAL OF PROJECTS
PROJECT APPRAISAL: THE BARE BONES
PREPARATION AND PRESENTATION

1
Choice and approval of projects

The preface referred to three important groups who are interested in projects – promoters, professionals, and financiers. This is of course a simplification of all the interest groups involved in getting projects operational. However, even confining ourselves to these three stereotypes we can begin to imagine the variety of circumstances in which decisions are taken on projects. We need to understand these before proceeding further, since they set the limits within which parties at each stage make their decisions.

Promoters

Decisions about projects are commonly thought to be influenced heavily by 'political' factors. There is thought to be something unchallengeable and sacrosanct about decisions taken in the name of 'politics' as opposed to those taken on economic, technical or financial grounds. In fact, the term 'political' tends to get attached to any factor that cannot be classified as economic or technical. More to the point, some 'political' factors are good and valid, others are weak and invalid.

So it sometimes can happen that decisions by politicians that cannot be rationalised in any other way come to be described as 'political' and that is supposed to end the discussion. But of course a politician has to respond to pressures and, to survive, to show benefits from his government accruing to those groups considered important. There has to be some attempt at a regional balance of benefits, which explains why projects arise in regions which may not be the best locations on purely economic or technical grounds. Politicians will want to bring projects to their village or region; governments will wish to mollify a disaffected area by the promise of new economic benefits. Particularly sensitive are border regions, especially thinly-populated ones, where the government is keen to establish some economic activity in order to fend off possible secession or territorial claims by neighbouring countries.

Proposals for other projects, though often veiled in the language of economics or ideology, are basically to be explained by politics. For instance, the phrase 'benefits for the poorest', used to justify a feeder roads scheme, or a low-income housing project, may be used to justify a project whose real aim is to grant the wishes of a particular political constituency. Projects begun as part of a drive for 'self-sufficiency in food' may be due to pressure from a farm lobby. Projects to substitute domestic production for industrial imports may be partly motivated by a wish to reduce the power of the importing and merchant class, especially where they belong to minority groups. Projects requiring the creation of large new institutions (e.g. irrigation boards, river development authorities) give the politician a base for the exercise of patronage. This view may be considered cynical – but only if one regards economic and technical factors as somehow higher and purer than political ones. To the student and practitioner of politics, there is nothing cynical about the practice of politically motivated actions.

In all countries politicians are frequently said to have very short time horizons.

It is said they are interested in projects with quick and visible results; what appears to be important is to be seen to make a start on projects in order for the politician to consolidate a reputation for decisive action; completion is less of a priority, even when the country can afford it. This helps explain the common phenomenon of countries starting far more projects than they can afford to complete – this being perfectly 'rational' for the politician faced with the problems as he sees them.

The politician's desire for rapid and visible progress in starting projects is echoed by the natural interest of the bureaucrat and his minister. The success of ministries is often judged by their ability to fully spend their budgets: any shortfall is taken as a reproach, and could lead to the finance ministry slashing their future allocations. Moreover, the ambitious minister or senior official will wish to expand his ministry's spending, or – in a more stringent economic climate – defend his department against proposed cuts. Such people will be more concerned to seize on a project that is ready for quick implementation than to wait until a better, or 'the optimal', project is conceived, which might entail further studies and delays. One should not underestimate the appeal of the second-best project in such circumstances.

The existence of a number of foreign financiers, including aid donors, anxious to commit funds to a country is a situation which can be capitalised on by a shrewd politician. To maximise investment, projects will be put forward that are likely to appeal to the particular preferences of the donors, or whatever is deemed fashionable – basic needs, rural development, self-sufficiency, transport problems of the landlocked, etc. Most aid donors and investors prefer to fund projects which have been subject to a reasonable feasibility study. They will not normally cover recurrent costs, nor do they favour a large proportion of local costs. Thus it makes sense for a country to present to investors new projects with a high foreign exchange component, that have been studied in detail, preferably by a foreign consultant.

It is often easier to get funds for completely new plant and equipment than to vote recurrent budgetary funds to keep up and to maintain existing capacity. Nevertheless, although new projects can ease a current budgetary shortage their future claims on budgetary revenues can be a cause for concern. It is not uncommon for new projects to be formulated by a ministry that does not have responsibility for recurrent costs or manpower implications – e.g. the ministry of planning as opposed to the ministry of finance.

It is rare for a project to be entirely new. Most projects have a history. Many, indeed, have been around for a number of years in one form or another, waiting for the solution to a particular technical problem, sources of finance, or the right combination of political forces. Such projects are often closely identified with particular individuals and have come to be important in the aspirations of the localities concerned. It may not be possible to reject, or radically modify, such projects. The areas of choice lie in modifying, delaying or phasing, and the appraisal has to be shaped accordingly. This is not to deprecate the value of appraisal in such circumstances.

Whether the project is already partially prepared or is to be worked up from scratch, a decision has to be taken whether to appraise it further. This entails a feasibility study, or in the case of large complex projects, a pre-feasibility study. (Where the feasibility study could cost several million dollars, it is a large 'project' in its own right, and needs to be preceded by a pre-feasibility study.)

Although it is tempting in moments of uncertainty and indecision to call for 'a proper study', such a study is never a neutral thing. The process of examining a project arouses expectations and creates momentum. The decision to have a feasibility study done is almost as important as the decision to implement the project. The difference is that the study decision is always made on much scantier data. Feeding in the lessons of experience ('rules of thumb') at this stage can have a high pay-off, more so than refinements to the study itself. Rejecting a proposed study on a doubtful-looking project is more important than adding sophistication to the appraisal itself, provided the decision is based on sound experience and specific background knowledge.

Consultants

Consultants might be thought of as independent arbiters, applying high standards of professional knowledge and experience to solve problems and to pronounce on projects. In most cases they are brought in precisely because of these qualities, to help the client overcome a genuine technical or economic problem. But there is always the danger that consultants may be invited to study projects in order to lend weight to the views, already formed, of the client, or to permit responsibility to be avoided where unpopular decisions have to be faced.

There is also the danger that so-called 'consultants' can be too closely linked to equipment suppliers, so that they have a material interest in pronouncing a project good and worth proceeding with. Even *bona fide* consultants may shrink from condemning a project if they know that this would lead the client to appoint another, less reputable, firm that would come up with the 'right' result. The consultant's terms of reference may also predispose the result to be favourable.

Even a consultant with a completely free hand and full access to data may not be able to perform a thorough analysis. In many instances, the analysis has to be based on incomplete data, gathered under a time constraint. Tasks such as compiling a regional development plan consisting of a collection of small projects, planning a network of secondary or feeder roads, or devising a system of village wells have to rely heavily on selected criteria, since a full examination of the individual components is not possible.

It is for these reasons that reputable independent consultants sometimes find it difficult to carry out an objective investigation.

Financiers

Much finance is ostensibly tied to individual projects. Obviously there are many ways in which lenders and donors become associated with particular projects. A common approach is for a mission to visit the country to reach broad agreement on how the money is to be allocated, and to set in motion feasibility studies and appraisals of the projects that are provisionally chosen.

This decision 'in principle' will probably be qualified by a saving clause requiring the projects to be technically and economically satisfactory. For all this, the initial tentative allocation of funds to projects is crucial, partly because of the exploratory resources which it commits, and partly because of the expectations that it arouses. However, the decision is sometimes taken on the basis of little evidence in the course of a visit that may last only a few days. Senior politicians and ministers – acting for either party – can also make decisions which foreclose future choices. While it is true that both financiers and recipients choose projects for a mixture of motives, the availability of guidelines for the selection of projects would help both parties in realising their aims.

Like ministries, financing organisations also have budget allocations to particular purposes and countries, and one of the tests commonly applied to an executive is his or her success in committing funds and spending them. This is another reason why commitments to projects can be entered into hurriedly, and this too underlines the importance of sound preliminary inquiries, prior to the full appraisal stage.

*

In an ideal world – which is to say one devoid of all the pressures and imperfections that make life interesting – projects would slowly crystallise in the light of growing knowledge, and would eventually assume a sufficiently definite form to enable an appraisal to be carried out. This appraisal (or feasibility study) would sift the good projects from the bad, and could be used to rank projects in order of their merits or match good projects with the investment budget available.

The brief discussion so far has tried to impugn this pure model of the evolution of projects – which often underlies theoretical discussion of the methods of project appraisal. Projects see the light of day in many ways and the sort of guidelines that are the subject of this book are powerless always to circumvent the strong political and personal motives that are often present.

Experience has shown, though, that the intelligent use of guidelines can result in better projects. Where lack of information or time, or the small size of projects, does not permit the normal thorough investigation, rules of thumb (or guidelines) can help to improve the decision and make it possible to achieve the objective at a lower cost.

Further reading

B. D. Giles, 'Economists in Government: The Case of Malawi', *Journal of Development Studies*, January 1979. (This is a rare account by a former adviser to an African government of the circumstances in which government planners operate, and the limits to the exercise of traditional project appraisal.)

Nurul Islam, *Development Planning in Bangladesh*, C. Hurst & Co., 1978. (A study of the process of adjusting to the political and administrative realities of decision-making.)

2
Project appraisal:
The bare bones

A project is an organism for converting resources (inputs) into end products (outputs) whether we are talking of the production of cement or the supply of medical services. Some projects 'convert' more efficiently than others; some projects indeed waste resources in the absolute sense if the value of the output they produce is less than that of the resources they consume. It follows that the basic aim of project appraisal is to measure the inputs and outputs involved and to devise a system of relating them to each other. Hence the name of one popular method: **cost–benefit analysis***. Where benefits cannot be measured, or where it is not acceptable to do so, the objective becomes one of defining the aims of the project and trying to satisfy them at least cost. This is **cost-effectiveness analysis**.

The main ideas

The most important concept is that there are normally a number of ways of carrying out the aims of a project. It is rare for a project to be a unique solution – normally the form of the project chosen is the best among a number of plausible ways of tackling the problem. Hence it is important to be aware of the **alternatives**, some of them radically different from each other, and to ensure that each of them has been carefully and fairly analysed before coming up with a recommended solution. In considering a solution for a town's growing demand for electric power, for instance, there is a choice between building a dam and a hydroelectric power station, on the one hand, and expanding or building more thermal power generators. There are many permutations, e.g. dams and generators of different sizes, used in different combinations, and they can be run through computers to test their technical and economic efficiency.

Perhaps a little less obvious is that an 'alternative' which could be tried is to adjust the structure of power tariffs to discourage peak demand, and encourage off-peak consumption in such a way that existing capacity can be run more fully, and delay the time when new installations are needed. Another possibility is to postpone a given project, or to break it up into phases that correspond more closely to the build-up of demand. At the extreme, one alternative is not to do the project at all, which implies that the existing situation will be allowed to deteriorate, or else that possible gains from the project will be forfeited. Doing nothing is preferable to doing a project that wastes resources; however, the point to stress is that the costs and benefits of doing nothing (sometimes called the **'without' case**) should be accurately and fairly specified in order to bring out what difference would be made by carrying out the project.

Just as there are alternative ways of tackling a development task, so the resources that go into a project have alternative uses. If they were not used

---

*See glossary for explanation of terms used in this book.

up in a particular project they could be used for other purposes, some of which would also have a positive rate of return. For instance, the land claimed for a steel factory could be used for housing, or for grazing cattle. Its skilled labour could get work elsewhere. Its unskilled labour may have the choice of going back to work on the land. Locally produced raw cotton used in a textile factory could be exported in unprocessed form. Where such resources (inputs) have alternative uses they can obviously not be regarded as 'free' or as uniquely earmarked or destined for the project in hand. Each input has an **opportunity cost**, and should contribute in output to the project at least as much as it could produce in the next best alternative use. Experience shows that ensuring that opportunity cost is always and systematically invoked is one of the best contributions economists can make in these cases.

For countries with few resources and possibilities for productive investment, but with available capital (e.g. from oil production, or foreign aid) it should never be forgotten that the capital itself has an alternative use, namely for investment abroad. Risk-free investments are possible on the international capital market yielding a rate of return in foreign currency that is, within margins, predictable. In certain cases this could be a more reliable source of future income for a country's inhabitants than investment in a project with a high chance of failure.

Time is a crucial dimension when assessing projects and in making comparisons between them. One project might have a large flow of benefits almost immediately, but have all its investment cost concentrated in the first year or two (e.g. purchase of railway locomotives to relieve a rail transport bottleneck). Another project might have long delayed benefits, but have investment costs that are also spread out over a number of years (e.g. an afforestation scheme). How can a comparison be made? An equally common problem is to make a comparison between a project with a high initial cost but a low running cost, and an alternative with a lower initial cost but a higher running cost (e.g. a hydroelectric power scheme compared with a thermal electric plant). In both cases a true comparison can only be made by allowing for the time factor, tracing the incidence over time of costs and benefits, and using an appraisal method that takes this into account.

The concept is to **discount** costs and benefits. The rate at which future amounts (both of costs and benefits) are discounted can be viewed as a negative rate of interest. The holder of money needs compensation for parting with it for a period, forgoing the consumption that he could enjoy. This compensation is interest, which is added to the amount at the end of the period. But take the opposite situation, where a person is offered the same sum of money, but can take it either immediately or in a year's time. Since the sums are nominally the same, and there is no compensating interest, most people would take the money immediately. The sum offered in one year's time is worth less, by at least the amount of interest that could be obtained in lending that sum for one year. The rate of discount measures how much less a sum is worth by each year that passes. The net present value (NPV) of an investment diminishes the more remote the return, and the higher the rate of discount. This is raised on page 9 under 'Decision rules'.

Thus, a project that offers large benefits which only appear well into the future could be disregarded in favour of one that offers more modest benefits right away, depending on how the discounted flows work out. Likewise, a project with investment spread out over a number of years would be favoured over one costing the same which required funds to be spent immediately, since the former would look cheaper if the investment stream were discounted.

A vital concept in cost–benefit analysis is the difference between nominal, or financial, values, and economic ones. A private investor is interested in the actual money costs and returns on his project, and reacts to the net effect on his or her bank balance. A government, however, needs to see through the financial rate of return to perceive the economic costs and benefits to the economy. There are several major differences between the concepts of the **economic and financial rates of return**:

i. Economic costs differ from financial ones. They try to measure the real, or resource, cost to the economy from undertaking a particular activity. Where inputs are subsidised, financial costs will be below economic ones. Where inputs are taxed, financial costs will exceed economic costs. Sometimes the extent of the subsidy or tax is concealed, e.g. when an item is supplied by a monopoly or loss-making nationalised industry. Where, because of minimum statutory wages or trade union pressure, wages are set at a certain level, but workers would have been willing to work for less, the financial cost of labour may exceed its economic cost. The economic value of an input is sometimes referred to as its 'shadow' (or 'accounting') price.

ii. Likewise, economic benefits are not the same as financial revenue. This is most obvious where benefits are not measurable, e.g. in water supply projects, or where they are measurable but do not directly accrue in financial form, e.g. road user cost savings. In both cases a notion of consumers' surplus may be used to approximate benefits. But the difference may also arise where output is sold in a protected market, or conversely where exports are disposed of at an inferior (over-valued) exchange rate. In such cases output, like costs, can have a shadow or accounting price reflecting its true social value.

iii. The government may wish to take account of various forms of 'externalities' which the private investor can safely ignore. If a particular activity is highly profitable, but bankrupts hundreds of small producers, this is of little concern to the private individual's financial rate of return, but could be of interest to the state, especially if these other producers are likely to claim on public funds. Conversely, a project may generate benefits for third parties which are not reflected in the financial rate of return to the investor.

Where money costs and benefits in an economy are distorted in various ways, a common approach is to value a project's elements according to their international or **'border' prices**. This entails working out what they would cost if imported or what they would realise if exported. This is often a healthy corrective to the arbitrary price-fixing in many economies.

The other important idea is that of **uncertainty**. The notion is widely understood, but the method of allowing for it in appraising and comparing projects may not be. Uncertainty really has two components: the range of possible outcomes, and the likelihood of any one happening. Consider a low-risk project such as distributing bulk power to households which are metered, and where there is an efficient electric power utility. There are not very many things that might happen to spoil this project. Moreover the likelihood of even any one of these things occurring (e.g. delay in supplies of cable) may be low. Thus there is a high degree of certainty attached to the 'central' or most likely outcome.

On the other hand we could take the case of a high-risk project for the cultivation under irrigation of crops new to an area. There are many possible outcomes, from a resounding success to a dismal failure, depending on responsiveness of farmers, reliability of water, effectiveness of drainage, the timely availability of fertiliser and pesticides, whether there are delays in land-levelling and preparation, prices received by farmers for their crops, etc. Furthermore, these are not theoretical possibilities – there is a definite chance of each of these outcomes actually occurring, and particular disasters – or successes – could overlap and reinforce each other. Such a project is uncertain, both in the sense that there are many possible outcomes, and because there is a good chance of any one of them happening.

One crude method of allowing for uncertainty is to demand a higher rate of return from the riskier projects (e.g. by applying a higher cut-off discount rate – see the next section, page 10). This is analogous to the private entrepreneur who regards profits as the rewards for risk-taking, and requires a higher profit from riskier projects. However, it is more satisfactory to work out the rate of return from the **most probable outcome**. The method is to describe the various possible outcomes (or combinations of events) and to try and attach a probability to each occurring. Each outcome is thus weighted by the probability of it happening, and they can all be added up to produce a central, or most probable, rate of return. However, policy-makers will be interested in knowing the likelihood of the extreme outcomes occurring, especially the chance of complete disaster.

Finally, **sensitivity analysis**, which is further discussed below, tries to pinpoint the events which would have the greatest effect on the outcome of a project. Experience shows that projects usually turn out very differently from what was expected. This may seem like worldly-wise nihilism, but that is not the intention. It is an argument for imagination in conceiving and testing all the important events and changes that would make or break the project.

Decision rules

How can these ideas be brought together to enable decisions to be made on projects? The procedure which is common to all the decision rules is that of discounting, which enables streams of costs and benefits to be compared on an equal footing allowing for the years in which they occur, and which can reduce both streams to a single figure, namely **present value**. The annex to this chapter (page 16) contains a simplified explanation of this procedure.

These decision rules apply equally to economic and financial analysis (indeed, the notion of discounted cash flow was first developed for use in private companies).

Cost-effectiveness is a criterion for judging the most efficient way of performing a given task. Whatever other decision rule is applied, the chosen method should normally also be the most efficient, that is, the cheapest, way of meeting the objectives of the project. Where the project has no measurable (quantifiable) benefits, the cost-effectiveness criterion is the main one to apply. It is very simple, consisting of calculating all the costs, both capital and recurrent, of a project, applying the appropriate shadow prices, and discounting the resulting stream to obtain a present value for costs. This procedure is repeated for the main alternative ways of carrying out the project, and the one with the lowest present value is chosen. Note that this criterion assumes that all the alternatives being compared can carry out the project equally well. If, on the other hand, there are quality differences in the service being supplied the basis of comparison is invalid.

It follows that cost-effectiveness is a valid decision rule for such activities as the supply of drinking water to a group of villages – where the scope and quality of the service to be provided are closely defined. One can then select the cheapest among the various alternatives as the 'correct' solution without any qualms. However, one would hesitate to apply the same procedure in comparing, say, site and service housing schemes with the construction of cheap prefabricated dwellings, since one would not be comparing like with like, and each would claim to be providing distinctive benefits.

Cost–benefit analysis may be done using three main decision rules. The major difference is between the **internal rate of return** (IRR) criterion and the other two, **net present value** and **benefit–cost ratio** (BCR). The IRR is the discount rate at which the streams of costs and benefits are equal.

The higher the IRR, the better the project, so projects with a higher IRR are to be preferred to those with a lower IRR. The IRR method has the convenience that it enables a comparison to be made between the rate of return of projects and the minimum, or cut-off rate, that the government or sponsoring agency may stipulate, and rates of return on other feasible investments. Thus an electricity corporation may be set minimum target rates of return of, say, 10%. The IRR criterion enables it to accept and reject projects that come out, respectively, above and below 10%. The concept is also intuitively attractive to people who think in terms of private rates of profit, even though the two ideas may be different in other important respects.

The IRR can be defined as that discount rate at which the **net present value** of a project is zero. The IRR and NPV are thus linked by definition. The NPV is simply the difference between the discounted streams of benefits and costs. It is the value, discounted to the present, of doing the project rather than not doing it.

Note that the NPV can only be worked out from a pre-determined discount rate. This needs to be the same for each project being compared. One approach is to set a more or less arbitrary rate (say 8%) and apply it to each project, choosing that with the highest NPV. Another and better approach is to estimate what real rate of return is available on investments in the private sector, and to require all public investments to achieve at least the same. Best of all, where it is done, is to accept the government's own estimate of the minimum acceptable rate of return on public investment, and use this as the discount rate.

One frequent, and false, objection to the use of NPV is that a large project will, other things being equal, have a larger NPV than a smaller one, and on this criterion would always be chosen. The smaller project could have a higher IRR but a lower NPV, and could therefore be rejected. There are two ways of countering this, one theoretical, the other practical. The theoretical response is to say that if all projects that could be undertaken with available public investment were appraised and ranked according to size of NPV, the best choice would be that collection that maximised NPV. In this event, several smaller projects which in aggregate had a higher NPV would be chosen over a single larger project. However, this reply is valid only if all possible projects are known and appraised. Since this is unlikely in practice, a useful check is to apply the benefit–cost ratio as a criterion to supplement the NPV.

The **benefit–cost ratio** is the ratio between discounted total benefits and costs. Thus if discounted total benefits are 120 and discounted total costs 100 the benefit–cost ratio is 1.2:1 (and the NPV is 20). This ratio enables us to distinguish projects whose NPV is high because it is large from projects that have a genuinely high rate of return (IRR). Note that the BCR, like the NPV, should never be quoted without stating the discount rate that has been used.

In most cases, the IRR, NPV and BCR will give the same result and will produce the same ranking of projects according to their attractiveness. There will be a few cases where the use of the IRR on the one hand and the NPV and BCR on the other will produce different results, and these oddities have attracted a disproportionate amount of academic controversy. In general, where the government is using some sort of target (minimum, or cut-off) rate of return on capital, maximising NPV should be the criterion, with the BCR as a supplementary check. However, to some people the IRR is more meaningful and in the last resort the decision-maker will choose the most easily comprehensible formula.

The information that goes into producing these results can also be used to throw light on the desirable timing of the project. Even if the analysis shows that the project is worthwhile, there may still be a case for delaying it a few years. Where the project caters for a growing demand, it may be desirable to delay its inception until that demand has caught up. Sensitivity analysis (see following paragraphs) can show the optimal timing of the start. As a rougher guide the **first-year rate of return** criterion can be used. The rate of return (in the simple sense of the ratio of discounted net annual benefits to investment costs) is computed for the first year of operation, and if this exceeds the cost of capital (opportunity cost) it should go ahead on time. If it is less than the cost of capital this implies that the overall rate of return would improve if the project were delayed.

Some presentational points

The use of a single number to capture all the merits of a project (such as IRR, BCR or NPV) is sometimes criticised for 'wasting' information and concealing aspects of the project which should be exposed to the decision-maker. Having reduced the merits of a project to a manageable form, in order to ensure comparability with other projects and alternative uses of national funds, the appraiser should be prepared to expand the numbers for two main purposes. First, it is normally useful to know how the result would be affected by changes in crucial data like sales, costs, etc. This is the province of **sensitivity analysis**.

Sensitivity analysis attempts to show which variables affect the result of the appraisal. This is useful information for those people responsible for the project since it may be possible to influence the crucial variables so as to make the project safer. The analysis simply consists of running the rate-of-return calculation through on different assumptions about the key variables – e.g. costs, construction period, sales, price, crop yield, etc. These data can either be altered one at a time, or in combinations, with each run being compared to the result of the 'base case' or 'central estimate' of the rate of return. In order to limit the complexity of the analysis it is customary to vary the data by 10% or 20%, although more variation can be done if larger fluctuations seem plausible.

This is to be distinguished from **risk analysis**, which uses a probability approach. Sensitivity analysis can show, for instance, that the world price of a crop is the datum that will make or break the project, and can show how low the price would have to fall to produce a negative rate of return. It would be the task of risk analysis to indicate the probability of such a price coming about.

The second reason for expanding the result is to spell out the **effects of the project on different groups** of the population, or on different aspects of the national economy. This is sometimes referred to as the 'effects method', after the analysis pioneered by the French economists Prou and Chervel. This approach is to distinguish certain groups in the population – say, landless rural labourers, small farmers, large farmers, urban consumers – and show for each one the incidence of costs and benefits. It would also show clearly how costs and benefits accrue to the national budget and the balance of payments.

Do not be deceived

Readers of project appraisals come to recognise certain common sleights of hand by which the authors try to hide fundamental weaknesses in the proposal. One of these is an excessive stress given to the **'multiplier effects'** of the project on the rest of the economy. The concept of the multiplier is a perfectly respectable theoretical tool, devised during the Great Depression of the 1930s, to describe the repercussions on output and employment that may arise from an act of investment in an economy with a great deal of under-utilised capacity. It is unlikely to be applicable in most developing countries, where idle capacity is not widespread in the economy, and where aggregate demand is not the major constraint on the growth in output. In these conditions, income arising from an act of investment is more likely to draw in imports, or press in an inflationary way on internal supply bottlenecks, than to cause a generalised boost to output and employment.

The same caution should extend to the use of the concept **'linkages'**. Linkages are the effects of the growth in output or investment in one sector on output, investment and employment in other sectors. This can arise in sectors 'upstream' or 'downstream' from the one in question. Upstream effects appear when firms in one sector, like steel, start buying more of the output of another sector, like iron ore. Downstream effects arise when the output of a sector improves the supply and price of raw material used in another sector, so encouraging investment in the latter (in the above example, where increased output of steel encourages the metal-fabrication industries). Of course, virtually every project has some linkages (except those that import all their requirements and export all their output) but some projects score better than others. It is the duty of the project's advocates to show that there would be stronger beneficial linkages from their project than from others. (The word 'beneficial' is used deliberately, since sometimes a project has a harmful effect on other sectors, e.g. when it forces up the price of local resources that are used by others.)

Another problematic concept is that of the **zero shadow price of labour**. The notion is that where a resource, like labour, is unemployed, or under-employed, the 'real' cost of using that resource is not its actual price (e.g. wages) but the amount by which output is reduced in its alternative occupations. If there is no alternative occupation – if labour is unemployed – or if the alternative occupation produces very low output, then the 'real cost' of employing it could be zero, or some cost lower than the ruling price (wage).

This is theoretically sound. The difficulty is identifying in the real world circumstances where it is appropriate – and safe – to insert values for labour which are less than the going wage. In the popular view developing countries are full of unemployed and under-employed workers. The observation is normally made in cities, or in the vicinity of industrial plants. Many such people are waiting to see if they can obtain work, and if not they return to their farms. Many are the 'educated unemployed' holding out for a job they feel is worthy of their talents.

People need to have resources to live off if they are wholly unemployed. It is common for a labour surplus in the cities to coexist with labour shortages in agriculture, either all year round, or more especially during the seasonal peaks for labour requirements. These shortages, e.g. when everyone is busy on his or her own plot, also affect other activities in rural areas, like road construction. Consequently, use of zero shadow wages in rural areas is not advised, and rates much less than the going wages should be used with caution. (Apart from making a project look unduly attractive, the inappropriate use of shadow wages favours unduly projects that are labour intensive compared with those that are less so. If there is not a labour surplus this practice makes the labour shortage even worse.)

In assessing the true benefits of a project, as well as its net costs, one has to imagine what would happen without it. Net benefits consist of the difference between the situation 'with' the project and the situation 'without' it. An honest appraisal thus requires a careful and accurate specification of what would really happen if the project were not undertaken. Even honest men may differ in the speculative business of constructing an imaginary future without the project, and unscrupulous promoters can exploit this imprecision to the full. It is very commonly argued, for instance, that in the absence of a proposed project, a road will cease to be passable to vehicular traffic, or a factory will break down completely. Thus the benefits from proceeding with a project of rehabilitating the road, or re-equipping the factory, can be shown to be enormous, if not infinite, since the alternative is virtually zero benefits. However, it is normally more realistic to postulate gradually declining benefits and increasingly onerous costs of maintenance in both cases rather than the doomsday scenario we are often confronted with. The so-called **'without' case** must be carefully specified.

Finally, **too much precision** in presenting the results of an appraisal can conceal dubious analysis. The decimal place implies a scientific precision which the analysis rarely deserves.

A pocket checklist

The chapters that follow go into detail about the approach to be followed in choosing projects in particular social and economic sectors. As a preliminary, we can mention some basic elements common to all types of project.

The investigator should first satisfy himself or herself that the **objectives**, whether economic, social or political, of the project are likely to be acceptable to the authorities. This may seem rather obvious, but sometimes a proposal which emanates from one part of the government is not acceptable to some other part of the government responsible for finance or implementation. One must recognise that putting up project proposals can have domestic political implications.

A quick check should then be made on the four fundamental elements of the project – output, input, technique and management.

There should be a clearly established market for the project's **output**. This is just as true of hospital beds, secondary-school leavers and agricultural research as it is for fertilisers. Demand should be effective, namely backed up by purchasing power and willingness to buy. 'Need' alone is not enough to secure the success of a project. (As an example, a textile mill in an African country was justified with reference to consumption of cloth per head of the population compared to that in other African countries. There had been no proper market survey and no firm evidence of effective demand for the product.) It should also be remembered that many projects provide only an intermediate product (e.g. research information, maps, soil surveys) which need to be analysed against the effective demand of the final users, e.g. farmers.

All projects need **inputs** – what economists call complementary factors of production. These comprise investment goods like plant and machinery, raw materials, bought-in components, skilled and unskilled labour, management, recurrent credit, etc. At a human level, inputs can consist of students (in the case of schools), doctors and nurses (in the case of medical facilities), research workers (in the case of research projects), etc. It is a near-universal tendency in developing countries to plan social infrastructure – like schools and hospitals – without securing sufficient skilled staff to run them. In one African country a magnificent new hospital, equipped with six operating theatres, is standing empty and unused for shortage of staff and finance, while the existing old hospital is bursting at the seams.

Inputs are converted into outputs by means of a **technique of production**. This technique can be embodied in hardware, like a blast furnace, an organisation, like a technical college, or know-how, as in the production of a new farm crop. In all cases techniques should be feasible and well-tried. A poor developing country is not an ideal place to test out a prototype. If farmers are being asked to produce a crop not hitherto grown in that locality, the introduction of that variety will need very careful preparation, trials, demonstration, credit, etc. An industrial technique should be appropriate, suitable to the capacity of locally-available technicians and workers.

Management is critical. Whether the project is located in a firm, farm, school, ministry of works, or satellite station the nature of the institution, the quality of its staff, its sources of finance, and its operational remit are vital data to check out. One should be particularly assiduous in looking at proposals requiring the creation of new institutions. New agencies are often created to by-pass the problems inherent in existing administrations – but they can be a source of new and intractable problems, not a relief from existing ones. The track record of the managing institution should be gone over carefully. This is especially true of public enterprises with a record of losses and political involvement. In project proposals, such agencies are often represented as being on the verge of turning over a new leaf. This may be no more than a hope.

Is further appraisal worthwhile?

The proper appraisal of a project can take time and lock up considerable resources. The appraiser should try and assess at each stage whether further appraisal is necessary, and if so in how much detail. For instance, the proposal may have gone beyond the point of no return by the time it is passed over for examination. If it is not too late to appraise with a view to making changes, are the changes likely to be large enough to justify the effort? Is the project likely to be blocked in any case by political factors?

Is the appraisal required purely for purposes of window-dressing a decision already taken? If more data is necessary, how easily and quickly could it be obtained, and how would the delay affect the project? Is there a deadline for the decision, and if so is it a serious one or a matter of bureaucratic convenience?

It should be re-emphasised that the purpose of an appraisal is not just to help decide whether a project should or should not be implemented; it can also help to improve the design of a good project or suggest ways in which an unacceptable project can be redeemed. This is why it is undesirable to rush project appraisal, or take short cuts, even if the appraiser believes that the project would go ahead anyway.

Further reading

There are a number of first-class texts on the subject of cost–benefit analysis and project appraisal. They are divided here into two groups, those exploring the issues at a methodological level, and those offering practical guidance.

Methodology
E. J. Mishan, *Cost–Benefit Analysis*, Allen & Unwin, 1971.

I. M. D. Little and J. A. Mirrlees, *Project Appraisal and Planning for Developing Countries*, Heinemann, 1974. (The best known textbook on project appraisal. An expanded version of the book produced by the OECD in 1969, *Manual of Industrial Project Analysis in Developing Countries*.)

The United Nations Industrial Development Organisation, *Guidelines for Project Evaluation*, UN, New York, 1972. (UNIDO's alternative to the OECD manual mentioned above, written by A. K. Sen, S. Marglin and P. Dasgupta.)

L. Squire and H. van der Tak, *Economic Analysis of Projects*, Johns Hopkins University Press for the World Bank, 1975.

Practical handbooks

Ministry of Overseas Development, *Guide to the Economic Appraisal of Projects in Developing Countries*, HMSO, 1977. (An attempt to apply the Little–Mirrlees methodology to devise practical guidelines. Contains detailed checklists of essential data for different sectors.)

E. V. K. FitzGerald, *Public Sector Investment Planning for Developing Countries*, Macmillan, 1978. (Oriented rather more for students than for officials. Contains case materials and essay topics.)

Commonwealth Secretariat, *A Manual on Project Planning in Small Economies*, London, May 1982.

Annex: Discounting

Discounting entails working out the net annual flows of costs and benefits for each year of the project's life and applying the appropriate discount factor to each annual flow. The summation of these flows produces total discounted costs, and benefits. These can be regarded as the present values of total costs or total benefits. The difference between the two discounted flows of costs and benefits is net present value, which epitomises the project's rate of return.

An example will make it clearer. Imagine an oil company is about to sink a well costing £10 million, spread equally over two years. Their best information is that, once open, the well will produce oil for five years and then dry up. The cost of operating the well will be £0.5 million per year. An appraisal of the project would take the form of a simple discounted cash flow analysis, and the data would be set out as follows:

					£ million
Year	Costs	Benefits	Net benefits	Discount factor at 10%	Discounted net benefits
1	5.0	0	−5.0	0.9091	−4.55
2	5.0	0	−5.0	0.8264	−4.13
3	0.5	1.0	0.5	0.7513	0.38
4	0.5	3.0	2.5	0.6830	1.71
5	0.5	5.0	4.5	0.6209	2.79
6	0.5	7.0	6.5	0.5645	3.67
7	0.5	3.0	2.5	0.5132	1.28
				NPV	+1.15

'Net benefits' are simply the difference between annual costs and benefits. The 'discount factor', in this case for 10%, is obtained from published discount tables for each of the years of the project. The 'discounted net benefits' are obtained by multiplying the net benefits by the discount factor for each year. The sum of the annual discounted net benefits streams is the net present value (NPV in the table). If it is positive, it indicates that the project has a positive rate of return, and *vice versa* if it is negative.

The same data can be used to produce an internal rate of return (IRR). This is the discount rate at which the cost and benefit streams are equalised, or at which the NPV becomes zero. If a calculator or computer facility is not available, the IRR is obtained by a process of trial and error using different discount rates until the NPV becomes zero. In the above example the IRR is 13.58%. It should be noted that a positive IRR is quite compatible with a negative NPV, where the IRR is less than the opportunity cost of capital.

Many books on project appraisal contain practical examples of discounting and some contain discount tables. One of the pioneering works in the application of the discounted cash flow method to private company investments, which is still worth reading, is:

A. J. Merrett and Allen Sykes, *Capital Budgeting and Company Finance*, first published by Longmans in 1966.

The World Bank's publication, *Compounding and Discounting Tables for Project Evaluation* (Washington DC, 1973), is useful for practitioners.

There are now many simple computer programs for discounting and the calculation of NPVs, and some calculators have this facility.

3
Preparation and presentation

Once a decision has been taken to investigate a project in more detail, the focus of attention shifts somewhat away from choice – the prime subject of this book – towards the preparation and presentation of projects for approval. These processes include appraisal, which was discussed in the previous chapter and which will not be raised again here. The immediate question is a blunt one – once choice has been exercised and some kind of decision in principle taken to proceed with further investigation of a project, is not the further elaboration of the project a mere formality?

Obviously this is too simple – and cynical – a view. Although the early decisions on a project – however innocuous – have a disproportionate importance to the final shape of the scheme, there are many things left to be decided during the processing of the project and at each stage careful presentation and preparation are necessary to bring out, and help settle, these points. Thus, in a power project the fundamental decision to proceed with a scheme of a certain size may already have been taken but there are vital technical and economic questions to be settled that require careful analysis, such as the source of energy (oil, coal), the type and size of each generator, the period over which each unit is introduced, whether a revision in tariffs is necessary, etc.

In addition to these decisions about the nature of the project in hand, the way in which the project is presented can be important for future projects of a similar kind, and for the future monitoring and evaluation of the project. It can, for instance, through sensitivity analysis, show the crucial factors which will make or break the project. This gives important signals to those concerned with checking the progress and reviewing the results of the project in the future.

The analogy of a dog show comes to mind. The attitude of the judges towards the animals parading before them makes no difference to the number or nature of canines on view (although it is obviously vital to which of them get the prizes), but it can influence the outcome of future shows if the dog fanciers start breeding for the features preferred by the judges.

Preparation

Assuming the project has been identified the extent of further investigation will depend on a number of considerations. Of course, the basic aspects – political, managerial, economic, technical, financial – need to be adequately covered in every case, but different clients (or users, or promoters) have different requirements, which means that some aspects have to be covered in greater depth and sophistication than others. An analysis done for a development bank will have to cover financial aspects very thoroughly. Projects prepared for aid agencies normally dwell heavily on socio-economic matters. An industrial client will require full coverage of marketing, technical and managerial aspects. Major items of public investment (motorways, airports, coalfields) demand extensive treatment of environmental effects.

Preparation also needs to take account of the approval procedure of the sponsor or financier. Some agencies, especially in the public sector, have elaborate and formal procedures for approval in order to satisfy public opinion, parliamentary scrutiny, or (in the case of international agencies) the curiosity of member governments. The World Bank, for instance, has a highly formal, elaborate and thorough process of approving projects through its executive board, necessitating extremely careful and comprehensive preparation. The British Department of Transport also has standard and thorough procedures for approving new road construction, partly to satisfy public opinion and partly to cover itself against charges of inconsistency, arbitrariness, or bias from the many possible interested parties. The British Overseas Development Administration likewise imposes on itself a well-defined and rigorous procedure for approving the larger aid projects. Other bodies, for instance merchant banks and development banks, may have simpler procedures requiring briefer preparation, and rely more on their judgement of the calibre of associated institutions, partners, or sponsors.

To illustrate the point that different clients have different requirements for information, consider the case of a former British minister of transport. He presented a case to the Cabinet for closing down a railway line in a remote part of Britain, justifying this with a full cost–benefit analysis, and a financial analysis showing the heavy losses, and supporting it with proposals for providing alternative and cheaper modes of transport for the local inhabitants. At the end of his careful exposé the silence was broken by the plaintive realism of a blunter colleague, 'But, Prime Minister, the line goes through four marginal constituencies!' The line was reprieved.

The final part of the preceding chapter mentioned the elements that need to be covered in any appraisal – demand, technique, supply of material, finances, etc. To adequately cover all these points the team assigned to prepare the project should normally contain people representing several disciplines. The leader should be an experienced person who can expect the loyalty of other members and command respect both from the promoters (donors, financiers) and from those at the 'receiving end'. This person should have some negotiating skills. The team should also contain the 'bread and butter' professionals like engineers and economists. Sector specialists can be added where the size and complexity of the project require, such as agronomists, financial analysts, geologists, etc. An excessively large project team can be cumbersome, fissiparous and intimidating, and therefore the claims of additional disciplines for inclusion in the team need to be weighed carefully, and it may be preferable to canvass such views either before or after the main field work.

Where, as is often necessary, members of the project team have to visit the location of the project, careful thought has to be given to the organisation of the mission in order to accomplish its objectives without wasting its members' time and unduly inconveniencing people at the receiving end. There are, of course, a large number of possible circumstances, and different project leaders have different styles of approach. An aid mission to a foreign government needs exceptionally careful thought since political and diplomatic nuances are involved in the various tasks. The team should involve the local government as fully as possible in the investigations, and this normally requires initial consultations at ministerial level, even if these are little more than courtesy calls, and round-up sessions with the people and agencies most intimately concerned with implementation. The finance and planning ministries should be made fully *au fait* with the team's progress and recommendations. Sandwiched between these essential initial and concluding sessions the team's time can be spent in its detailed professional work.

There are many cases of a project team being bemused by the enthusiasm of a particular minister or official, and founding its recommendations on such partial evidence, only to return to find that other important political or bureaucratic figures take a different view.

Presentation

The above remarks about tailoring project preparation to the needs of the approval procedure apply with even stronger force to the way in which the project is presented. Some agencies insist on standardised presentations with bulky supporting documentation, while others prefer shorter and more sharply focused papers.

Whatever the nature of the approval body, there must be an assumption that some – and possibly the majority – of the people who have to take the decision are non-specialists, and fairly busy. This argues for a clear and simple document with the accent on brevity, and containing the more detailed discussion of technical and specialist aspects as annexes to the main document. If the main text of the proposal runs to more than a small number of pages (the normal case) it should contain a summary and conclusions. A map of the project location is always helpful, together with other visual aids like diagrams and bar charts. Where values are expressed in foreign currency a rate of conversion into a more familiar currency should be included. In principle, the gist of the paper should be in a form that can be made available to other parties involved – e.g. the foreign government receiving the loan or aid, the local authority that will have to implement the work, etc. To this end, the document could be divided into two sections, one that can be distributed and the other containing information and views meant for the approval body only.

Where the submission or project document contains conditions for granting the loan or starting the project, it is unwise to include them without having cleared them first with the parties affected or those required to implement them. It sometimes happens that conditions are written in largely for the cosmetic purposes of the approval body, but if there is a real likelihood of their not being accepted by the people at the receiving end the promoters have an awkward choice of accepting non-compliance or withdrawing the project. Conditions should not be included if the promoter or financier is half-hearted about following them through.

It is helpful if the submission clearly draws out the effects of the project on different parties and – in the case of a project involving governments – on the wider economy. Benefits (and costs) should be shown for profits, wages, farmers, imports, exports, government finance, etc. This is without prejudice to the appraisal methodology that is used. Likewise the economic discussion should include sensitivity and risk analysis (see preceding chapter) in order to accentuate the most important factors governing the success or failure of the project. This analysis should be used to demonstrate which government policies are likely to have greatest influence on the outcome of the project (pricing, tariffs, procurement, incomes policies, etc.).

One possible schema of presentation is as follows:

Summary and conclusions.

Brief description of project. Objectives. Main features.

Background. History. Circumstances in which agency became involved. Previous attempts. Political factors.

Technical aspects. Justification of proposed technology. Cost-effectiveness. Appropriateness to local conditions. Details of trials, etc.

Economic appraisal. Demand/market. Cost–benefit analysis. Sensitivity and risk analysis.

Financial aspects. Costs of construction and operation. Revenues. Cash flow. Effect on balance sheet. Treatment of inflation and contingencies. Arrangement for cost overruns. Exchange rate assumptions. Sources of funds, etc.

Inputs. Arrangements for securing land, labour, management, machinery, materials, imports, etc.

Managerial/administrative set-up. The institution that will install and operate the project. Its track record, organisational structure, relations with government, morale, etc. System of management responsibility and financial control.

Other aspects. Environmental and social angles.

Arrangements for construction.

Implementation responsibility.

Plans for monitoring and evaluation.

Special conditions. To be agreed with co-operating parties.

Finally, the document should contain the more detailed **annexes**, such as those on technical, economic and financial aspects. These should be 'keyed in' to the discussion in the text, otherwise they may be ignored.

We have assumed that the responsibility for writing up and presenting the project falls to the project team leader who carried out the preparation and appraisal. This is normally a logical choice. However, some agencies prefer that the final document should be written, or at least edited, by people close to the approval body, who know the approach that the latter is looking for and can anticipate problems perceived by 'headquarters' better than those 'in the field'. Field workers, who can justly claim to know the project and the circumstances of its implementation, often get irritated by what they construe as 'head office interference' in their submissions. However, this may be necessary to ensure the smooth passage of the project through the approval stage. At the very least, 'head office' should keep the right to do fairly drastic editing.

ROADS
RAILWAYS
PORTS
AIRPORTS
POWER

E C O N O M I C

I N F R A S T R U C T U R E

4
Roads

A road may strike one as a project totally different in character from a productive project like a textile factory. Roads are among the oldest, least controversial, and most widely accepted artefacts of government. Although they are more technically complex than they appear to the layman, their purpose is well understood and their benefits are available to all.

However, there is more in common between a road and a textile factory than the non-economist might think. A road produces benefits to its users and taxpayers and there are ways of valuing the benefits quantitatively. If these benefits exceed the costs of investment and upkeep, the road is held to be justified. Thus the decision rules that apply to other projects – NPV, IRR and BCR – can equally be used for roads. In practice, much use is also made of the 'first-year rate of return' criterion to determine the timing of the investment.

Of course there are important differences between roads and other projects. Not all the benefits appear in direct monetary form. Savings in travellers' time, for instance, can be valued, but only in a rough manner, and the travellers themselves may not value them in the same way. Even travellers' cost savings – on fuel, tyres, vehicle upkeep, etc. – do not appear at once in their wallets. Thus a sizeable part of road benefits is notional.

This is one reason why it is normally impractical to charge people for the use of roads. Although tolls can be levied on certain key routes and crossings (e.g. bridges, French motorways) they cannot be employed very widely without adding to administrative costs, delaying traffic and discouraging travellers. Since an important object of building roads is to encourage people to use them in preference to more congested or dangerous routes, and since benefits are measured in proportion to the number of users, it is self-defeating to charge for road use if that seriously discourages travellers.

A related point is that the cost of someone using the road (as opposed to the cost of putting it there in the first place and maintaining it) is very low. The wear and tear on the road surface from the passage of a car is tiny (though this would not be true of an army tank or a juggernaut lorry), thus the authorities have no strong reason for charging road users, at least not so long as the road is not congested.

All this explains why the benefits from using roads cannot be converted directly to money through road charges. This chapter explains some of the notional devices for measuring benefits and, more generally, some of the yardsticks for taking decisions in this sector.

Alternatives

The need for a new road may seem self-evident to its advocates. In cities by-passes are advocated as the only way of reducing inner-city congestion and accidents. Farmers see the upgrading of earth tracks to all-weather standard roads as the only way of guaranteeing that their products are marketed all the year round. Politicians see improvements in roads with neighbouring countries as being of strategic and political importance, and the best way of cementing regional ties.

These people may be right, but it is important to ask if there are cheaper and easier ways of achieving the same objectives, or whether there are constraints which will continue to apply even if a road is built. For instance, inner-city congestion can be tackled by improved traffic management – traffic lights, one-way streets, bus lanes, or even – as Singapore has shown – charging motorists for entry during peak hours. These measures are all cheaper than the alternative of building by-passes, and very much less costly than building urban freeways.

The alternative to building all-weather access roads for farmers is to improve crop storage so that produce can be held until travelling conditions improve. In any case, unless marketing conditions are good, and viable arrangements are in place, the construction of feeder roads will not generate the expected traffic.

Although trans-national routes have an evident appeal to politicians and all those concerned with regional cohesion, hardened travellers will attest that the state of the road is often the least obstacle to travel between adjacent countries. This is more true of commercial traffic than it is of individual travellers. The frustrations and delays of customs procedures, diplomatic requirements, and sheer bureaucracy can more than offset the advantage of an improved road. Studies of the Trans-Africa Highway show that the very low level of traffic on the route is not due primarily to physical travelling conditions but to the existence of these delays and difficulties – which amount to the lack of will of neighbouring countries to encourage movement between themselves.

Assessing benefits

We have shown that the benefits from building roads cannot be lumped together into a single monetary measure, such as sales or tariff revenue. The types of benefit to be discussed in this section are disparate. Estimates of their economic worth can be made, but it is important not to gloss over the different kinds of benefit that go into the measure of aggregate benefits.

The types of benefit normally considered are direct savings on the costs of operating vehicles, economies in road maintenance, time savings by travellers, the reduction of accidents, and the wider effect of the road on the economic development of the region it serves. Let us examine each in turn.

i. Vehicle cost savings
When an improved road is built the owners and users of vehicles profit from reduced costs of transport. Higher average speeds can be maintained, with fewer gear changes and braking, hence there are savings on fuel consumption. Tyres last longer on the improved surface and there is less wear and tear on the suspension and the body. These savings are undeniable, and are quickly perceived by road users in the form of lower outlays.

This is not to say that such savings can be accurately predicted. They depend on the type of vehicle, the way it is driven, the type of road surface, the route alignment, the climate, etc. There is no substitute for local assessments carried out in the country concerned comparing vehicle performance on the existing roads with that on roads similar to those about to be built. Many studies of large road projects incorporate such direct estimates of cost savings. However, some useful estimates of standard costs for different types of vehicles on specified types of road are available in publications of the Transport and Road Research Laboratory (see section on further reading, page 35).

It is common to distinguish vehicle cost savings according to the circumstances in which they arise. The easiest to estimate are those accruing to existing users of the route. Next come savings enjoyed by travellers diverted from other roads, or other modes of transport, onto the road in question. Their cost savings are also a matter of direct estimation, though the extent of the diversion can be a matter for speculation. The most tenuous kind of saving is that accruing to traffic which is generated by the existence of the road, and which did not exist before the road was built. Apart from the difficulty of predicting the size of this generated traffic there is the theoretical problem of attributing 'savings' when there were no prior costs. The solution normally recommended is to count as a benefit half the cost savings from generated traffic. (See the annex to this chapter, page 36.)

ii. Economies in road maintenance

An old road, with a deteriorating surface, needs increasing amounts of maintenance if it is to continue serving its intended purpose. A broken bitumen road calls for repairs to potholes and eroding edges, while earth and gravel roads need continuous attention to restore the surface after damage caused by climate and the passage of vehicles. Compared to this, the construction of a new bitumen road can produce immediate savings on recurrent upkeep – although constant attention is just as important for this type of road as for the others.

Although maintenance costs are only a small fraction of the initial investment cost of the road, they are an important item in the budgets of many countries, and savings are greeted with relief. This is all the more true where investment costs are covered by foreign aid donors, while maintenance falls on local finance.

A gravel road carrying 100 vehicles a day may need grading ten times a year and re-gravelling every three years or so. A bitumen road needs routine maintenance to repair potholes as they occur and keep drainage channels clean, periodic maintenance to reseal the surface, and strengthening from time to time so that it can continue to carry traffic satisfactorily.

Maintenance costs are commonly expressed as a percentage of the initial capital cost. An earth feeder road that is little used might need annual maintenance outlays of only 0.6%. A gravel road carrying 200 vehicles per day might need 10%. A sealed bitumen road with 200 vehicles per day could require 2% outlays, but the higher capital cost could go some way to equalising absolute maintenance costs compared to the gravel type. As a generalisation, maintenance costs for anything other than feeder roads can vary between 2% and 5% of the capital costs. Where they fall in this range depends mainly on traffic usage, and to a lesser extent climate and topography.

Most of the annual spending on maintenance is on labour and materials. In all cases transport is required for the workers and the materials. Gravel roads need graders, roller, tippers and a water truck. Earth roads mainly need grading equipment. Sealed bitumen roads need a pre-mixing plant, rollers, tippers, and bitumen distributors. Routine maintenance, grass cutting, drain cleaning and minor patching can often be done effectively by hand labour, while periodic maintenance and improvement – grading and re-gravelling of gravel roads, and patching and resurfacing of bitumen roads – inevitably require specialist equipment.

Maintenance need not happen every year – this depends on the age of the road and the type of surface. It is desirable that earth roads should be cared for annually, otherwise the surface soon deteriorates. The same is true of gravel. But sealed roads should only need resealing every five years or so, though patching may need to be done more often. As in so many other spheres, small regular spending on maintenance can obviate much larger outlays to rescue the initial investment.

We should not, however, blind ourselves to budgetary realities. It is sensible for the government of a poor country to insist on high standards for roads financed out of foreign aid, since this relieves the local budget of maintenance outlays for a breathing space of a few years. By the same token, because maintenance can be delayed from one year to another without utterly disastrous consequences it is tempting for a hard-pressed finance minister to economise on this item rather than some other element of the budget. The cumulative effect of such skimping is that road maintenance departments are frequently poorly staffed, badly trained, and demoralised compared to other departments dealing with new investment. Maintaining roads calls for good organisation above all, and thus training staff is especially important.

In stating the motives of government departments towards maintenance and the related issue of road standards, we have suggested some areas that should be particularly watched by financiers or consultants. Pressures for road standards that are higher than justified should be resisted since they draw investment funds away from other priority areas and undermine the creation of proper maintenance departments, which are unavoidable in the long run.

iii. Time savings
An improved highway enables the traveller to save time. This can sometimes be of direct monetary benefit – as when a quicker journey means there is no need to stay overnight in a hotel, or to buy a meal *en route*. Usually, though, time savings are not tantamount to direct cash savings. It is difficult to express in monetary terms the satisfaction a traveller obtains from a quicker journey, or from being able to leave for work half an hour later in the morning. Surveys can be made of travellers to ascertain what they would be prepared to pay in order to obtain certain time savings – but this subjective approach is not the same as achieving hard cash benefits.

The hardest evidence of the value of time saved arises where travellers have the choice of alternative modes of travel or routes, with differing times taken, and opt to pay more for the one that is quicker. For instance, commuters in a city may be able to choose between a slow bus journey and a speedier train journey, and one could represent the extra cost of the latter as the value placed on the time saved. Even in this relatively straightforward case, other factors may intrude, like comfort, frequency, accessibility, and convenience. Outside cities, it is rare to be able to test people's travelling preferences directly in this way. Time savings can save costs directly in a commercial firm, e.g. when a trucker is able to reduce the size of his vehicle fleet.

The conventional approach is to make the simplifying assumption that the value of working time saved is equal to the average income of travellers for the unit of time in question. Surveys can show which socio-economic group different kinds of travellers belong to, and time savings are valued according to the hourly income of each group. But what of time savings that occur during the traveller's leisure time? Or time savings during working hours that are taken out as extra leisure? There clearly should be a distinction between working and leisure time savings, and the latter are very difficult to evaluate.

Another obvious question to ask is whether the expected time savings occur at a time of day and in a place such that they are likely to be used productively. Moreover, is the amount of time saved sufficient to be capable of productive use? An hour is one thing, but ten minutes saved at the end of the working day of a salaried commuter is a totally different proposition.

Enough has been said to appreciate that the valuation of time savings is a tricky business. It is reasonable to make such estimates and count them in the benefits of urban travellers, or highly paid road users of any kind, but there are cogent objections to using them in areas of little economic activity, where it is not clear that the savings would be productively used, or where people behave as though time savings are not very important to them. In general, one should be very suspicious of cases where the justification for a road relies heavily on time savings rather than the more tangible user cost savings. Time savings are best viewed as a welfare bonus coming on top of more direct benefits.

iv. Reduction in accidents

Road improvements, especially in urban areas, are often justified in terms of reducing the number, severity, and cost of accidents. The two main problems facing appraisers are to determine whether increased safety is likely to occur, and if so to put some monetary value on this benefit.

Accidents are, by definition, unpredictable. Although one may reasonably point out that certain conditions tend to lead to accidents, and reinforce this viewpoint by referring to historical accident rates, it is rarely easy to foresee how a change in circumstances – like building a new road or introducing a one-way system in a town – will reduce the incidence or the severity of accidents. It is even possible for 'improved' road conditions to lead to an increase in accidents through increasing the average speed of traffic.

A few things can be said with confidence. Raising traffic speeds in towns is likely to increase the incidence – and probably the severity – of accidents. Widening roads, other things being equal, will reduce accidents, and so will reducing the number of junctions on rural roads. Accidents will also be reduced if pedestrians and animals can be separated from road traffic. Reports of the Transport and Road Research Laboratory (see section on further reading, page 35) provide some guidance in this matter.

As for valuing the 'savings' from reduced accidents, we are on firmer ground in considering damage to property and vehicles than damage to life and limb. The shorthand method of treating accident costs for vehicles is to include vehicle insurance costs as an element of vehicle operating costs, on the ground that these rates cover claims on insurance companies in the event of accidents.

It is more difficult, and controversial, to put a value on life and limb. People's subjective valuation of their own lives, or those of relatives or friends, will differ from society's valuation. In order to preserve their own lives – e.g. in the event of a kidnappers' ransom demand – individuals would borrow the largest sum they could possibly raise. To society, however, the value of a life in economic terms is the value of the net output that the individual would produce over his or her remaining life. Only by a rare coincidence would this be the same as the sum for which a person insures himself or herself. Thus there is no uncontroversial measure of the value of lives saved.

Personal injury, stopping short of death, also imposes a cost on society, namely the loss of production during hospital confinement and convalescence, and the direct cost of medical treatment. Private insurance and social service payments can reduce the incidence of such costs on the individual.

The line of least resistance is to take insurance values as a proxy for lives, limbs and loss of work. The problem is that this involves massive aggregation of widely differing personal circumstances. Also, in poor countries many road users will not have life or accident insurance. The moral is that the appraiser should be sceptical of road projects where a large part of the alleged benefits consist of savings from accident reduction, especially where injury to people is concerned.

v. Induced benefits
Roads are often credited with miraculous effects. Virgin areas can be opened up to population and economic activity by building an all-weather access route. Whether in the Highlands of Scotland or in tropical Africa people who claim to know the local scene swear by the importance of roads. Without roads, they say, there can be no economic development; many go further and claim that roads *per se* induce economic development.

This is why one cannot ignore the induced benefits of road construction. The problem is not primarily one of measuring these benefits. They arise in forms already discussed – in operating cost savings by traffic on existing tracks or those diverted from other routes, in time savings, in cost savings over other modes (ferries, aircraft, etc.). Once a benefit can be identified and verified there are fairly straightforward ways of measuring it and entering it into a cost–benefit calculus.

This is not to dismiss measurement problems completely. There are some benefits that do not materialise primarily via gains to traffic. For instance, a road may stimulate agricultural production for on-farm consumption, or it may make it easier for the population served to use the social and medical facilities in the area. There is no objective way of measuring social and medical benefits. However, the stimulus to agricultural production can be tackled by allotting an arbitrary – but generally small – proportion of the increase in net farm output to the improved transport. Improved transport alone is unlikely to produce all the benefits. Increased amounts of other inputs are necessary, like labour, credit, land, equipment. Ideally a careful study should be made of the constraints to production in each situation, and a cost–benefit analysis done of a comprehensive package of measures to improve production – including transport. Since this is scarcely likely to be feasible in most cases, the short-cut method is to postulate a reasonable increase in net farm output, and to attribute a proportion of this to the improved road transport.

The greater problem is to decide when induced benefits are likely to accrue and how important they will be. One should be suspicious of projects that are justified by reference to induced benefits in circumstances where these are not likely to arise. *Prima facie*, one would expect induced benefits to be important where access roads are being built to connect an area to the existing transport network for the first time, and where there is of course no traffic at present. A similar situation is where seasonal tracks are being upgraded to an all-weather surface, and where existing traffic is very low.

Obviously in such cases it would be impossible to justify the road on the normal basis of cost savings to existing users, or to traffic diverted from other routes (since no alternative routes exist). All the benefits have to be loaded onto induced ('generated') traffic, plus gains that cannot be attributed directly to traffic like increased output, reduced stocks, access to social facilities, etc. How likely are these gains to materialise?

There is not much point in putting a road into a barren and thinly populated area and expecting a big stimulus to agriculture. Resources available need to be consiu. ed, and whether road transport is really the binding constraint on development. Some resources can develop without roads – cattle can be evacuated on the hoof, timber can be floated down rivers, etc. Light aircraft can be a perfectly economic way of serving isolated communities. We should not lose sight of the possibility that in difficult terrain the cost of maintaining the road could exceed the value of annual benefits, thus causing a reduction of national income. As for social benefits, there are plenty of examples of road construction accelerating the depopulation of an unappealing region.

In weighing the likelihood of these events, the appraiser can take account of the resource endowment of the region to be traversed by the road, the size and distribution of the existing population, the number of vehicles, the extent of marketed production, the importance of transport costs in the marketed value of produce, the possibility of seasonal storage of produce, the degree of cultivation of cultivable land and the existence of other constraints on development that road building will not remove. It should also be possible to gauge people's potential inclination to travel by looking at the propensity to travel by similar groups elsewhere, the extent of rural–urban migration, the existence and distribution of community, social and medical facilities and the population's desire to have access to them. That roads can produce social costs and disruption should always be borne in mind.

One possible approach to judging whether road building is warranted in small communities is to relate the capital cost of the road to the number of vehicles or inhabitants and to assess whether the resulting additional output would be sufficient to service a loan of that size.

Forecasting demand

Almost all road projects rely on an estimate of future traffic in order to justify new road construction or improvements. As we have seen, the amount of generated traffic is especially hard to predict; even the growth of existing and diverted traffic is difficult to foresee with any confidence. Leaving aside the case of feeder roads in virgin areas, discussed above, all forecasts must start with knowledge of the amount of existing traffic along the route in question, and the vehicle 'population' in the areas to be served. The former depends on good historical traffic counts, and the latter on vehicle inventories or censuses.

A traffic count should show the number of vehicles in each of several categories (passenger car, light lorry, heavy lorry, bus, etc.) that used the route over a 24-hour period. To ensure that the results are representative, the count should be an average of readings taken over at least one week, repeated several times in the year. This is necessary in order to smooth over diurnal, weekly and seasonal influences. The count should be up-to-date. The counting points should be spaced along the route so as to avoid being unduly influenced by local traffic. In particular, the counting points should start far enough away from towns to avoid getting suburban traffic caught up in the trawl. In general, repeating counts rather than extending their duration improves reliability.

Composition of traffic is an important detail; heavy vehicles suffer much higher operating costs than light, and so stand to gain very much more from improvements. At the same time, they punish the road much more than light vehicles. This means that a road built with heavy vehicles in mind must be constructed to sturdier specifications. It also implies that costs can be saved by prohibiting certain types of vehicle from using the road. The important feature here is axle loading, not the length or capacity of the vehicle (though total weight is obviously relevant to the design of bridges).

Studies done on road building in the past throw light on the factors which in practice affect the growth of traffic. The size of the vehicle population is an obvious factor. If sales, and imports, of vehicles are growing rapidly, this is a favourable omen. If existing vehicle users are unable to buy spare parts, e.g. because of strict import controls, one would expect a growing number of existing vehicles to fall out of use. If the growth of traffic in the past has been associated with unduly cheap petrol, one should distrust historical trends and predict slower growth once petrol prices catch up with the world price of oil. Particular countries may have policies towards the distribution of population or agricultural production that will affect traffic growth. For instance, if the government seeks to encourage the growth of villages along the route, this will affect traffic. But if the state resolutely keeps the price of agricultural produce down to uneconomic levels, or if the marketing board persistently fails to deliver seed or fertiliser on time, these factors will prevent the hoped-for farm benefits appearing.

Cost-effective solutions

Once it has been decided to build, or up-grade, a road in order to fulfil certain objectives it is essential to make sure that construction is cost-effective. In order to conserve national resources – for example, for use on roads else-where – the chosen solution should be the cheapest one that fulfils the objectives.

Costs depend on a number of features of the route. The nature of the terrain is crucial – it obviously costs more to build through mountains and swamps. Soil strength, which depends on geology and rainfall, influences the type of foundations that need to be put in. Climate affects the surface and drainage works required, especially if the road is subject to frost, ice, or heavy rain. Construction costs also depend on the proximity of basic materials to the site. The transport of earth (for embankments), gravel, etc., over long distances can be expensive. All these factors mean that one should be careful about relying too much on figures of cost per kilometre without consulting experts about the peculiarities of the route in question.

The other main influences on costs relate to traffic. The expected volume of traffic, taken together with the types of vehicles and their axle loading, will determine the required strength of the road and its surface. Normally a bitumen road is only warranted at traffic volumes of several hundred vehicles per day. This rule of thumb is no substitute for a detailed examination of each proposal, but it suggests that an exceptionally close look should be taken at proposals for bitumen roads with a traffic density of, say, forty vehicles per day.

Finally, the design speed – the average speed for which the road is designed – vitally influences costs. Most countries lay down national design speeds for their road network, varying according to terrain. The design speed is especially important when planning roads in mountainous areas. It affects, for example, the alignment – the curves that are acceptable in order to maintain the desired speed. In a mountainous area it could be highly expensive to insist on curves gentle enough to keep up high speeds. The alternative is to accept tight curves in certain situations and to warn traffic with signs and road markings. Design speed also affects width and gradient. In short, an inappropriate design speed can be an expensive liability to the local ministry of works.

The planner or engineer who keeps cost-effectiveness in mind is constantly on the lookout for ways of making savings and improvisations. In upgrading schemes, for instance, it will be observed that some parts of the road are liable to deteriorate more rapidly than others, hence 'spot improvements' are the alternative to a full-scale upgrading. It makes sense to concentrate on stretches where the traffic is greatest. The design speed can be compromised in a few places in return for large savings – e.g. a few curves that do not conform to the prescribed standards. Since bridges are more expensive per metre than roads, it might save money to build a more circuitous road to avoid a river crossing. Sight distances would be increased by removing rocks as an alternative to altering the road curvature.

Labour-intensive techniques

Where labour is in plentiful supply and is willing to do construction work at the prevailing wages it has been found that some of the tasks of road building can be performed using labour-intensive solutions as partial or total substitutes for machinery. There is no such thing as *the* labour-intensive solution, since road building falls into a number of clear stages (modules), at each of which there is a choice between an array of different ways of performing the job. At each of these stages, the choice of technique is influenced by the relative cost of labour and capital, and by the efficiency with which the work is organised.

Research and trials in developing countries have demonstrated the scope for substituting labour for capital in certain stages. This can be the cheaper solution when wages are below a certain level in each country. However, even in such cases the assumption is that labour can produce a result to a satisfactory standard and, more important, can be effectively managed by foremen. In practice, mobilising and supervising large numbers of workers on a road construction site is difficult, and a potential source of cost and waste. Moreover, labour-intensive methods normally take longer than the alternatives; they delay benefits, and require more working capital during the construction period – in countries where credit can be very costly.

These remarks are aimed at enthusiasts for labour-intensive solutions concerned with the laudable aim of mopping up unemployed labour. There are certainly opportunities to substitute labour for machinery, but they are rarer than is commonly supposed, and require intensive planning and management – themselves not plentiful. There is probably more scope for labour-intensity in road maintenance, especially of earth and gravel surfaces. In some countries villagers are made responsible for the upkeep of sections passing near their dwellings, in return for an annual payment. Such an arrangement combines the three desiderata of local involvement, incentive, and labour-intensity. (See section on further reading (Allal and Edmonds), page 36.)

Appraisal without data

This is a species of the general predicament, planning without facts. Quantitative data necessary to measure the likely benefits of the road are likely to be scarce and of doubtful quality. If benefits cannot be estimated from the outset, an alternative approach is to take the likely cost of the road, calculate the level of benefits that would be necessary to justify it, and judge whether such benefits are likely to arise.

Pointers to the scale of benefits are the size of the population served by the road, its average income, the number of vehicles in the area, the kind of products being transported, the number of hectares of cultivated land, etc. One then knows how much benefit would be required to produce a first-year rate of return of, say, 10%, and it may be possible to judge how likely this is in view of the factors mentioned above. If, for instance, it needed a 10% increase in net farm output, or a reduction in user costs of 30%, or an annual rate of traffic increase of 6%, these levels might be judged reasonably likely, while much higher required benefits might be judged implausible.

Some practical points

A growing body of evaluation reports enables us to compare the way road projects turn out with what was originally expected of them. The following are some of the main factors that influence their outcome:

1 It is futile to regard roads as a 'good thing' as such, and to imagine that they will automatically generate enough traffic to justify their construction. Other conditions must be present if traffic is to grow as part of the general development of the locality.

2 The build-up of traffic often departs from forecasts, and can be either less or more than predicted. Appraisers should be sceptical of the traffic forecasts that are given them, which are often the work of interested parties. It is important to check whether past trends onto which the future is extrapolated are not abnormal, and that traffic build-up is not going to be frustrated by general economic conditions or government policies. However, in many countries there is a strong trend favouring road transport at the expense of other transport modes.

3 The influence of a new road on regional development is not always positive. It often leads to the polarisation of economic activity in the larger centres, and can even accelerate depopulation. Much depends on the social and economic attractions of the area in question.

4 In planning a national network it is normally sensible to expand outward from the densely trafficked routes.

5 Economic returns (the IRR) are likely to be highest for rural access roads, but the realisation of these returns is beset with the greatest risks. Most of the benefits of such projects will accrue to traffic which does not yet exist. Appraisals involving such generated traffic become very speculative.

6 Traffic cost savings are not always passed on to users. Truckers and bus companies may maintain charges, depending on the strength of competition. This will trap the proposed benefits at the first layer of the local economy.

7 The effect of road improvements on income distribution and social equality is often adverse. The poorest usually do not own vehicles, nor are they major transport users. Changes in land use are frequently to their disadvantage, as when landholding becomes more concentrated or cash crops replace food. On the other hand women very often benefit in their roles as auxiliary construction workers, traders and consumers.

8 Claims for increased safety and health should be treated warily. If the average speed of travel increases, the incidence of accidents may increase rather than the reverse. Visibility is a key factor in safety especially when it concerns pedestrians and traffic entering from side roads. As for health, although people's access to health posts and hospitals will improve, the spread of diseases and epidemics could also be accelerated.

9 Cost overruns are almost universal. This is commonly due to inadequate surveying of the route, poor estimation of the required quantities of materials and changes in specifications after commencement. Delays greatly add to inflation. These are not always the contractor's fault, and in the presence of strong inflationary pressures the use of a fixed-price contract could merely bankrupt the contractor and lead to further delays.

10 Local bureaucratic organisation is vital to timely completion, but, by the same token, it can contribute disproportionately to costly delays. Planning and appraisals should take account of the relevant bureaucratic capacity and competence.

11 Staged construction is a useful device. Where local finance is limited and/or the future growth of traffic is uncertain, the development of a road can proceed in stages. A common sequence would start from an improved earth road, with better alignment, base and drainage, to which gravel can be added later as traffic builds up, and finally the surface can be sealed with bitumen.

12 In densely populated countries with an apparent surplus of labour the employment of labour-intensive methods of road construction is theoretically attractive and is often advocated. There has been much research into this topic and practical manuals have started to appear (see section on further reading, page 36). Common problems with labour-intensive techniques have been a longer construction period, difficulties of managing a larger labour force, seasonal variations in the availability of labour, and the 'backward sloping supply curve of labour' (where increased earning prospects lead to workers working less because they can accumulate the desired capital sum more quickly). Some processes are eminently capable of being performed

in a labour-intensive manner, but much depends on the cost of labour, the type of road, and the way the work is organised.

13 Poor road maintenance is a universal bugbear, and has led to the premature deterioration of surfaces, the failure of user benefits to materialise, and the waste of investment. Funding and staffing shortages are crucial, but hitherto all parties have found it convenient to concentrate on new construction at the expense of keeping up the existing network. The alleviation of this problem should be given the highest priority.

Checklist of main questions

1 Background

i. Physical and geographical features of area
Relevant features of terrain, relief, drainage, soil, rocks.
Climate.
Vegetation.
Major economic activities.

ii. Population
Numbers. Trend. When was the last census?
Distribution. Location of main urban centres.
Occupational distribution.

iii. Transport system
Outline of transport network (tracks, roads, railway, river, air).
Volume of existing movements. Has there been a recent traffic census?
Relevant features of government's transport policy.
Organisation of local road transport industry.
What alternatives are there to the project? Have they been explored?

2 The project

iv. Brief description
Summary of project.
Antecedents.
Is there a feasibility study? Who has done it?
Who is pressing for the project, and why?

v. Technical aspects
Nature of project (new road, up-grading, repair and rehabilitation, maintenance, bridging, etc.). Any major structures?
Design features: geometric design; design speed; materials.
Strength and longevity; maximum axle load.
Type and quantity of materials required. Volume of cut and fill.
Is gravel, sand, bitumen, etc. available locally?
Is the method of construction (specifically the balance between mechanisation and labour-intensity) appropriate?
Maintenance requirements.

vi. Costs
Capital costs (distinguishing local and imported items). Equipment, labour and materials.
Recurrent costs: regular and periodic maintenance; resurfacing and rehabilitation.
How do costs per mile compare with those elsewhere?
Is the proposal cost-effective? Is there evidence of over-design? Is staged construction with progressive up-grading feasible?

vii. Traffic

Volume of existing traffic. Has there been a recent traffic census? Is it reliable?

Breakdown of traffic. Vehicle type. Passenger/goods. Motives for trip.

Projected growth. What is the basis for these forecasts? (Simple extrapolation of recent trend, or more sophisticated modelling.) How sensitive are the results to the state of the economy, the implementation of other projects, policy measures, etc?

Estimates of traffic diverted or generated by the project.

viii. Benefits

User cost savings. Are these direct estimates, or are they adapted from those used elsewhere?

Time savings.

Maintenance savings.

Other direct benefits, e.g. reduced accidents or congestion.

Induced and indirect benefits.

Results of cost–benefit analysis. How dependent is the IRR on generated traffic, time savings?

Are the benefits likely to be widely distributed? Who will be the principal gainers? What factors are likely to frustrate the realisation of the benefits?

Net financial impact of the project. What will be the gains in fiscal revenue, e.g. from tolls, extra licence fees, road taxes, fuel taxes, other revenue? Will these offset the initial and recurrent costs of the project?

ix. Managerial and institutional aspects

Capability of public works (or roads) department. Its record in constructing and maintaining roads. Its complement of foremen, skilled workers, equipment, workshops, and depots. Its annual budget. Availability of unskilled labour.

Competence of contractor. Record. Financial viability.

Nature of contract. (Fixed price, cost-price, target cost? Are there penalties for cost or time overruns?)

Will there be a supervising consultant?

Are the design and method of construction familiar?

What arrangements are being made for maintenance?

Further reading

The following is a tiny selection from the vast literature on the planning and appraisal of roads. As in the text, the emphasis is on the circumstances of developing countries, though the discussion has relevance to rural road building in developed countries too.

The Transport and Road Research Laboratory of Britain's Department of the Environment has done much research and has published a large body of reports and guides. Rather than try and select particular publications here, it is urged that readers interested in exploring topics in greater detail should contact TRRL direct (Old Wokingham Road, Crowthorne, Berks RG11 6AU).

Planning and appraisal

D. Bovill, I. Heggie and J. Hine, *A Guide to Transport Planning within the Roads Sector in Developing Countries*, HMSO, 1970.

World Bank, *The Economic Analysis of Rural Road Projects*, Washington DC, 1976.

M. B. Grieveson and J. T. Winpenny, *Leading Issues in Aiding Road*

Development, a paper produced for the Conference of the Institution of Civil Engineers, 'Criteria for Planning Highway Investment in Developing Countries', London, May 1982. (The collected papers produced for this conference make varied and interesting reading.)

P. G. Hill, *A Synthesis of Rural Road Evaluations*, an ODA Evaluation Report, 1982. (A paper written for a series on evaluation experience in different sectors, sponsored by the OECD, Paris.)

World Bank, *The Road Maintenance Problem and International Assistance*, Washington DC, 1981.

Practical manuals
M. Allal and G. Edmonds, *Manual on the Planning of Labour Intensive Road Construction*, International Labour Office, Geneva, 1977. (A detailed illustrated guide.)

United Nations Economic Commission for Africa (Addis Ababa), *Maintenance of Unpaved Roads – Practical Guidelines for the Maintenance of Roads in Africa*. (A simple and practical illustrated guide.)

Annex: User cost savings on generated traffic

The only satisfactory way of explaining this point is by recourse to a demand curve relating the amount of travelling done to the cost of so doing. In the figure (page 37) the vertical axis measures the cost of travel in, let us say, pence per mile. The horizontal axis provides some measure of the amount of travelling done along the road in question, say the total number of vehicle-miles. The curve DD is then the demand schedule showing how much travel is done at different levels of cost. (At lower levels of user cost obviously more travel is done than at higher levels.)

Along the unimproved road surface the cost to road users might be OC^1 and at this level OT^1 amount of travel is undertaken. When the road is improved the cost of travelling falls to OC^2. To simplify, let us suppose that the increased travel T^1T^2 is done by new travellers. Then we can say that people who used the road in its unimproved state have made road user savings equal to $C^1D^1XC^2$, and enjoy a total 'consumers' surplus' equal to the area under the demand curve, DD^1XC^2.

But what of the new road users, represented by T^1T^2? We infer from the shape of the demand curve that some of the new road users, those closest to T^1, would have been willing to travel at cost levels only a little less than OC^1, whereas the marginal travellers, those closest to T^2, needed the full cost reduction to induce them to make the journey. In a sense these marginal travellers have no cost savings.

The convention is to regard T^1T^2 as generated traffic and to attribute a cost saving represented by the area XD^1D^2. This is half the unit cost savings attributed to existing traffic OT^1. The commonsense interpretation is to say that we split the difference between the cost savings to those road users who were virtually happy to travel at the old costs and those who would not have travelled at all except at the new lower costs.

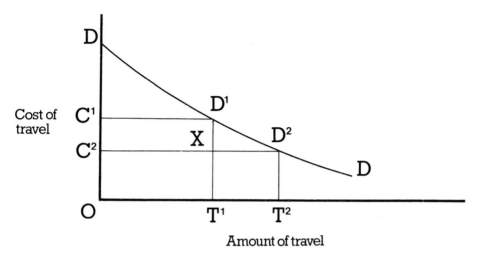

Amount of travel

5
Railways

The world's railways have been almost everywhere in decline over the last two or three decades. The Golden Age of the train is long past. Few railways have been built in recent decades and most systems now run at a loss, in some cases of epic proportions. In developed countries railway networks are being trimmed back, and (in North America) private companies are merging and rationalising their operations.

This might appear a discouraging background against which to review new railway projects. However, it is possible to believe that the tide which has recently moved so decisively in favour of the automobile and road investments may now ebb a little and enable the railway to regain the ground which it has lost.

The crucial factor is, and will remain, the rapid increase in the cost of fuel, which penalises road transport more than rail. In addition, the bad state of many railways means that there will be no shortage of proposals to repair, rehabilitate and re-equip rail systems. Moreover, railways retain an edge when it comes to transporting large volumes of bulky matter over long distances, and hence there will be a continuing flow of railway projects in connection with mineral developments (e.g. iron ore in Brazil, coal in Mozambique).

Distinctive features

Railway systems are best at hauling bulk loads (or large numbers of passengers, such as commuters) over long distances between places with a high payload concentration. Conversely, roads are suited to carrying relatively small unit loads of freight or people over shorter distances to and from locations that are more dispersed and with a smaller concentration of business. It follows that if a transport system is being designed from scratch to haul bulk freight over long distances (e.g. iron ore from an interior mine to the coast) a railway will normally have the advantage.

Railways benefit from economies of scale in the transport of goods and people. The other side of the coin is that starting-up costs tend to be much higher than those of road transport.

These costs reflect the high level of technical and adminstrative complexity in a rail system, and its expensive equipment and infrastructure. (This also means that appraising a railway demands more information and technical advice than does a road.)

Another difference from roads is that railways are managed by large, expensive and often highly centralised administrations. These are responsible not only for the technical efficiency of the whole system but also the sorting and movement of freight, passengers and trains.

One of the major economies of scale is the low unit operating cost arising from economies in the use of fuel. The advantage of railway over road in fuel usage increases according to the size of the load and the distance over which it is carried. This is the main reason why, in this age of expensive oil, we can expect the railway to regain some competitive ground.

The railway is on strongest ground in carrying freight. However, the above remarks apply to some extent when carrying passengers too. The attraction of trains is greatest for passengers travelling a long distance (e.g. between major cities), or where many passengers want to travel shorter distances and frequent services are therefore possible (e.g. commuters to work). Even so, most people travel to and from work by road, and commuting by rail is only common where very high concentrations of commuters are found, namely in very large cities.

The main parts of a railway system

What cannot be emphasised too much is that a railway forms a complex system of facilities, the operations of which are highly interdependent. The weakest link is likely to form the constraint on increasing the capacity of the whole system. By the same token, a change in one part of the system (e.g. an increase in the number of wagons) will throw strain on some other part and so emphasise the weaknesses of the least efficient areas.

The capacity of a railway system to carry passengers and freight depends on four main factors. First, the 'base area' facilities, comprising terminal facilities and marshalling and sorting capacity. Second, the 'line capacity', namely the ability of the permanent way to carry trains. Third, the number and type of locomotives and rolling stock. Fourth, railway management and its workforce.

i. The base area

Let us intercept the circular flow of traffic at a terminal such as the docks. Goods unloaded from the docks are transported by wagon to **sorting sidings** where the wagons are sorted for dispatch to the depot. The **depot** (or goods yard) is responsible for bringing traffic onto the railway line and each part of the depot is responsible for dispatching goods to a particular set of destinations. At the depot goods are sorted into full wagon loads going to certain destinations. Bulk traffic, such as petrol or minerals, may not need sorting at all and can pass through to the main line.

After the wagons have been sorted into full loads they pass to the **marshalling yard** where they are made up into packs to form trains. These trains are then shunted to the **railhead** where departure times to destinations are co-ordinated by a railhead regulating station. The railhead is also the point where incoming full trains from the main line terminate. The trains are shunted to the depots where they are unloaded and the goods sorted and dispatched to terminals.

This process of sorting, loading, marshalling and dispatching of trains is complicated and time-consuming. Shunting can account for up to 40% of engine-hours. The efficiency of the base area is fundamental to the performance of a railway system, and explains why so much stress is put on improving wagon turn round time. It is often in this area that a railway system's biggest capacity constraint lies. Within the base area the capacity of the whole is determined by that part, whether depot, terminal or marshalling yard, with the lowest capacity. Like an army, a railway marches at the speed of the slowest.

Since sorting and marshalling are so costly and time-consuming the greatest economies are obtained moving a heavy volume of bulk traffic to a single destination. The opposite case – shifting small consignments to a great variety of destinations – is not an efficient use of a railway and this is a zone where it is most vulnerable to road competition.

One of the golden rules of railway operation is that the movement of empty or half-full wagons should be minimised since there is no payload. There are high returns to an efficient system of wagon and locomotive distribution.

ii. Line capacity

In progressing from the base area to its destination the train enters a realm where line capacity is the limiting factor. As the name suggests, line capacity measures the maximum number of trains of a specified tonnage that can run over a particular line at a given speed. Line capacity depends on a number of elements, discussed below.

The movement of trains along the track is controlled by a system of signalling known as **block working**. A blockpost is a place, normally a cabin, containing the instruments by which the blockman controls the movement of trains into the next block system. There are two possibilities: under the principle of absolute block working no other train is allowed to enter a section (block) already occupied; permissive block working, on the other hand, allows more than one train to be in the same block section at a time – but this generally only applies to freight trains.

Signalling improvements can increase line capacity by enabling a greater number of trains to safely use the line. This can be readily appreciated by considering the most primitive form of signalling, where the train driver stops at each blockpost to check with the blockman that the next section is clear. The more block sections there are on a line the more trains can safely use it, but at the expense of reduced speed and more stops. This is where signalling improvements can help by obviating the need to stop, improving communication between blockmen, etc.

There is an enormous choice of equipment for signalling and communications, and the standard chosen will depend on the type and number of trains that pass over the line. Passenger trains warrant a higher standard of such equipment than freight.

As anyone who has played with a model railway will know, trains going at different speeds along the same length of line pose problems to the line controllers. The speed of the slowest train on the longest section (block) is the bottleneck on line capacity. A fast train can travel at high speed only if the forward track has been cleared of slower trains (e.g. by moving them into loops). This normally means less freight and fewer passengers carried per day. If it is desired to increase the number of train movements along a stretch of line the options include reducing the length of block sections (and associated signalling improvements) and increasing the speed of the slowest train.

It is not clear whether the **gauge** of the track limits wagon axle loading, but it certainly affects the speed at which trains can travel. The wider the track

40

the faster a train can pass round a corner. Standard gauges vary between countries, but there are three broad categories: narrow gauge ranges from 2 ft to 2 ft 6 in., medium from 1 m to 3 ft 6 in., and broad from 5 ft 3 in. to 5 ft 6 in. (British standard gauge, 4 ft 8½ in., is different again.)

The choice of gauge will depend partly on the need for compatibility with existing gauges and equipment (such as the wheel span of locomotives and wagons) and partly on the type of goods intended to be carried. A wider gauge can permit either greater speeds (important for perishable goods) or heavier loads. The reconciliation of different gauges on interconnecting systems can be made by building a third rail.

Measurements of alignment and gradients are vital in determining the line capacity. The degree of **curvature** of the track affects the speed of the train and the grip of its wheels on the track, both of which can considerably reduce the train's performance and increase the cost of maintaining the track. The degree of **gradient** also makes a lot of difference to the load that can be hauled on a track. A 1-in-50 gradient is tolerable, while a 1-in-25 is very steep.

Line capacity on single-line tracks can be increased by building **loops** which allow approaching trains to pass, or allow a faster train to overtake a slower one. The loops must be long enough to accommodate the longest trains used in the system. The length of loops can limit the length of trains passing along the line, and in India for example this is a major constraint on line capacity. Constructing double tracks is another way of increasing line capacity; this also reduces the risk of head-on collisions.

The discussion so far on line capacity has been based on the assumption of a reasonably busy line. However, there are many railway systems in developing countries that have no more than two or three trains a day in each direction. In such cases the constraint is unlikely to be in line capacity.

There is an alternative way of increasing the carrying capacity of a line, and that is to increase the tonnage that can be carried by a train of a given length. This requires a discussion of the factors governing the **axle loading** of a train. If we leave until later the question of the wagon specifications, an increase in axle loading depends on the state of ballast, sleepers, rails, fishplates and bridges.

The point of **ballast** is to distribute the weight of the train uniformly over the surface of the ground, to hold sleepers in place, to drain water from the track, and to lend some elasticity to the road bed. The minimum depth of ballast under the sleeper is 7–8 in. in Britain; in general the greater the depth of ballast the heavier the loads the train can carry at high speeds.

Sleepers transfer the train's weight from the rail to the ballast. As axle load increases sleepers have to be stronger and/or closer together. They can be made of timber, concrete or steel. The old method of joining rails to the sleeper was to use a 'chair' which gripped the rail and was then bolted to the sleeper. A recent development is to use a **rail track clip**; this is cheaper and easier to fix than the other, and is rapidly becoming the norm.

The character of the **rails** influences the carrying capacity of the line. A stiff rail can economise on the number of sleepers and track labour. The quality of the **fishplates** joining the rails together is also important since these are, literally, the weakest link in the system. The advent of **welded track** has a lot of impetus. This method of production increases the capital cost of the rails, but reduces the cost of maintenance and makes for a smoother run. It does, of course, eliminate the need for fishplates (and their upkeep). Welded track is laid mechanically, which is more expensive and demands more precision than the manual method.

Finally, **bridges** can be the limiting factor in any scheme to increase line capacity. Bridges are expensive to rebuild, widen or strengthen, and can limit the axle loading of locomotives and rolling stock, as well as restrict the number of tracks and the width and height of loads.

iii. Locomotives and rolling stock
It is the locomotives that give a railway 'sex appeal' and attract the schoolboys of all ages. While the enthusiast may harp on a loco's speed and gracefulness the essential design features are more mundane. The axle loading and wheel arrangement (4–6–4, 4–6–2, etc., as every train-spotter knows) determine the tractive power that the loco can exert, and hence its grip on the track. The second feature is its power (in h.p.) and the range of speeds for which it was designed. Thirdly, its trough pull, or draw-bar pull, capacity determines how much a loco can safely pull without its frame buckling.

The four main types of locomotive are steam, diesel, diesel-electric and electric. In recent years there has been large-scale replacement of steam locos by diesel (though there are some countries – e.g. in Southern Africa – where steam locos are being brought out of retirement). We can thus start with a comparison of steam and diesel traction.

Steam locos can burn coal or oil, while the smaller ones can use wood. Coal-burning locos use large quantities of high-grade coal in an uneconomical and dirty manner. Oil-burning steam locos consume a cheaper type of oil compared to diesel. Wood-burning locos are running up against a growing shortage of timber along the line of rail, caused by widespread deforestation. The trend back to steam locos, discussed elsewhere, is towards the oil-burning types in East Africa, and the coal-burning units in Southern Africa. Maintaining steam is relatively straightforward, but a very dirty job. Steam engines increase the costs of maintaining and cleaning buildings, bridges and other structures affected by the corrosive action of steam-laden smoke. Steam locos rupture track more quickly than diesels because of the thrust of the piston on to the rail.

In favour of steam is the capital cost, which is lower than that of diesel or diesel-electric. They are easier to maintain, and some countries have the capacity to make their own replacement parts. Furthermore, the cost of fuel is moving against diesels, especially in countries with their own plentiful coal supplies. There are a lot of steam engines left in the developing world, especially in Asia and Southern Africa. Countries with a serious shortage of foreign exchange, their own coal, and their own workshop repair facilities, are starting to reconsider the wisdom of phasing out their steam locos. (It is, incidentally, worth running a steam loco until the boiler cracks before considering replacement.)

Diesel engines are more efficient in their use of fuel. Moreover, the fuel consumption of a steam engine is related to the number of hours in steam, whereas that of a diesel depends on hours in service. The diesel can be cut off where operations are intermittent, as in shunting. When it comes to maintenance, the diesel needs less but it requires more skill.

Diesel engines come in two main types. The ordinary diesel transmits power mechanically to the wheels via gears. In the **diesel-electric** the diesel engine drives a generator which in turn drives an electric motor. Since there are no gear changes the movement of diesel-electric trains is smoother than that of ordinary diesels. For the same reason there is less damage to couplings and freight and a more economical use of fuel. They can also employ electrically-assisted braking systems.

Diesel-electric locos can be viewed as mobile power generators, whereas **all-electric locos** pick up power from the country's grid. The two kinds of loco have similar efficiency, in the sense of using energy to haul a load. However, the cost of producing the power can vary greatly, and electrification of lines makes most sense where a country has resources to generate bulk power very cheaply. This can offset the initial higher cost of electric locomotives, and the cost of transmitting power along the track (whether by overhead line or electrified rail).

The electric train also has distinctive technical features. It can overload itself by drawing extra electricity from the system for periods up to one hour. This enables it to accelerate quickly from a standing position, which can make a difference to line capacity where there are many stops (e.g. on a commuter line). Electric locos contain far fewer parts than a diesel-electric one. They are also more reliable and need less maintenance than diesels. The loco is lighter, because it contains no engine and can therefore travel faster. However, for the same reason it does not have the same grip on the track as other locos when pulling heavy loads.

In short, the higher initial cost of an electric locomotive can be justified in circumstances where the grid is supplied with cheap bulk power, where the line is busy, where the train has to stop and start a lot, or where the track has steep gradients and many curves. Whether or not electrification spreads in future will depend on the trend in the cost of diesel fuel compared to the other sources of electric power. However, its price will have to increase a lot before fuel costs become a significant factor – at present they rarely account for more than 5% of all operating costs.

Turning to **wagons**, their design has to be a compromise between high capacity, which produces economies of scale, and a more modest size which is more likely to be filled and which does not involve the waste of pulling half-empty trains. Apart from size, a wagon's important design features are its draw-bar pull capacity (i.e. how much tension it can take without buckling) and its axle loading.

Wagons come in many shapes and sizes. The most common is the fixed four-wheel box wagon. There is also a low-sided variant. Closed wagons of different kinds provide better security for goods and protection for perishables. Eight-wheel bogie wagons, which can be either open or closed, are larger and can pass around corners without the risk of derailment. Flat wagons are designed for carrying logs, and more recently containers. Side-unloading, or bottom-unloading, wagons are intended mainly for minerals. Tank wagons, for carrying liquids, are expensive to buy and also to run, since they are designed only to carry one type of product and are thus likely to travel empty in one direction. This may also be true of other specialised wagons, such as refrigerated trucks.

To state the obvious, a wagon is a link in a train. The length of a train is limited by the bar pull capacity of its wagons, which must not buckle from the pull of wagons behind. The strength of the couplings acts as a similar restraint. Increasing axle loads of particular wagons in an attempt to increase the size of unit loads may encounter limits from the size of bar pull capacity.

Brakes form another limit on a train's length and axle load. Many freight trains have no brakes on the wagons, and depend on the brakes of the locomotive and those of the brake van. If such a train is too long or overloaded it may not be able to stop safely without derailing. There are two main types of brake, vacuum and compression (or Westinghouse). The vacuum brake limits the train's length since the vacuum can only be maintained for a certain distance. This is a constraint on the length of Indian trains, for example. On the other hand the compression brake imposes no such limit. Improvements to a train's braking system may enable it to travel faster and thus increase line capacity as well as improving safety.

iv. Management and workforce

Railways are usually managed and run by a central authority. The system is highly interrelated and each part of the system is vulnerable to events in other parts (as commuters, experienced in hearing reasons why their train was late, will testify). Such a structure demands an efficient administration and well trained personnel, especially technicians and engineers. Poor management shows itself in many ways, e.g. padding payrolls with unsuitable people, failure to mobilise stock effectively, neglect of maintenance of stock and permanent way, payment of wages and salaries which are too low to attract competent technicians, etc. In these circumstances management will often ask for more equipment, where the real problems lie deeper. Poor management is probably the major single reason for the decline of the railways in many countries.

Railways need a large workforce comprising a wide range of skilled and unskilled categories. In Pakistan, for instance, the railway is the largest public employer. In developing countries salaries and wages can account for up to 35% of all operating costs. This accentuates the importance of good personnel management, an appropriate level and structure of incomes, and an active training policy.

Unfortunately the size of the railway as an employer often makes it a political milch cow. Governments lean on railway management to employ as many people as possible (usually on political or social criteria) while holding down the level of wages and salaries and compressing salary differentials. Labour unions often find the railway a tempting power base and interact with weak managements to exploit the railway for their sectional purposes. Road transport does not suffer from this exposure and has fewer or different problems. The growing natural advantage of road transport for certain types of goods has been aided by the railway's organisational problems, to produce the transfer of business to roads that we have witnessed over the last few decades.

A specific management task that is often neglected is proper **maintenance** of all parts of the system. This depends on the administrators developing a routine for inspection, maintenance and overhaul. These tasks call for highly skilled technicians – much more so than for roads. Poor maintenance can reflect a shortage of skilled workers, in the sense either of a national dearth or of insufficient numbers presenting themselves at the wage offered. But it can also result from a shortage of cash or foreign exchange. A railway running a financial deficit may be tempted to cut down on its maintenance budget since this can be done without immediate ill effects. But it is not long before the railway pays for its neglect – at compound interest.

Benefits from railway investments

There is no point in stretching the analogy with roads too far, since it should be clear from the above that railway systems are complex and have some unique features. Nevertheless, there are similarities between investing in new track and up-grading a road, on the one hand, and buying new railway wagons and investing in a fleet of lorries, on the other.

For instance, rehabilitating a railway track produces benefits which will be familiar to readers of the last chapter, namely:

  i. Savings from maintaining the old track

 ii. Savings in the operating costs of locos and wagons over the improved track

iii. Savings in time (which passengers would be willing to pay for, and which in the case of goods trains show up in crew wages and possibly fuel). If these are significant enough the system may be able to manage with fewer trains

 iv. Fewer accidents, especially where passengers are involved

  v. Indirect benefits to economic activity in the region served by the railway. Many railways were built ostensibly to open up certain parts of the country.

In many cases a conventional cost–benefit analysis can be done along the above lines. Where this is not possible, the criterion should be that of cost-effectiveness. For instance, it is frequently not possible to do full justice to the impact of a specific improvement on the entire network using cost–benefit analysis. We recently decided that improvement to a railway bridge in Southern Africa could not be warranted purely on the grounds of measurable direct benefits. Some improvements were going to be necessary in due course to keep step with changes affecting the whole system, so the exercise became one of seeking the most cost-effective solution meeting the system's future requirements.

Unlike in the appraisal of road investments, savings in the operating costs of railway 'vehicles' are not normally foremost among the benefits. In railway projects far more stress is put on the effect of the project on line capacity. The reason is that on a railway direct operating costs are less important relative to overall system costs and to the value of the cargo.

The benefits of the main types of railway investments are reviewed below.

Track rehabilitation
The possible benefits of track improvements are:

i. Reduction in track maintenance costs

ii. Decrease of wear and hence of maintenance costs of locomotives and rolling stock

iii. Speed increases, which decrease the staff, locomotives and rolling stock required for a given traffic. It may alternatively increase the capacity of the line, enabling it to haul more goods and passengers

iv. Increased permissible axle loads which result in either hauling more goods and passengers, or hauling the same amount of goods and passengers using less rolling stock

v. Increased safety, which implies reduced loss of life and limb, reduced loss of goods, and fewer repairs to locos and rolling stock.

Signalling
The principal effects of improved signalling are:

i. Staff savings, resulting from the introduction of automation and centralising of signalling. The effect of simply increasing signalling may be to increase the required number of blockmen

ii. Increased safety, which can be quantified as a decrease in accident costs

iii. Increased train speeds, resulting from more rapid signalling actions, or simply increasing the speed at which trains may safely proceed. This increases staff productivity, utilisation of traction and rolling stock, and line capacity

iv. Increased line capacity due to the ability to operate trains closer to each other.

Telecommunications
The benefits of more or better telecommunication equipment may be estimated as follows. First, from records of accidents and accident costs estimate those accidents which could have been avoided by the proposed telecommunication equipment together with the corresponding cost saved. Secondly, examine the records of delays on the railway system in general, and estimate the likely reduction in delays attributable to the new equipment. In a recent report on Sri Lanka one third of total delays on a particular line was attributed to poor telecommunication equipment.

One can also estimate the induced benefits due to the improved telecommunication system, that is, how much of the increased traffic over a particular line can be attributed to the improvement in the telecommunication equipment.

Additional locomotives and rolling stock
Benefits arise from increasing the system's capacity to haul loads. There may also be savings in fuel and other operating costs. Where the fleet is being increased, there may well be an increase in associated costs, as in the following:

i. Increased cost of track maintenance and renewal

ii. Increased cost of signals and means of control

iii. Additional handling and marshalling facilities

iv. Additional staff to operate, load, and control locomotives and wagons

v. Time delays due to increased congestion on track

vi. Increased maintenance facilities for rolling stock and locomotives.

Containerisation
Containerisation has become very fashionable on railway systems as a quick way of transporting full loads. While the benefits can be substantial, one must ensure that the system can cope with containers:

i. There must be the right type of flat wagons with sufficient axle loading and draw-bar pull capacity

ii. The track should be capable of carrying such loads

iii. Flat wagons should be able to carry these containers through all the tunnels

iv. The distance between the rails should be sufficient to allow two trains carrying containers to pass

v. The existing stock of locomotives should be adequate to haul these containers

vi. The railway system should have the right sort of handling and marshalling facilities in the base and terminal areas to handle containers.

Improvements of repair and maintenance facilities
The benefits of such an investment will be to reduce the number of 'defectives' (both locomotives and rolling stock). It may either be regarded as equivalent to investment in second-hand locomotives and rolling stock equivalent to the reduced number of defectives at any one time, or may be calculated from the 'value' of increased transport of goods and passengers resulting from an improved supply of power and rolling stock. Investment in maintenance machinery may lead to reduced staff costs and reduced maintenance costs as well as improving the quality of maintenance generally.

Investment in yards, depots and general marshalling and handling facilities
Such investments may improve the turn-around times of wagons, resulting in time savings and increased through-flow of cargo. Handling costs may also be reduced together with damage to the cargo handled. However, it is necessary to emphasise the relationship between such investments and the existing condition of the railway. Investments in yards and depots may require not only additional staff in order to achieve the objective of handling and dispatching more goods per day, but also additional rolling stock, locomotives, and telecommunication equipment. The increased amount of goods being hauled over the track may also require track improvements, higher maintenance costs, improved signalling, etc.

Electrification

The largest potential benefit comes from fuel savings, provided cheap bulk electric power is available. For countries without sophisticated repair workshops, and short of skilled mechanics, another important benefit from electric traction is the saving on maintenance.

Acceleration is also better, which is an important feature on passenger commuter services or on track with many bends and gradients.

On the cost side, electric locomotives are more expensive than others. The electrification of the track is also a heavy outlay, and may necessitate changes to bridges and tunnels as well.

Important practical points

1 The theoretical benefits from the project will be thwarted if the system is not operated to its full potential because of financial, managerial or other weaknesses. It is unrealistic to postulate 'optimal' performance when estimating benefits. A railway is a complicated system and the bottlenecks and constraints that exist at large will come to bear on changes made in one part of it.

2 Railway management often orders new equipment, especially rolling stock and locomotives, as the easiest way of improving performance, when the real bottlenecks lie in other directions that are potentially harder to remove. It follows that in many instances the need for expensive new equipment could be avoided by (admittedly painful) adjustments to operating practices and policies.

3 Many, perhaps most, railways are in a parlous financial state and many of their weaknesses can be traced to poor cash flow, inadequate investment finance, insufficient allowance for depreciation, poor access to foreign exchange, etc. These in turn can be related to inadequate tariffs, kept down for short-term political and social reasons, the need to maintain uneconomic services and the inability to trim an excessively large labour force.

4 In extreme cases, the above problems interact, producing low morale on the part of management and labour (not to mention travellers). This can alienate the railway staff from the purposes of the project. In some poor countries it can lead to intentional or accidental damage through theft and misappropriation of railway materials.

5 The proliferation of different types of stock and equipment greatly adds to the problem of operating a system. This is a common result of an indiscriminate uptake of aid and subsidised credit from different supplying countries.

Checklist of main questions

1 Summary of project
Type (track rehabilitation, new line, rolling stock, etc.).
What alternatives have been investigated?
Has there been a feasibility study? If so, give brief details.
What will be the sources of finance for the proposal?

2 Features of national railway system
Length and geographical coverage of track. Number of separate systems.
Quantity and condition of rolling stock, locomotives.
Sources of motive power.
Volume of annual traffic of freight and passengers.

Size of managerial and labour force, in main grades.

Organisation: function and constitution of railway authority.

Finances (statutory obligations, sources of recurrent and investment finance, operating results, cash flow, subsidies).

3 Performance indicators

(There are a large number of possible indicators, and different railway systems publish different data. However, the end-product of the various individual pieces of data should be: average availability of locomotives and rolling stock; productivity of available locomotives and wagons in miles or kilometres; average turn-around time; average wagon load; number of traffic units per employee; average speed of trains; etc.)

4 Traffic

i. Freight: recent trends in tonnage handled, main individual items, average length of haul, receipts.

ii. Passengers: numbers carried, average length of journey, receipts.

What forecasts have been made of future traffic in these two categories? Are they based on simple extrapolation, or more sophisticated modelling of the principal factors generating traffic? What assumptions are made about fares and charges? Do they allow for competition from other transport modes?

5 Technical features

Condition of the various components of the system.

Main physical parameters (gauges, length of single or double track, load-bearing capacity, gradients and curvature, type of locomotives and rolling stock, etc.).

Identification of main bottlenecks and constraints on system.

Features of the proposed investments.

Implications of the investment for other parts of the system, and for recurrent maintenance.

6 Costs associated with project

Capital and recurrent, by major type.

Foreign exchange and local outlays.

7 Benefits claimed

(The precise type of benefit claimed will depend on the kind of investment, whether a new line or the rehabilitation of an old one, the addition of locomotives or rolling stock, the repair of a major installation like a bridge, improvement in signalling, purchase of breakdown cranes, etc.)

Additional revenue from extra traffic.

Savings in operating costs of existing traffic.

Savings in maintenance.

Reduction of accidents.

Who will be the major beneficiaries? Will cost savings be conveyed to the users? Alternatively, will the extra costs of an improved service be recovered from users?

What are the economic and financial rates of return on the project?

8 Implementation plan

Have all the suppliers and contractors been selected and engaged? Has a critical path been drawn up for the work?

Will there be a major disruption to existing operations while work proceeds? Has this been costed and allowed for?

9 Managerial and labour aspects
Is management capable of efficiently operating the resulting system?
Are there sufficient capable and motivated managers?
Is the labour force going to be supportive? Has it been consulted? Are there going to be redundancies?
Is there a satisfactory career structure, salary scale, training programme?
Are arrangements for maintenance satisfactory?

Further reading

Most of the important writing on railways has appeared in unpublished manuals and reports, especially those of the World Bank. The ODA has also produced a number of project appraisals and evaluations, as well as financing some important consultants' reports. The single reference below is one of the few that will be readily accessible. This does not mean that ODA has a monopoly of work in this sector!

M. G. Foster and J. W. Knowles, *Railways Sector Appraisal Manual*, Overseas Development Administration, London, 1982.

6
Ports

Like an airport or a railway station, a seaport is a point where different transport modes intersect, and transfer from one to another takes place. Thus the degree of need for port services depends on trends and events in other transport modes like roads and railways as well as shipping. The international nature of a port also means that decisions about its capacity and shape are influenced by distant events – trends in world trade, decisions by foreign shipbuilders and shippers, etc. By the same token, an improvement in port services can benefit the foreigner (shipper, exporter) as much as the citizen.

Recent trends

In recent years ports have had to accommodate far-reaching technological changes. The main trend has been towards specialisation – the use of ships specially designed to handle certain types of cargo. In the 1940s and 1950s the movement began with oil, coal and grain, and has since continued with semi-bulk and general cargoes. The main types of cargo are the following: liquid bulks (mostly oil and oil products); major dry bulks (filling a whole ship); minor dry bulks (part of a ship load); unitised cargo (containers, wheeled cargo and cargo on specialised pallets); other dry cargo (traditional general cargo); and passengers and live animals (normally capable of getting on and off the ship on their own).

Specialisation exemplifies, and responds to, the increasing capital-intensity of cargo movement. The rise in labour costs that make up much of the cost of traditional methods has prompted the growing use of bigger ships and high-capacity handling methods. The growth in size has mainly affected tankers. Very large crude carriers of 250,000 d.w.t. are increasingly common, though at the opposite pole product carriers, tankers of 20,000 d.w.t., are holding their own. Conventional general cargo ships have changed much less. The new generation is not much larger than the classic Liberty ships of 11,000 d.w.t., though some general cargo vessels have been built up to 24,000 d.w.t.

The larger size and greater sophistication of ships represents a sizeable capital investment and explains the trend towards reducing the time spent by ships in port, and achieving higher handling rates for cargo. A ship, like a modern passenger aircraft, only earns money when it is moving. Large tankers typically spend twenty-four hours or less in port, and their cargo can be moved on and off at a rate of 10% of their deadweight per hour. Iron ore carriers can load at a rate of 3,000–10,000 tons per hour, and discharge at rather less. Handling rates for conventional general cargo vessels vary enormously, but usually within a range of 200–1,500 tons per day.

The pace in these technological changes is being set by the economic circumstances of the developed countries. The smaller and poorer developing countries have to adapt their port facilities to the type of ship being sent, or risk becoming backwaters off the main shipping lanes. One alternative to tooling up to cope with the largest container ships is to plan on being a feeder port linked to a larger port that is directly served by the container ships.

The growth of national shipping lines has provided developing countries with some mitigation of these trends. Such publicly-owned lines help to perpetuate the traditional types of shipping and, at one remove, the labour-intensive handling methods that are still feasible in many developing countries.

Benefits

Ports are part of a larger transport system. If as a result of some improvement in the port goods are able to move through more quickly, the transport system as a whole could benefit from more rapid throughput and lower costs. Likewise, if port improvements throw greater strain on bottlenecks elsewhere their benefits can be greatly reduced. This argues for a broad view, placing ports within the context of the whole transport and distribution system. This total perspective is not easy to achieve in practice. What it does imply is that the wider repercussions of port improvements are considered and that all the major constraints on the movement of goods terminating in ports are examined. Furthermore, improvements at one port can affect the movement of traffic through other ports in the country or those of neighbouring states.

The main benefits are normally derived from savings of time and reductions of costs. An improvement that reduces the time that ships spend either waiting to enter the port or alongside the wharf can save the shipowner large sums on wages and other operating expenses. Average ship turn-around time is a crucial factor in fixing freight charges: if turn-around time becomes excessive for a particular port the shipper is apt to levy surcharges, which are frequently passed on to the consumer. Other possible benefits include reduced breakage, losses of cargo, and pilfering or theft. These costs are especially great where cargo is transferred from the ship to the shore by means of lighters. Over the past decade or so a number of Caribbean islands have moved over from lighterage to deep-water berths. The new system is less picturesque but more beneficial to the users.

A congested port can be a major drag on the economy of a country. Delay in releasing exports can cost vital foreign exchange. Traders are penalised by the cost of holding stocks and demurrage charges on railway wagons unable to unload. Importers and distributors are unable to get their hands on essential consumer and investment goods in time. Development projects suffer when capital goods are held up in the docks. These points are vividly exemplified by recent events in Port Sudan and Dar es Salaam, and their effects on the economic life of the Sudan on the one hand, and on Tanzania, Zambia, Rwanda, Burundi and Eastern Zaïre on the other.

As in all projects, it is important to specify the 'do nothing' case accurately and honestly in order to identify the true benefits of a port project. The waiting time of a large ship can feature enormously in assessing benefits, and can be held to justify quite expensive improvements in berthage, etc. However, in practice ingenuity is used where there are port bottlenecks, and such expedients as temporary lighterage, the use of land transport from nearby ports, etc. are resorted to. This means that the cost of growing congestion should be treated with an eye to the alternatives.

Because ports have an international dimension, the benefits from improvement (and the costs of the 'do nothing' case) are split between foreign and domestic parties. The costs of ships waiting fall on shipping companies in the first instance. If waiting or handling costs become excessive the shipper may levy a surcharge, which could be wholly or partly passed on to the consumer. By the same logic, reduced congestion generates benefits which can accrue to either party or both. The port authority and shippers are also in a potential bargaining position over the level of port fees; improvements that lead to a quicker turn-around time create a consumer's surplus for the shipper which the port authority can attempt to tap by raising port fees.

The precise way in which benefits and costs are shared obviously depends on the bargaining strengths of the various parties. This is partly a matter of relative sizes, as when an important shipping line confronts a small island port. But the underlying factor is the economic concept of the relative elasticities of supply and demand in the investing country compared to the rest of the world. For example, if the investing country's exports are in highly elastic supply and its share of world trade in the exported commodity is small, the total benefit could exceed the initial transport savings as foreign buyers take advantage of the lower transport costs to increase their imports from the investing country.

In the export of iron ore, for example, the willingness of a shipping line to keep ships waiting, or pay higher port fees for an improvement, depends on the strength of demand for shipping iron ore compared with the convenience and cost of continuing to operate from the port in question. This depends in turn on the state of world demand for iron ore and the derived demand for shipping relative to vessels available.

Likewise for imports. Although port charges are not sizeable in relation to the final cost of most products, consumers might be in a position to resist higher prices from fees passed on from shippers (by surcharges) and port authorities (by higher fees). In other cases, perhaps the majority, higher port costs could be lost in a general inflation and consumer boom.

The assumption that transport savings are passed on is more reasonable in the long run than in the short. Even then, given the many other factors operating simultaneously which determine current freight charges (including inflation), a reduction in freight charges of the sort described above may only mean that freight rates will increase by less than they otherwise would. Further, freight reductions are sometimes averaged out over a route so that even if transport savings are fully passed on the investing country might gain only a portion of the benefits its investments had made possible.

It is worth repeating that potential benefits from improvements in specific areas of a port can be denied to the ultimate users if they are frustrated by bottlenecks further on in the system. If a big new container crane is installed that can handle 100,000 boxes per year this is wasteful if the area behind can only cope with half that number. It follows that one must not automatically assume that users would be prepared to pay higher port fees to reflect the savings they can expect from 'improvements' – if the improvements never materialise. Port users – shippers, railways, truckers, etc. – should be consulted at the earliest stage when planning improvements and assessing the scope for financing the investments by increased charges.

Forecasting demand

So often, forecasts are made by taking a trend from, say, the last ten years and extrapolating it into the future. This is always dangerous if applied uncritically, but never more so than in planning for port improvements. The overall growth of tonnage is less important to the planner than the type and size of ship likely to use the port and the kind of cargo it will carry. To illustrate the hazards of forecasting, imagine trying to predict the rapid technical changes that have occurred over the last two decades.

Ports are built to last, yet the decision to invest has to be taken with only a hazy idea about the expected amount and type of shipping. In principle, the appropriate investment policy in these circumstances is to proceed with a long-term plan of improvement in phases. This would be continually adjusted to allow for changing patterns of demand. Forecasting should ideally be a continuous process, with updated information being fed in on such items as:

  i. total tonnage handled, broken down by type (in particular liquid, bulk, and general)
 ii. average ship turn-around time
iii. average tonnage loaded and discharged
 iv. volume of tonnage by type of loading
  v. number of ships with their own cranes or ramps
 vi. average and maximum lengths and draughts of ships.

The origin and destination of cargo may also provide useful data to planners, though this may be more difficult to come by.

Planning port improvements

It is useful to view a port as a series of conveyor belts. Goods are continually flowing through it and the port's overall capacity is limited by that of the slowest conveyor belt. A bottleneck in one part of the port can very soon bring the rest to a standstill. Thus it is important to balance the capacity of the system's various components, and to appreciate that if the capacity of one isolated part (e.g. the wharf) is increased while the real constraint lies elsewhere (e.g. the railway's ability to take goods away) the original investment will be frustrated.

The need for port improvement normally shows up in the form of unacceptable congestion or queues of ships waiting in the roads. The facile solution is to invest in physical improvements like the construction of more berths or the installation of cranes. It is important to head off such premature 'technical' solutions by taking a broad view of the causes of the port's problems, which may well lie in inadequate facilities but equally might be traced to unsuitable tariffs or dock labour payment practices. The solutions could be sought in changes in policies as much as by altering facilities, e.g. by agreeing different schedules for shipping lines. Changing policies or operating practices are often more difficult and invidious than building more facilities, but in the long run can be more effective.

Simulation is a common tool for planning ports. A model is set up showing the demands on berth space, storage, etc., from certain assumptions about the number of ships calling, the average waiting time, and the periodicity of their calls. The variety of events can be imitated and manipulated on a computer program. However, the predictions of these often complex programs are only as good as the quality and reliability of the data they use, and sophistication can mask a weak data base and genuine uncertainty about future events. (If computerised modelling is justified, the World Bank's Central Projects Department can supply a well-documented computer program.)

Planning physical improvements is pointless without an assessment of the ability of the port authority to manage, or cope with, the changes. This is especially true where the changes require closer control in order to maximise their impact. It is often tempting to recommend more highly mechanised facilities. But if they require radical changes in management and the alteration of hallowed labour practices such changes will put increased demands on management and risk being unsuccessful. Rather than plan improvements on the assumption of adequate management, still less 'optimal' management, it may be prudent to recognise the inadequacy of management as a fixed factor and plan improvements around this.

This is not to condone low productivity. The question of the 'appropriate' level of productivity is relevant to port planning when thinking about cost-effective ways of meeting projected demand. Clearly, if productivity doubles, then only half as many berths, forklift trucks, warehouses, etc. will be required. The experience of ports in similar countries can be used to establish a probable particular level of productivity. This can be a useful comparative yardstick, and in particular can be used to check whether productivity assumptions are too optimistic. Equipment manufacturers tend towards optimistic assumptions about the productivity of their equipment in use, for instance by assuming 'best practice' operation. The introduction of new equipment may even reduce productivity during the transitional period because of teething troubles on the side of management or labour.

Nevertheless, productivity is taken seriously as a planning tool. There are various ways of measuring it, the most common being to relate throughput to either labour or equipment, though financial measures can also be applied. One measure is the quantity of tons of cargo moved per gang of workers. Another concept is the number of tons per crane. A rather different measure is the number of gangs of workers used per hatch or per ship.

These measures are all concerned with what goes on at the waterfront, whereas the performance of a port depends on how quickly and efficiently goods can be handled and moved off the wharves, through the warehouses and onto inland transport.

The level of productivity should not be treated as immutable within existing arrangements and the port's endowment of equipment, etc. It is a common error to take forecasts of future queues too seriously. Productivity can be changed by port management if the pressures are great enough. For instance, the time spent ashore by the crew can be reduced, or ships can be forbidden to take up berth space if they are waiting for repairs.

Investment proposals
Port investments tend to fall into one of four categories:

i. Improved access

Widening and deepening of navigational channels can permit either more traffic or vessels with a deeper draught. Because of the shape of vessels and the way buoyancy operates, deepening the channel by a few metres can have dramatic effects on the size and capacity of ships able to enter the port. Recent discussions about dredging the entrance to the port of Beira (Mozambique) assumed that lowering the sand bar by a few metres would permit access by ships of 25,000 tons, compared to the current limit of 5,000 tons. The same multiplication is also evident in the various plans for enlarging the Suez Canal. The benefits from such work will show up in reduced delays on the part of larger carriers, or access by larger ships, and in either event a tendency to reduce freight costs.

Tug boats may be justified, depending on the type of channel, currents, climatic conditions and traffic. However, tugs incur a considerable capital and operating cost, and are only warranted where sizeable reduction in damage and safety risk is likely.

Navigational aids such as buoys, beacons and lighthouses will enable more frequent use to be made of channels at night or in poor weather at less risk. The need for these investments will depend on the complexity of the port, the configuration of its channels, its currents and its climate. Radar control will become increasingly necessary as traffic increases and the value of ships rises. Skilled maintenance is required if these facilities are to produce their full benefits.

Breakwaters provide shelter from the elements, thus permitting the faster movement of cargoes. The basic technical choice is between the vertical and trapezoidal types and the decision depends on a knowledge of local conditions. The justification for any sort of breakwater rests on data about the frequency, type, and severity of storms, the type of shipping operation and its seasonal frequency.

ii. Increased berthing facilities

The provision of more berthing capacity by increasing the length and draught of quays, wharves or jetties is related to expected demand, but not in any very simple way. It is not sufficient to merely project total expected tonnage calling at the port; some indication is necessary of the size of ships likely to call, the periodicity of their arrivals, and their average length of stay. The worst prospect for port planners is of a given tonnage arriving in a few large ships all bunched together. Capacity would need to be created which would have a low year-round utilisation.

Planning techniques are available, using elements of queueing theory and simulation based on random numbers, to convert data on shipping sizes, arrivals and loading/unloading times into the demand for berth space. The future operations of the port are simulated on a computer. If ship arrivals are not negotiable or predictable from a shipping schedule they can be represented using Monte Carlo random number analysis. Average, or maximum acceptable, waiting and loading/unloading periods are fed in to produce the demand for peak required berth space.

The answers thrown up by the simulation should not be used in a mechanical fashion. If the model shows unacceptable queues building up at certain times there may be a way of managing the traffic stopping short of building an expensive new berth, e.g. the use of lighters, double-shift working. Also queues can be caused by factors other than the lack of berth space.

iii. Improved cargo handling
There are few ports that can afford to neglect modern handling equipment. Labour-intensive methods of handling have their attractions in terms of maintaining employment, as well as being picturesque, but require discipline and management if loading and unloading are to be done at a speed which avoids port surcharges by shippers. A degree of mechanisation is normally essential.

However, there is a depressing tendency of ports, especially in developing countries, to order excessive amounts of equipment. A surprising number of port managers seek solace in fifty more forklift trucks when their real problems lie elsewhere. Everywhere in Third World ports fleets of idle equipment testify to over-ordering, and the absence of the managerial, labour or financial resources to use or maintain the hardware. Whenever a proposal for equipment is being examined, care should be taken to check that a special central workshop will exist, manned by qualified workers and with stocks of spares.

iv. Land transmission
This category includes storage for loaded and unloaded cargo and the inland transport of goods. Storage and transport can pose problems that are more intractable than those of waterfront operations, and often constitute the real bottlenecks to throughput. Storage and transport are clearly related; inadequate storage of the proper kind can add to congestion and hamper efficient transport, while poor onward transport can lead to an excessive amount of goods in storage. Either way, the flow of merchandise on to and off the quays is held up.

Sometimes the culprit is the delay caused by bureaucratic procedures involved in clearing imports and exports, which can keep goods lying around for months exposed to damage, theft and deterioration. At other times inland transporters may keep goods in warehouses at the port as a deliberate means of passing the trouble and cost of holding goods on to the port authorities. The guilt could equally well lie on the other side, as when inadequate port storage and the slow movement of goods keep cargo tied up in railway wagons, thus immobilising them.

It follows that a careful analysis needs to be made of the reasons for delays and congestion and the real prospects for overcoming these constraints. Some ports may occupy cramped sites, with inadequate hinterland available for increased storage and transport, and in such cases relocation may be the only feasible long-term solution (e.g. Port Sudan is to be superseded by Port Suakin and Karachi eventually by Port Qasim). Where an increase in container traffic is projected plenty of storage space is required, though it does not have to be immediately adjacent to the port, and there may be labour cost advantages in locating it away from the port area.

Organisational aspects
Efficient organisation and management are crucial to the successful operation of a port but beyond that truism it is impossible to be categorical about the best arrangements for every situation. Ports are so important for any country that it is rare to find them left to the unfettered actions of private enterprise.

On the other hand management needs a high degree of operating flexibility and this makes it undesirable to try and run ports as government departments. There are a variety of organisational types between these extremes. This variety appears not only in comparing ports in different countries but also in ports within the same country (compare the variety of authorities in Britain for instance).

What the various types have in common is a Port Authority with considerable day-to-day autonomy, but normally working within guidelines or statutory requirements laid down by the government. Even where a Port Authority exists with clearly defined functions the area within which its writ operates may be divided with other agencies. For instance, the government may be responsible for the access of ships to the port.

As a general principle, planning and regulation ought to be separated from management. Thus one approach would be to vest a central body with the powers of planning, investment and tariff regulation. The justification of such powers would be that a port is a monopoly and the general public has an interest in the way it operates. Management, however, should be performed at a lower level, preferably by statutory port authorities. The point here is that management should remain in the hands of a group that can build up experience and whose authority is not continually being undermined by outside interference.

Important practical points

1 Before planning completely new installations the scope for raising the productivity of existing ones should be fully explored. Developments in Karachi since the start of the new Port Qasim show the extent to which a traditional port can raise its operating performance faced with competition from a new potential rival.

2 Before ordering large amounts of new equipment, port authorities should be sure that this is not a palliative masking deeper problems which are causing low productivity. In a badly managed port improvements in sector A could easily be frustrated by a bottleneck in B.

3 Although the costs of improvement fall on the port authority, most of the benefits accrue in the first instance to port users, and in particular visiting vessels (which often belong to foreign lines). This underlines the importance of cost recovery from the beneficiaries. The port authority also has the choice of keeping ships waiting (if this is only going to be an occasional event) rather than make expensive investments in new wharves that are not going to be fully used.

4 The most likely scenario is that new installations will have to be managed and operated by much the same team of managers and workers. The issue of whether they can really handle the changes is thus central. If doubts persist, it may be more sensible to plan any changes around the existing capability of management and labour force, even if this means the lowering of sights.

5 Port installations have a long life and a long planning period is necessary. This makes realistic traffic forecasts vital. The power of compound interest is such that a few percentage points on a growth rate, sustained for fifteen

years or so, can lead to facilities that are either grossly excessive or inadequate. In projecting the growth in the volume of trade it is unwise to crib uncritically from development plans, which are often exercises in rhetoric. It is equally important to identify the likely types of cargo and ship sizes. Data can be fed into a simple model to predict likely berthing needs.

6 Relocating ports, as opposed to making improvements to existing ones, implies an alteration in the balance of political and economic power which can evoke intense opposition from vested interests. The patronage and revenues that go with a port are highly prized by politicians.

7 It is essential to fully consult all port users, and not just those making all the noise, before finalising plans.

Checklist of main questions

1 Background

i. The national ports system
Number and location of main ports.
Volume and trend in national maritime trade.
Principal imports and exports.
Constitution, organisation, regulation and management structure.

ii. The port in question
Hinterland.
Organisation and finances.
Main physical features; structures; equipment; layout.
Staff, management, labour force.
What are the main problems? Where are the bottlenecks?
Is there evidence of congestion? Are the shipping lines operating surcharges?
Are its landward links satisfactory (e.g. storage, transport)?
Productivity indicators – handling rates, throughput per man, etc.

2 The project

iii. Summary of project
Type: improved access; enlarged berthing; better cargo handling; improved
  storage; layout and transport.
What reasons have been given for the investment?
Which parties have taken the initiative?
What alternatives have been considered and explored?

iv. Demand
Current volume and composition of cargo, main items.
Number of ships in various size categories. Average length of stay.
Forecast of future requirements. What is it based on? Is it sheer extrapolation
  from the past? Have special factors been operating? Does it assume diversion
  from other ports?
Has there been a simulation of ship arrivals and departures to guide investment
  in wharf space and other facilities?
What assumptions are made about tariffs? What are the level and structure
  of current tariffs, and when were they last adjusted?

v. Technical aspects
Geographical and geological features of land, shoreline, and seabed. Prevailing
  and maximum winds. Tidal range.
What are the results of site investigations? Have there been test borings?

Details of proposed new or altered structures, e.g. wharves.

Dredging requirements, both initially and periodically.

Adjustments necessary elsewhere in the port to accommodate the changes being made.

vi. Costs

Capital costs: land; dredging; structures; buildings; equipment. How much in foreign exchange? How is it being financed?

Recurrent costs: materials, fuel, labour, dredging, etc.

On what parties do the costs fall?

vii. Benefits

Main types of benefit: time savings; cost reductions; reduced losses; quicker throughput.

Who do the benefits accrue to?

How is it proposed to recover them? What will be the financial benefits?

What are the expected economic, and financial, rates of return?

viii. Implementation

Which organisations will perform the work? What is their track record? Do their contracts contain performance incentives?

Is there a schedule of implementation, with a critical path?

Will there be disruption to normal port operations during implementation, and if so how will it be coped with?

ix. Organisation, management and labour

Will radical changes be required in the way the port operates?

Are labour problems anticipated? Will there be redundancies?

Will a new port managerial structure be required?

Further reading

Port Development. A Handbook for Planners in Developing Countries, UNCTAD TD/B/C/175, United Nations, 1978. (An excellent comprehensive guide to port planning.)

R. Oram and C. Baker, *The Efficient Port*, Pergamon Press, 1971. (A useful practical guide to port planning.)

Jagjit Singh, *Operations Research*, Pelican Books, 1971. (For an introduction to queueing theory and Monte Carlo simulation.)

E. Bennathan and A. A. Walters, *Port Pricing and Industrial Policy for Developing Countries*, Oxford University Press, New York, 1979.

7
Airports

Some of the issues that arise in choosing and appraising airport projects resemble those already discussed in the context of seaports. There is the choice between installing infrastructure capable of handling all types of aircraft (ships) arriving at inconvenient times, or of negotiating for the rescheduling of arrival times and/or accepting visits from smaller aircraft (ships). Again, the question of the division of benefits – and sharing of costs – between national citizens and foreign airlines (shipping lines) arises in an acute form. But there are important differences. In airport planning the safety factor is paramount and it is not easy to incorporate this factor into cost–benefit analyses.

Of all items of economic infrastructure, airports are perhaps most subject to 'political' or prestige influences. This is hardly surprising, since the airport is the preferred gate of entry and exit for VIPs, and first impressions or parting glimpses weigh heavily. Hence many airports are unexpectedly smart and sophisticated. Fears may be expressed that, unless a new airport is built, or improvements carried out, airlines will not continue using the airport and the country will be condemned to second-class status in air circles. Both the political and the prestige arguments can be valid up to a point, but the frequency with which these arguments are deployed is striking, and extravagant proposals are the bread and butter of airport planners.

Benefits

If improvements to airports are made, users should be prepared to pay more in fees and charges. If investments make possible a greater throughput of traffic, the revenue to the airport authority will go up. However, such revenue should not be confused with *real* benefits from airport investments, still less added to them, since charges are simply a way of capturing and recovering part of the real benefits which users enjoy. Increases in revenue certainly have a place in the decision, but the best place to deal with them is in the financial appraisal, otherwise there is the risk of double-counting.

The real benefits are of several possible kinds:

i. *An increase in the capacity of the airport* to handle passengers and freight. This is analogous to investment in a factory to enable it to produce a higher level of output. The beneficiaries are all those people and air freighters who are enabled to use the airport. Apart from allowing a larger number of planes, passengers and parcels, the investment might also permit larger aircraft to use the airport. This enables airline operators to tap economies of scale, which can be passed on to travellers by lower fares and to freighters by lower tariffs.

ii. *Improved convenience, costs and comfort* of existing traffic. A quicker turn-around time for aircraft provides the most tangible gain in the form of savings on aircraft overheads and crew time. If it also reduces time spent in the air, circling or 'stacking', there will also be savings in fuel. At

61

a less tangible level, improvements to the standard of service which mean greater convenience for airline operators and more comfort for passengers confer benefits which might, if significant, form the basis of increased fees or passenger taxes. At the margin, they might also make the difference between an airline or charterer using the airport or not. But in the last resort it is difficult to put a value on the benefits, clear enough to passengers, from having a pleasant terminal with enough seats, or having a quick and efficient system for delivering luggage. Time savings are more tangible.

iii. *Improved safety* is a special case of ii. All transport systems have to concern themselves with the safety of their passengers and crews, not to mention that of third parties, but in the case of air transport the safety factor has the status of a holy cow. Many airport improvements are justified with reference to 'improved safety', some with better reason than others. The fact that lives are at stake does not mean that each and every citation of the 'safety argument' should be accepted uncritically, since some are valid and others are not.

We might linger over two of the above benefits which are more elusive and controversial than the others, namely time savings and safety. There is no argument over **time savings** accruing to aircraft and crew members which arise as cash savings to the airlines. An aircraft is a costly investment and airline operators like to maximise its time in the air carrying payload. Delays on the ground due to inefficient handling and servicing can upset schedules and waste crew time. Inefficient handling in the air can waste both time and fuel while aircraft wait to land. The elimination of these difficulties means that the massive overhead represented by the cost of the aircraft can be spread over a greater number of trips, thus increasing profit.

Time savings for passengers cannot be evaluated financially in the same way. The conventional belief is that air travellers are high-income passengers who place a high value on minimising the time spent on their journey. This is probably true only of a minority of air travellers in these days of cut-price fares, package tours, and the international migration of workers. There are certainly some routes, such as short-haul services between European cities, or between North American cities, that are largely patronised by business travellers and on which significant time savings are highly valued by passengers. But, as in the case of road investments, such time savings have to be predictable, be large enough to be significant, and occur during business rather than leisure hours (unless employees are compensated for travelling in their own time).

In principle, the only time savings that should be counted are those for which travellers would be prepared to pay extra. This is a severe test, since most flights are made up of a mixture of people flying for different motives, only a minority of them valuing time savings sufficiently to be willing to pay more. Moreover, fares on most scheduled flights are still governed by international agreements, and the level of fares bears no close relation to direct costs, distances, or duration on any particular route. Thus it is difficult to reflect time savings in higher fares.

It is, however, perfectly feasible for airport authorities to try and recover the cost of investment by means of higher fees charged to airlines using them.

Safety is a factor that is sometimes deployed in the hope that it will end all argument. Opponents of a scheme that is put forward for 'safety' reasons can be portrayed as callous individuals who put money before lives. They may well be, but they are also entitled to point out that many investments put forward for 'safety' reasons have as their main objective the saving of airlines' time!

By any standards, air travel is very safe. In the last few years an average of fewer than 1,000 people per year have been killed out of a total number of 600 million passengers on scheduled routes. Over the last two decades the annual average number of crashes involving fatalities has been 20 to 30. This impressive safety record could not have been achieved without heavy investment in sophisticated equipment to guide and control aircraft movements in the crowded airlanes of the developed world, where it is not practical to rely on purely visual methods at high closing speeds. However, such equipment may not be necessary in circumstances of much lower traffic density, good and predictable visibility, and an amenable site. Many developing countries have one or other of these advantages.

All airlines have standard operating procedures which, if followed, obviate the need for some types of equipment. To take one example, if an airport does not have night landing facilities aircraft are not allowed to approach it unless they have enough time and fuel to return to an airport that has. Thus, investment in night landing facilities is purely an economic proposition, permitting airports to operate round the clock and airline companies to make landings at more convenient times. There are no safety benefits as such.

Our argument is simply that some claims for safety are valid, while others are invalid and merely cloak economic factors. Where there are clear and compelling arguments for an investment on safety grounds this is reason enough, and does not need to be dressed up in spurious reasoning based on the 'economic value of lives saved'. It is not recommended that this last criterion be employed.

In the first place, it is even more difficult for airport investments than for roads to predict how a given improvement will result in fewer deaths, or injuries. Air accidents are very much rarer than road accidents and therefore the statistical basis does not exist for predicting accidents based on the observed historical association between circumstances and events. An investment *might* prevent an accident, which *might* have involved deaths, which *might* have occurred next year or in thirty years' time. How many deaths, or injuries, is difficult to predict. This is impossibly shaky data to fit into the usual cost–benefit analysis, even without introducing the second major difficulty, that of valuing lives saved or injuries prevented. This takes us into deep water, both philosophical and economic, and is best avoided.

Benefits discussed so far are direct, meaning they accrue at once to the users of an airport, whether or not they can be expressed in monetary form. They may give rise to further benefits if new activity is engendered that was not previously possible or profitable. These benefits might be labelled 'induced', or 'indirect' or 'downstream'. For example, an airport investment might lead to a profitable trade in airfreighted spring vegetables, the development of a thriving international conference business, more frequent business visits, or the growth of tourism. It is difficult to ascribe the whole of the value-added from this extra activity to the airport investment, and to attribute only part of it makes the appraisal very arbitrary. The only satisfactory procedure is to include the cost of the airport investment in the appraisal of the larger scheme – e.g. the whole tourism development project – where the airport improvement is closely related to the other activity and the latter is sufficiently large.

Types of airport investment

Proposals can be roughly divided into six varieties:

i. Landing strips, taxiways and aprons
The length of runway that aircraft need for take-off (landing requires less) is a function of aircraft type, weight, air temperatures, surface wind speed and direction, and degree of runway gradient. The required strength of the runway is mainly related to the distribution of the aircraft's axle load, qualified by frequency of use and other factors.

Once a minimum runway strength has been attained, further strengthening is not an issue in safety. Touch-down is the most dangerous time in landing but the pressure on the runway is less at this moment than when the aircraft is stationary or taxiing. The maintenance needs of runways are determined by factors similar to those operating in the case of roads, namely frequency of use, weather conditions and load pressures. Maintenance can be piecemeal, as required. Complete resurfacing of an asphalt runway may become necessary at intervals of between eight and twenty years, and more frequently if maintenance has been poor. Resurfacing as a means of strengthening the runway may also be required if a new aircraft, with a heavier load on the pavement, is being introduced. Good maintenance is very important to runway safety, since an uneven surface on which pools of water may collect can be dangerous.

Such is the cost of building long runways to take the largest jets that alternatives should be carefully considered. It is common to find small countries arguing that they need long runways in order to be served by wide-bodied jets, which are necessary for developing a tourist industry. This may be true, but if such landings are infrequent it might be worth exploring the alternative of operating smaller flights out from the main dropping-off point in some neighbouring country.

ii. Terminals, and their contents
There is no clear rule of thumb for the right size of a terminal, although in the case of an expansion the existing facilities can be used as a norm. The amount of space required is clearly the prime influence on costs, and the largest demand on space is normally that for departing travellers. If airlines can be persuaded to share counters less space is required. Small airports are especially vulnerable to 'bunching' by large aircraft, as anyone can testify who has been in the lounge when two jumbo jets arrive together. The obvious alternative to building an expensive terminal large enough to cope with peak demands, which is grossly under-used for the rest of the time, is to try and arrange with airlines that arrivals and departures occur sufficiently far apart for comfort and convenience.

Among the more common pieces of equipment included in airport expansion plans are electronic arrival and departure indicator boards, and baggage handling systems. It is banal, but true, to state that such equipment is all too prone to break down in the conditions of many developing countries. It is not uncommon to find porters walking along belts and carousels recently installed but immobilised by anything from a shortage of spare parts to a local power failure. The same is true of sophisticated indicator boards, and not just in developing countries! Again, the pressure placed on such terminal equipment by the bunching of arrivals and departures can often be eased by re-arrangement of airline schedules, which may justify more modest installations.

iii. Fire-fighting equipment

The International Civil Aviation Organisation (ICAO) requires that no landings and take-offs should occur without such equipment being present, the amount and type being dependent on the nature and frequency of aircraft movements. The expense of buying and maintaining a modern capability and training manpower can be considerable, and this should not be treated as a mere residual item.

iv. Airport approach aids

There are several types. **Non-Directional Beacons** (NDBs) are inexpensive pieces of equipment which enable aircraft to locate the airport and also facilitate *en route* navigation. They are standard equipment for all commercial airports and essential for safety, as well as efficient navigation. In conditions of atmospheric static, however, NDBs can be unreliable, and even unusable. In such conditions VORs (**Very High Frequency Omnidirectional Ranges**) come into their own, indicating the direction of the airport and providing static-free navigational guidance. In the absence of static interference they should be regarded as an economic investment enabling the pilot to locate the airport more quickly.

VASIS (**Visual Approach Slope Indicators**) is an arrangement of lights at the beginning of the runway which enables the pilot to tell when the aircraft is on the correct glide path for landing. It is a very useful and inexpensive visual aid. The **Precision Approach Path Indicator** (PAPI) is a similar concept, but with panes of light on one side. It is internationally accepted as an approach aid and is also inexpensive.

Distance Measuring Equipment (DME) tells the pilot the distance of the aircraft from the DME installation. Taken together with the information on bearing provided by a VOR this gives an accurate indication of the aircraft's position which can provide greater safety if the aircraft's altimeter fails to work. The combination of VOR and DME can be used as an approach aid for landing in circumstances where ILS is not required (see below). VOR and DME are often treated together in operations.

Instrument Landing Systems (ILS) are relatively expensive devices which provide precision approach guidance to aircraft that can be used to very low weather limits. The installation can be even more expensive if the approach is hilly. Land may have to be levelled or the runway re-aligned simply to put in the ILS. There are three types, the simplest being Category I. Category III permits virtually 'blind' landing. As a generalisation, international airports all possess ILS, but depending on the prevailing weather and density of traffic smaller airports – including many in developing countries – need to make out a very strong case for having Categories II or III. Where the weather is normally clear, the approach terrain is flat and traffic is light, ILS is not vital.

Air operators and pilots always press strongly for installing ILS. Parties who do not have to bear the cost of a device have nothing to lose by pressing for installations which the airport may not really need. There is, however, a little more to it than this. The possession of ILS can increase an airport's ability to take landings in poor weather, thus obviating the need for diversions which are costly and inconvenient to airlines. Thus ILS can be seen as a help to the economics of airline operations, which the airport should be able to recoup through landing charges. It is not primarily a safety device, since in the absence of ILS international air safety regulations require the aircraft to divert to the nearest safe airport. (ILS is only a safety investment if pilots are apt to risk a landing in order to avoid a diversion.)

v. Navigational aids

These consist of the various kinds of radar. Aerodrome radar (**Airport Surveillance Radar**) has a limited range of thirty miles up to 10,000 feet, and is normally installed at minor airports to give approach guidance where other aids such as VOR/DME or ILS are not available. Approach radar (**Precision Approach Radar**) has a range of sixty to seventy miles up to 30,000 feet, and is normally used to control the flow of arriving and departing aircraft, and where ILS is available can sequence traffic on to the ILS localiser. **Terminal Area Radar**, with a range of 200 miles up to 40,000 feet, is used to control traffic where for safety reasons there has to be surveillance of climb and descent for all flights. This is required when, for instance, several airports are being used in that area, where there are complicated routeings, where high-performance military aircraft enter the airspace, etc. Finally, *en route* radar (**Air Route Surveillance Radar**), with a maximum range of about 200 miles, is used to guide aircraft flying over the installation.

The value of primary radar can be increased by the addition of **Secondary Surveillance Radar** (SSR). With SSR, each aircraft is fitted with a radar transponder which responds to ground signals, conveying a stronger signal back, together with data on the aircraft's height and identification. SSR saves effort both for the pilot and the ground control and makes possible instant identification of the aircraft. If there is any danger of a collision this is vital in order to signal danger.

Although radar is primarily an investment in safety it can provide economic benefits from reducing delays and diversions and from producing more efficient routeing of aircraft.

vi. Night landing facilities

Aviation Ground Lighting is required for all night operations and by day when visibility is reduced. Its cost and complexity can vary enormously. The simplest system is that of emergency flares which can be used in minor airports lacking proper night landing facilities. Next come simple portable lighting sets which are battery operated, only cost a few thousand pounds, and are suitable for infrequent night landings. At the top end of the range come lighting systems to complement ILS facilities, and the expense of which increases according to the category of ILS. The most expensive, at several hundred thousand pounds, is that to accompany ILS Category III, permitting landing with a cloud base of thirty metres and visibility of 400 metres.

The main arguments for airport lighting are economic, namely the possibility of using the airport facilities round the clock for the arrival and departure of aircraft during the night, and the avoidance of diversions for aircraft that arrive later than they planned. Safety is not usually the main factor, since departures from an airport without night landing facilities must allow for the aircraft to return to the airport during daylight should that be necessary. Thus there is minimal risk of an aircraft being caught out and having to land, at night, at an airport lacking proper lighting. However, safety can be a factor where day visibility deteriorates through a tropical storm, dust storm or fog, though even then diversions are possible.

International standards. Who benefits?

Not a few extravagant proposals are justified with reference to international standards (specifically those of the International Civil Aviation Organisation). ICAO *desiderata* are drawn up by experts, and are of two types, the standards and the recommended practices. Both apply mainly to international airports, and there is room for much discretion in applying them to the smaller national airports.

ICAO standards are the rarer of the two, and relate to such issues as the type of fire services required for each type of aircraft, the width of the runway in relation to its length, and approaches and take-off areas. There is no legal obligation on governments to implement these standards, and many governments do not.

ICAO recommended practices have less authority, and span a wide range of operations. They identify 'best practice' techniques which need to be considered *ad hoc* depending on the circumstances. Pilots and airport users, not to mention equipment manufacturers, often invoke ICAO recommendations in support of particular investments. As already noted, it often costs them nothing, and they gain benefits. If the costs of making an improvement can be passed on to users, and if those users are willing to bear the higher charges, then it is reasonable to heed their entreaties. Since IATA members have increasingly been paying for services at airports their pressure for elaborate facilities has been tempered by economic reality.

In practice, airport charges normally form a small proportion of an airline's flight operating costs (typically 2%–4%), and where a choice of airport exists, the operator is more inclined to choose on the strength of geographical location and passenger generating capacity than with reference to charges.

This means that airports should be able to recover the costs of improvements through airport charges, provided the facilities confer benefits, and that the charges are reasonable in relation to what rival airports are making. Landing fees, calculated in relation to the aircraft's weight, are normally the largest charge, and include many associated services. But there may also be levies specifically for parking, ground services, hangarage, night landing, passenger services, overflying, navigation services and various other facilities.

An established airport should be able to cover its operating costs and contribute towards the recovery of its overheads. Although the host country may adopt a policy of running the airport at a loss in its initial stage in order to encourage traffic, or build up tourism, there is no case for prolonging such a policy which amounts to a subsidy to air travellers from the rest of society. Countries which do subsidise their airports are often those least able to afford to do so.

Matching capacity with demand

Airport authorities are apt to justify their proposed investment with reference to 'operating requirements'. Despite the hint of inevitability in this term, the forecast of requirements is nothing more than a forecast of demand, and this is sometimes very crude.

Moreover, the bias in the forecast is nearly always in one direction, on the high side. Airport operators, like those of other public services, have to coax resources out of a reluctant treasury or finance ministry, and there is often an element of over-bidding in their claims for recurrent cost support or permission to raise loan capital. Airport staff, especially technical people, desire the best and most modern facilities and equipment. There may be an unconscious element of wishful thinking in demand forecasts which envisage large numbers of big aircraft converging on the airport – in bad weather of course – thus requiring the installation of sophisticated, and rather expensive, facilities. It is therefore important that appraisals of airport investment do not take as sacred the 'operating requirements' conveyed by the airport authorities. An independent prediction of demand should form part of the appraisal.

Capacity should be planned in relation to expected use of the airport. This depends on future trends in the type and size of aircraft, the number expected to call, the extent to which their schedules coincide, and the number of passengers and amount of freight arriving and leaving. As with seaports, once these data are received and checked they can be put into a computer and manipulated by a programme to suggest the peak capacity that should be installed. If peak demand is excessively large in relation to normal throughput, there is a case for trying to negotiate some demand spreading.

An airport can form a complex system, but it is helpful to distinguish three main types of capacity: the surfaces used by aircraft, passenger facilities, and landing and navigational equipment. Surfaces – runways, taxiways, parking aprons, etc. – should be geared up to the type and number of aircraft passing through. Passenger facilities, consisting of terminals, baggage handling equipment, restaurants, etc., obviously need to be planned according to the throughput of arriving and departing passengers, and the flow of transit passengers. Navigation and landing aids are more difficult to relate to the size of future traffic and there is a lot of scope for discretion. The standard of facilities at comparable, and long established, airports may sometimes be used as a guide.

Airport planners do have a problem in foreseeing the future demand for their services. Traffic forecasting is exceptionally hazardous for this mode of transport in view of the rapid changes occurring in aircraft technology and the difficulty of foreseeing over particular routes how the changes in real fuel costs will balance against the increasing world competition in low fares. Ideally, long-term forecasts should be continually up-dated, and particular acts of investment should not create expensive hostages for the future. This is easier said than done, but if there is the choice between progressive and incremental improvements and wholesale new investments, the former should be preferred where rapid technological change is happening.

Some practical points

1 Safety arguments adduced in favour of investments in new equipment need to be carefully weighed. They may conceal other motives, such as a desire

by airlines to land at more convenient times or by airport authorities to operate round the clock.

2 For smaller countries the alternative to building a large new runway is to operate feeder flights from the nearest landing place for large aircraft. International Civil Aviation Organisation (ICAO) stipulations, whether standards or recommended practices, are in no way obligatory, and there is room for discretion in applying them to the smaller national airports. In considering proposals based on such stipulations, it is pertinent to ask which parties are pressing most strongly and whether they would be willing to pay higher fees to recover the cost of the equipment.

3 There is nothing sacrosanct about 'operating requirements' submitted by airport authorities, which are based upon forecasts of the use to be made of the airport, and are only as strong as those forecasts.

4 In considering the amount of passenger facilities to be installed, it should not be forgotten that an alternative to building new installations is to attempt to reschedule arrivals and departures to stagger the burden on the airport buildings and passenger spaces.

5 Where the installation of new facilities or the provision of new services will confer benefits on airport users, there is no reason why airport authorities should not attempt to recover the costs from users. People benefiting from airports are very rarely those in the poorest elements of society and there is no reason why they should expect to be subsidised.

6 Particular attention should always be paid to the maintenance of new equipment and to the arrangements being proposed for training local staff in its use. For most items of airport investment maintenance and operations costs are a major factor, and tie up scarce management and technical skills.

Checklist of main questions

1 Country background
Pattern of civil aviation traffic in recent years.
What is the national network of facilities?
Is there a national airline?
Have civil aviation requirements been looked at comprehensively, e.g. through a master plan?

2 Summary of the project
Type of investment proposed.
Costs, both initial and recurrent.
Arrangements for construction and implementation.

3 Traffic levels
What have been the recent levels of traffic, with passengers and freight?
Is there a pattern of daily, weekly or annual peaking and bunching?
What level of traffic is projected?
Has there been an independent forecast of demand?
What scope is there for altering the periodicity of arrivals and departures?

4 Benefits
What principal benefits are claimed, and what is the relative importance of time-savings, economies in cost, and safety?

Which of these can be quantified and attributed to different types of user and operator?

5 Cost recovery
What will be the financial impact of the project on the airport authority?
What charges does the airport currently levy?
Have all possibilities for increased income been investigated, and have users been consulted?
Specifically, is it proposed to recover any cost savings from airlines?

6 Implementation
Has a contractor been approached, or engaged to carry out the work?
What is the nature of his contract?
Has equipment been ordered? Were tenders obtained?
Has an implementation schedule been drawn up? Will there be interruptions to the airport's normal operations? Have the costs of the latter been fully allowed for?

7 Management and labour
Is the airport management familiar with the facilities being proposed, or will special training be required?
Will the new facilities require more labour or will they be labour-saving? In either case, are any problems foreseen?

8 ICAO standards
Is the project justified by reference to ICAO standards or recommended practices? Are these applicable to local circumstances?

9 Downstream facilities
Has thought been given to the effect of the airport's improvements on the increased throughput of passengers and freight and the extra pressure they will exert on transport, warehousing, and hotels, etc. further downstream?

Further reading

The ICAO has produced a number of handbooks and manuals on the planning of airports and aerodromes. Many of these are available as United Nations publications.

The British Civil Aviation Authority (45 Kingsway, London WC2B 6TE) is another source of authoritative reports on the planning and design of airport facilities.

The ODA's Project Data Handbook on *Airports and Navigational Aids*, although it was produced in 1974, contains much data that is still relevant.

David Beaty, *The Complete Skytraveller*, available in Magnum Books (Methuen Paperbacks Ltd), is a handy paperback containing a vivid and readable account of how airlines and airports operate. The author was an airline pilot and, briefly, an official in an aid agency.

8
Power

In this chapter we explain some of the elements in the decision to supply electric power. This is a complicated topic, in which decision-makers will soon find themselves resorting to the specialised expertise of electrical engineers schooled in designing power systems. The sources mentioned in the section on further reading (page 83) will take the reader a little further but eventually an army of technicians, economists and financial analysts stands unavoidably astride the critical planning path.

A large part of the complexity of this subject arises from the fact that power is often supplied and distributed in large interconnected systems (the grid). This means that a decision to add to or alter part of the system has to be considered in the context of the whole, and some modelling, which is best computerised, is inevitable. However, the exposition of the elementary points is aided if, to begin with, we consider the supply and distribution of power to an isolated system, say a town or a district, which does not rely on the import of power from, or export to, adjacent regions.

The chapter will not concern itself with fixing the level and the structure of tariffs. This subject has excited much theoretical commentary, and strictly speaking investment criteria cannot be discussed in isolation from electricity pricing. However, the typical situation that this chapter addresses is where tariffs are given and outside the power of the decision-taker. Readers wishing to explore this complicated issue will find that the sources in the section on further reading provide excellent guidance.

A major source of power is multi-purpose dams which also serve to control river flow and provide water for drinking or irrigation. Dams are major investment projects with enormous technical, economic and environmental effects and it is impossible, and would be foolhardy, to consider them fully here (though the subject crops up again in the discussion on irrigation in chapter 15). Hydroelectric schemes raise the issues of allocating benefits between power, agricultural, flood control and recreational benefits, as well as the priorities for the use of stored water between these various uses. These are difficult and complicated issues. Hence the subsequent discussion, although relevant to the capacity of dams to generate power, does not pretend to offer guidance on the decision to build the dam in the first place.

Alternatives to power investments

Electric power is obviously not the only source of heat and light. Heat can be provided from solar appliances, wood, dung, gas, etc., and light from gas- or oil-fuelled lamps. Although in many circumstances electricity is superior to these other forms, they do exist as widely available alternatives and provide a yardstick of cost and convenience that electricity has to beat. This is particularly true in isolated communities where the cost of installing a generator or connecting to the nearest system would be very high.

Power can also be 'imported' from neighbouring regions and countries. Where economies of scale exist in exploiting a large dam, it may be cheaper for a country to rely on its neighbour than to install its own capacity. In Southern Africa, Zimbabwe has long imported power from Zambia, and Mozambique from the Republic of South Africa. Less obviously, products embodying a lot of electricity, the classic case being alumina and aluminium, can be imported as an alternative to generating power to process the raw material at source.

An alternative to creating new capacity is to use existing capacity more intensively and efficiently. Supply systems are normally planned to cater for peak demand, which varies considerably during the day and between different times of the year. Much of the time capacity is standing by, under-used. If peaks can be reduced, by spreading demand more evenly throughout the day or year, a given amount of capacity can be made to go further without new investment. A flexible tariff structure, encouraging off-peak consumption, can help to achieve this, which is a far more economical way of accommodating demand to supply than by putting in new capacity. Likewise, savings on power losses in the system can delay the time when new capacity is needed.

What are the benefits?

The supply of power is a service to consumers, for which they are prepared to pay a tariff. The tariff revenue is not necessarily the same as the benefits, merely that part of the benefits which are recouped by the power authorities. Benefits to consumers arise from the convenience of using electric power compared to other sources of heat, light and power, which sometimes appear as cost savings compared with these other methods. Benefits to the economy arise from savings in real ('resource') costs, such as the use of cheaper fuel or a more efficient process.

Expected tariff revenue is a minimum measure of these benefits, but where there is reason to think that consumers would have been willing to pay more it is legitimate to count in consumers' surplus as well. This is measured as the excess of what they would have been willing to pay over what they are asked to pay. Where they were formerly paying more for an inferior supply, this provides a possible basis for calculating consumers' surplus on the new improved supply. However, it must be admitted that putting values on consumers' surplus entails extremely arbitrary assumptions.

This is just as true of industrial as of domestic consumers. Industrial users, or at least the larger ones, have the choice of installing their own generator or taking supplies from the public mains. Unless the public supply is grossly unreliable an industrial firm or commercial undertaking will often find it cheaper and more convenient to buy power from the public system. Again, the cost margin between the public supply and that of operating its own generator provides a basis for estimating the firm's consumer surplus from the project. (There are, however, cases of a firm running its own generator, and even selling its surplus to the municipality. This tends to occur where reliability is all-important – e.g. where the process relies heavily on heat – and where the public supply is not reliable.)

Where consumers – whether domestic, municipal, commercial or indus-trial – have geared themselves up to a certain level of power supply they obviously become very vulnerable to any interruption in that supply. Frequently power projects are not only concerned with catering for an increment in electricity demand (load), but also in making the present supply more reliable. All generators need to be taken out of service at intervals for maintenance. Where they are badly maintained and/or time-expired they are liable to break down and force the power authorities to reduce supplies to consumers by load-shedding (as it is politely known). This is inconvenient to domestic consumers, but it can be disastrous for industrial firms, especially those dependent on continuous power for assembly, process or heat. In these circumstances it is reasonable to credit the project with benefits from the avoidance of such losses.

In the remaining discussion it is convenient to distinguish the generation of power from its transmission and distribution.

1 Generation

In assessing the need for generating capacity, and the size and type of equipment, it is customary to follow this sequence:

i. Forecast the future **peak demands** (maximum load) and electrical energy requirements, together with a time profile showing when these occur

ii. Project the **firm* generating capacity** available over this period (existing 'nameplate' capacity, derated for age and condition, and subtracting the capacity of, say, the largest unit)

iii. Derive the difference between i. and ii. If there is a deficit this indicates the amount of **new firm capacity needed**, and the latest year by which it should be installed. Allow time for the generators to be installed – about two years for gas turbines and diesel plant, at least five years for other thermal plant, and longer for hydro. Allow also for expected 'system losses', the waste of power in transmission and distribution, as well as the internal consumption of power by the station itself. In total these can amount to 15%–30%

iv. Devise a **cost-effective solution** for the provision of capacity for the given period of time. This entails choosing the 'best' type of generator (diesel, steam, gas turbine, etc.), and the size and number of units. The optimal set is that which provides required firm capacity at the least cost, which should be interpreted as the least discounted cost of new capital plus total system operating costs, including fuel. A common technique is to use 'pairwise' comparison of alternative investments

v. The above least-cost solution should be tested by **cost–benefit analysis** to see whether it is a sensible economic allocation of national resources. First, tariff revenue can be taken as a proxy for benefits. If there are grounds for believing that tariffs understate benefits, consumers' surplus should be estimated and added. The latter should be performed with restraint, and the analyst should in any case ensure that the short-term financial position of the power authority is not jeopardised. It should be a source of suspicion if a relatively large consumers' surplus is required to ensure the project's viability.

It is worth dwelling a little more on two of the key elements in this decision sequence, namely forecasting demand, and choosing capacity.

*For explanation see page 77.

Forecasting demand

Where extravagant and excessive capacity has been installed, the root cause can often be traced to poor demand forecasts, in some cases prepared by those with a vested interest in supplying or operating the equipment. Demand forecasts should enable the power authorities to decide when new capacity is necessary, and what the increment in capacity ought to be. We say 'when' rather than 'whether' because the demand for power in a system rarely falls for long except in the short/medium term or where a community or region is left high and dry by economic developments elsewhere. Thus, given the finite economic life of power equipment,the decision is really one about *when* additions to capacity will be required. (A plausible answer could, of course, be 'not in the foreseeable future; postpone a decision until the need becomes much clearer'.)

The normal forecast for power should focus on the period two to ten years ahead to allow planners time to grasp the size of warranted new capacity, and the engineers time to order and install it. But alongside projections of annual peaks and average consumption, the forecasts should also tell planners something about daily and seasonal variations (and peaks). It is also important to form some judgement about the size of any existing excess demand for power which would have to be added to the growth in demand in assessing the need for capacity. There may, for instance, be consumers who are not yet connected, or who want to install power-using equipment in excess of what their present supplies could support (this is just as true of domestic consumers as of industrial firms). Regular black-outs and forms of load rationing are also evidence of present excess demand.

There are three basic approaches to forecasting demand. One is to extrapolate by assuming that the rate of growth in the recent past continues. This is the simpler method, and is based on examining a time series of figures on peak demand and energy consumption. (Both measures are necessary. **Peak demand**, expressed in kilowatts or megawatts*, indicates the amount of new capacity required. **Energy consumption**, expressed in kilowatt-hours or gigawatt-hours, is needed to forecast sales, financial revenue, and operating costs for such items as fuel.)

Extrapolation is very common and sometimes is even based on the average growth of consumption for the whole country, or the whole world (this explains why figures of 12% p.a. are so common). Unless it is to be misleading, extrapolation should take into account whether tariffs have been unduly low (thus encouraging consumption), whether future prices (of fuel and equipment) will increase in real terms, and whether new conditions will prevail in future (new factories to be built, the network of distribution extended). No extrapolation is going to be reliable unless it is accompanied by assumptions about future prices of fuels and power. If the power utility is currently making losses, or if it has recently faced stiff increases in fuel prices which have not been fully passed on to consumers, then future price increases might seem unavoidable. In the opposite case future tariffs may fall in real terms if the system is on the brink of being connected up to a grid fed by cheap hydro-power (depending on how high the connection costs are).

The limitations of extrapolation suggest the second forecasting method, which is to discover from past data what the main factors are in explaining the

---

*Megawatts = 1,000,000 watts (MW).

74

demand for power, and estimating how these factors are likely to behave in future. This is a sophisticated method, involving the correlation of demand with a number of explanatory variables, and using the relationships that are derived to predict consumption on various hypotheses about future trends. For instance, it may be discovered that in the past the consumption of power can be 'explained' (in a statistical sense) largely with reference to the number of individual connections, sales of electrical appliances, average annual temperatures, and the growth of industrial production. If a view can be taken of how these main variables are going to behave, the basis exists for a more accurate forecast of demand than extrapolation alone would produce.

The third forecasting method is a market survey of the prospective end-users to find out what their power consumption would be at certain plausible tariff levels. The estimation of a demand schedule for power is indispensable to the use of consumer surplus analysis. At a much simpler level, where a particular community is to be electrified, an estimate of demand can be made by direct observation of the number of households, dwellings, etc.

Choice of capacity
Armed with projections of reasonable expected demand, the planners' job is to choose that capacity which will supply the system at least total system cost (capital, fuel and other operating expenses). To simplify the discussion we are assuming an isolated power system, that is one which is not linked up to the grid. (The existence of a grid allows any system the choice of linking up – with associated costs of transmission and transformer stations – and 'auto-generation', i.e. creating its own generating capacity. For systems already connected to a grid there is a more complicated calculation for the power authority concerning the cheapest and most efficient way of increasing the supply capacity of the grid. There is also the option of importing power from a neighbouring country, and exporting to that country power which is temporarily surplus to internal needs.) Without pre-empting the later discussion about transmission and distribution, we should merely note here that in choosing generating capacity it is the least **total system cost** which is relevant, where the total includes the transmission and distribution costs related to each choice.

Although some countries have the option of nuclear power, the choice for most countries lies between hydro, steam turbines, diesel and gas turbines. Small systems (say, a few megawatts) normally have only one type, and this is commonly diesel. Larger systems can and do contain generators of different types. The decision is quite complicated and requires specialist technical advice, but the following may be proffered as guidance.

Hydro schemes are costly to install but very cheap to run. Because they normally require a large minimum investment some kind of grid (or a very large steady load, like an aluminium smelter) is a precondition of getting the economies of scale in the production of power that they permit. Once the initial heavy investment in the dam, hydraulic structures, and generators has been made, it makes sense to run them at maximum capacity since the extra cost of each kilowatt hour (kWh) produced is almost zero, provided sufficient water is available. This last proviso is important. The water that drives the hydro turbines has an alternative value as stored water for drinking or irrigation which may be lost by its release at a particular time. Where the water is

75

scarce, either in general or at a particular time, this will affect the 'merit order'* of hydro compared to the various kinds of thermal.

The decision whether or not to prefer hydro to thermal generation is strongly influenced by the discount rate used. The cost of hydro power is almost all capital cost incurred in the first few years, while the benefits accrue long into the future as there are no fuel costs. The higher the discount rate the less hydro is preferred because the benefits are more heavily discounted compared to the costs.

Of the various thermal alternatives, **steam turbines** are often preferred for the larger units of capacity (say, 30 MW to over 1000 MW, though the range is elastic). Where there is no available hydro, and load is of this size, steam sets are very often the cheapest way of covering base load, allowing for both capital and operating costs. The steam boilers can be heated by coal or residual fuel oil. For very large sizes, steam sets can of course be composite units made up of different sizes. They are very robust and reliable, and incur relatively low repair and maintenance costs. Although more expensive to buy and run than diesels they need fewer outages for maintenance, thus achieving higher availability.

Unlike the previous types, **diesel** sets can be easily started and shut down, hence they offer very flexible use in a power station. There are many different types and sizes (up to approximately 30 MW) and they are economic in two types of circumstance. One is as stand-by or peak load capacity in a large power station, where their flexibility offsets their relatively high cost per kWh. The other is as capacity for systems with quite small loads – say, below 30 MW, or the threshold at which steam starts to be feasible. Diesels are normally readily available, which is a factor in systems where a power crisis is looming. However, although their technology is not complex and is widely understood, regular maintenance (involving periodic shutting down and occasional stripping) is vital, and its neglect is the main reason for the depressing number of idle diesels littering power stations of the developing world.

Within the family of diesels there is a choice between high-speed sets, which are cheaper to buy but burn expensive gas oil, and low-speed sets which cost a little more but which burn residual fuel oil. The high operating costs of the high-speed diesels make them only suitable for intermittent service.

Gas turbines are available in a wide variety of sizes (say, 1 MW to 50 MW). Although they are among the cheapest sets to buy (measured as £ per MW installed) they are very expensive to run (they normally consume large amounts of gas oil). Hence they are normally only considered for meeting peak demand. However, they are relatively easy to get and quick to install, and many a power authority has resorted to them as an expedient, where more time or a more cost-conscious choice would have led to longer-term and cheaper solutions.

The factors governing the choice between types of generator could be summarised as follows:

i. The amount of capacity required. This is bound up with

ii. Total discounted cost of providing a unit of energy (kWh)

---

*Explained on page 77.

iii. Whether the capacity is required for base load or peak load coverage

iv. Availability and cost of motive power or fuel

v. The importance of easy maintenance.

An additional factor is the length of time for which the capacity is needed. Some systems have the prospect of being connected to the grid at a future date, at which time generators installed now will become redundant. Alternatively, demand might build up to a point at which a larger and more economical generator can be installed to cover the whole of demand. In both cases, there are advantages in putting in generators which can be taken out and moved elsewhere. Some diesel sets are specifically mobile, while others can be moved with a little more trouble.

We have discussed choice of different types of generator, but what of the choice of the size of each unit? There are many sizes available, so that 12 MW, to take an example, can be supplied by one unit of 12 MW, two of 6 MW, three of 4 MW, etc. The main consideration – assuming that economies of scale do not operate in this range – is the need for security of supply. All generators need routine maintenance, which usually entails shutting them down for a few hours, days or weeks (depending on the type of maintenance being done). A power station should have enough generators elsewhere to be able to cover peak demand even when its largest unit is out of action. This is even more apposite for unexpected breakdowns. The steps in calculating **firm capacity** are as follows: take the **'nameplate' capacity** in the power station, derated as appropriate for old equipment; allow for planned shutdown, e.g. for overhaul or maintenance, thus obtaining **available capacity**; finally subtract the capacity of the largest unit. Every system should have some slack in it to cater for unexpected events – which could be an unforeseen peak in demand as well as a breakdown in plant. This is the rationale for a **reserve plant margin** often found to be in the range 20%–30%.

However, there are costs in having too large a margin. The costs of holding excessive reserve capacity fall on the power authority and represent the capital which is locked up in the unused plant and the need to maintain it. The costs of insufficient margins are, on the contrary, borne by consumers who suffer from the various kinds of load shedding. In many developing countries, especially those short of technical skills and where there are delays in getting spare parts, it may even be prudent to allow for two or more units to be out of action in the calculation of firm capacity. Thus, in the above example, there would be a case for considering four 3 MW units as preferable to one of 12 MW or one of 10 MW plus one of 2 MW.

Where generators of a certain type and size have been installed power station managers and grid system operators have to decide when to bring the various generators on-stream. Here the main factor is the cost of supplying a marginal unit of electrical energy (kWh), which sets up a **merit order** for the units. Normally nuclear or steam turbine units are switched on first, followed by diesel and lastly gas turbine, which is only used for the last increments to the peak load. Hydro power is always used to maximise the thermal savings made by using the available water.

2 Transmission and distribution

Power is transmitted from the generating points to demand areas, and is then distributed to consumers. For distribution its voltage is reduced ('stepped down') at **transformers**. Power is produced and transmitted at relatively high voltages – anything between 33 kV and 500 kV. The typical household consumer is geared up to receive it at 240 V (or in some countries 110/120 V). Transmission and distribution are at different ends of the same process, and the distinction is usually drawn according to voltage. Transmission is usually regarded as the conductance of power at voltages at or above 66 kV, while distribution is at voltages at or below 33 kV.

Transmission at **high voltages** (say, 132 kV or above) has certain technical advantages, such as reduced voltage loss, as well as economising on overhead conductors ('wires' to the layman). However, it also calls for high pylons, costly insulation, and extra outlay on transformers and sub-stations. Leaving aside the problem of voltage losses, the cost of transmission increases with distance because of the need for pylons and conductors. A balance has to be struck between the economies to be obtained from connecting a demand centre to a cheap source of power, and the cost of getting that power to the consumers. One of the economies to be obtained from linking up systems, each with their own generating capacity, is the savings that are possible in system capacity requirements, since 'reserve' plant can be pooled. This is the essence of the case for setting up a **grid**.

The basic physical choice in a transmission project is between overhead and underground systems. The latter are much more expensive, requiring extra insulation and excavation work, and can only be justified for very short sections or unusual circumstances (e.g. submarine uses, or where there are overriding safety, security or environmental factors) – in practice this means urban conditions.

The essential problem of distribution is to devise a system which reaches all the consumers at least total cost. (In working out the economics of distribution it is conventional to start with the **economic bulk tariff** as representing the cost of power 'bought' from the grid at a particular transformer, and add the costs of installing and servicing the poles, conductors, transformers and switchgear that make up the distribution network. This is the cost against which benefits have to be set.) The physical layout of the system can be modelled to produce the optimal web, allowing for the fact that **voltage losses** increase when power is carried any distance at low voltages.

Rural electrification

This is a special case of transmission and distribution, in which developing countries have to decide on the pace and the extent to which they spread the power network to include rural consumers, who are typically very poor. A good example is the Egyptian government's rural electrification programme for the Nile Delta, inspired by the desire to bring the benefits of cheap bulk power (from the Aswan dam) to the poor farming villages of the Delta.

Many kinds of benefit are claimed for such a programme. Having electric power available would save the cost of traditional sources of heating and light, such as firewood, dung and kerosene lamps. Water could be pumped without the need for oxen power, thus saving land and fodder. It would help the development of rural industry. It could revolutionise social life in the evenings, and has even been invoked as a means of population control. Its effects on education are potentially very strong, as anyone who has seen students sitting reading under street lamps can testify. Certainly the advantages of electrification are easily seen by comparing those Delta villages with, and those without, power.

The main snag is that rural consumers pose particular problems of cost recovery. The costs of distributing power over the distances involved and the fact that the consumers are scattered usually make for high costs of supply. However, the rural consumers involved are often among the poorest members of the population and could not be expected to pay the full economic tariff (especially when the object of the supply is to get them to use this novel source of power).

These factors do not raise any special economic problems in justifying the investment. It is valid to consider consumers' surplus as the concept of benefits, since in most cases the electric power will be cheaper than existing sources and will produce economic savings. This is even more true of rural industries which were operating costly small autogenerators. Another point is that unit management costs fall sharply as the network expands because of market economics of scale.

It is the financial analysis which needs special care since it is undesirable to burden the power authority with new loss-making systems unless it has a strong overall financial position. If central government is willing to furnish a regular subsidy to cover the losses from rural electrification, or if the power authority is prepared to cross-subsidise from elsewhere in the system, this is a legitimate solution in view of the exceptional social value of rural electrification.

The economic tariff for this type of rural consumer would invariably be higher than that for urban or industrial consumers. Yet many countries find it convenient and politic to have a unified tariff structure for all users. And, as we have seen, the full economic tariff would cause hardship to poor rural users as well as discouraging greater consumption. Although the complexities of tariff-fixing should not be ignored (see Webb, in the section on further reading, page 83) a useful rule of thumb is that rural tariffs should be at least equal to the cost of operating and maintaining relevant parts of the system.

Even this cost may be beyond the ability or willingness of consumers to pay. In Bolivia some villages are not using the electricity system since they are unable, or do not think it worthwhile, to pay even the operating costs. In such cases some very low 'life-line' prices are applicable for, say, the first 50 kWh, with more normal rates applying to consumption greater than this.

But the number of rural consumers clamouring for connections is normally greatly in excess of the power authority's ability to satisfy them in any one year. The power network has to be gradually extended and filled in according to the utility's financial, technical and administrative constraints. Power should first be sent to areas with most existing economic activity, or which promise a rapid growth of demand from productive uses. These tend to be those villages already served by infrastructure and with reasonable agricultural potential, and where the villages are not too widely scattered. By the selective expansion of the network to such areas the utility can build up its resources and financial strength to enable it eventually to take on the remoter villages, or those in areas of low economic potential, which are going to depend on continued subventions from the rest of the system. In this context, it is worth remembering that where transmission and distribution costs are going to be very high the alternatives come into their own (e.g. autogenerators, diesel-powered pump sets, etc.).

Rural electrification entails spreading administrative and technical resources over a wide area. Therefore arrangements for the procurement and assembly of materials need to be carefully set up, and a system for the maintenance of far-flung rural networks set in motion.

Although rural electrification is sometimes justified as leading to the fuller utilisation of surplus generating capacity, it can nevertheless impose extra costs on the system. Quite apart from any extra transmission and distribution costs, it may bring forward the date when new generating capacity is needed. The above-mentioned Egyptian example is relevant. The electrification of the Delta was originally justified with reference to the surplus capacity of the Aswan Dam. This surplus has since been absorbed, and costly new generating capacity has had to be installed to meet the growth in load.

Important practical points

1 The extrapolation of past trends in demand is risky. Over the last decade there were several large increases in the real price of fuel, the most important cost in thermal generation. The general world recession of the late 1970s and early 1980s has also depressed trend rates of growth in demand, while the depressing short- and medium-term outlook for the poorer non-oil-producing developing countries will restrain power demand from all quarters.

2 Where the existing power system has been allowed to deteriorate pre-maturely, the rehabilitation of plant is an attractive alternative to new investment. Load spreading by encouraging off-peak consumption is another way of increasing consumption without making expensive new investments.

3 For interconnected (grid) systems the basic investment criterion is 'least total system cost'. The many possible alternatives need to be tested against this criterion, a task which normally will need to be done on a computer model. The basic comparison is between the cost of generation to serve a load centre, and the cost of transmitting power from elsewhere via the grid.

4 The neglect of maintenance is probably the largest single problem in power generation in developing countries. Many such countries simply ignore it. The notion of pre-emptive maintenance, which requires closing generators down after a certain number of operating hours, is a difficult one for many power authorities to grasp. Consequently machines are run until they break down, and since holdings of spares is often inadequate too, the sight of several generating sets out of action at once is depressingly common. It follows that simple and robust generators should be preferred to others, even if they are rather more expensive. However, this is no substitute for planned maintenance.

5 The choice between hydro and thermal generating alternatives hinges crucially on the discount rate used in the analysis. The higher the discount rate, the more it penalises hydro.

6 Mobile generators are a neat solution where a local system is in need of new generating capacity, but where an eventual link-up to a grid is likely. In practice, though, many mobile generators are so run down by the time they are no longer needed that they end their lives where they began them.

7 In estimating benefits, the notion of consumer surplus is most reliable where consumers already buy power from a higher cost source, or generate their own. The existence of alternatives adds greater veracity to the notion of consumer surplus.

8 In densely populated poor cities the loss of power by 'theft' is very common. It is difficult for the authorities to trace the many illegal connections that occur, which, together with the abuse of meters and bribery of collectors, can make a serious hole in receipts. One practical implication is that increased tariffs may simply lead to increased theft and evasion. However, illegal connections often result from frustrated people waiting for connections taking matters into their own hands, and a programme to extend distribution to all people wishing it can defuse some of this frustration.

Checklist of main questions

1 Demand (in area to be served)
  i. What information is there on consumption? (Recent trends in sales – in gigawatt-hours – daily and annual peak loads, fluctuations, load factor – ratio average load to peak loads, etc.)
  What is the breakdown of consumers (domestic, institutional, commercial, public, etc.)?
 ii. Are tariffs adequate? (History of recent changes.)
  Are they near an 'economic' level?
  Does the power authority have an obligation to adjust them in line with inflation?
  What financial obligations has the power authority (e.g. need to meet a target financial rate of return, to cover average cost, to cover operating and maintenance costs only, to pay a dividend to the government, etc.)?
  What is the structure of tariffs (industrial/domestic rates, peak/off-peak rates, etc.)?
  What is the typical power bill for different types of consumer, and what relation does it bear to their total incomes (or, in the case of industrial users, total costs)?
 iii. What projections have been done of future demand?
  What are these forecasts based on (simple extrapolation, or economic study of demand components)?
  Has recent demand been biased by unusually low or high tariffs, or unusual events?
  What assumptions are being made about future tariffs (or subsidies)?
  What view is being taken about future fuel costs?
 iv. What evidence is there of present unsatisfied demand?
  In what respects is present supply unsatisfactory to consumers?

2 Features of supply
  i. What are the main elements of the present system for generating, transmitting and distributing power?
  What proportion of consumption is from the public network rather than private generators?
  How many households have power connections?

ii. What is the capacity of the system (allowing for derating plant and any constraint the distribution system imposes on power delivered)?
What is 'firm capacity' and how does it relate to peak load?
iii. What plans are there for expanding the supply network?
What prospects are there for creating or enlarging the grid?
iv. What are the main constraints or bottlenecks in the present system and how will they affect the proposed investment?
v. What is the level of power losses in the system?
Can they be reduced?

3 Institutional aspects – the power authority
i. What are the constitution, powers, and statutory functions of the power authority?
In what respects does it have autonomy from its parent government department?
ii. What are its financial obligations?
In practice, what are the financial relations between the power board and the government?
iii. Are the different parts of power supply entrusted to different agencies (e.g. are generation and transmission separate from distribution, are there separate regional boards, are there private power utilities in certain areas)?
iv. How large is the power authority (annual turnover, staff numbers)?
Does it have a satisfactory staff structure, and adequate skilled and qualified people at the appropriate levels?
Does it have its own salary scales, or is it compelled to pay civil service rates?

4 Required capacity
i. What is a reasonable estimate of the growth of peak demand?
ii. What firm capacity will be available at various times in the future (allowing for derating old plant, and realistic outages for ageing equipment)?
iii. When are power deficits likely (difference between i. and ii.)?
iv. When should new equipment be planned and ordered (i.e. iii. minus delivery and installation period)?

5 Cost-effectiveness of solution
i. Is the proposed solution the most cost-effective of the alternatives considered (the method which provides power at least discounted total cost)?
ii. Is the generating plant the most suitable and economical in the circumstances (allowing for factors such as capital cost, fuel, ease of maintenance, whether for base load or peak, etc.)?
What is the specific justification for the size and combination of generating units?
iii. Has adequate thought been given to the availability of crucial inputs like fuel, water, maintenance labour, conductor wire, poles, etc.?

6 Benefits
i. What extra tariff revenue will result from the investment?
ii. Will there be any cost savings?
iii. Will there be fewer supply interruptions, blackouts, voltage reductions, etc.?
iv. Is it reasonable to add in consumer surplus (e.g. where consumers show evidence of willingness to pay more for reliable supplies, as in the possession of an autogenerator)?

  v. What kind of consumers will benefit from the investment?
 vi. Are social and public benefits being claimed?
vii. Has a cost–benefit analysis been done?
     What does it show?

7 Financial aspects
   i. What is the financial rate of return of the project?
  ii. What will be its overall impact on the finances of the power authority, allowing for the arrangements for repaying capital?
 iii. What are the project's inescapable operating and maintenance costs?
 iv. What prospects does the power board have of covering its capital charges? Will it need a government subsidy?
     Is it being required to cross-subsidise between different types of consumer?
  v. What is its collection record?
     What scope is there for tightening this up?

Further reading

Ralph Turvey and Dennis Anderson, *Electricity Economics: Essays and Case Studies*, a World Bank Research Publication, published for the World Bank by Johns Hopkins University Press, 1977. (An authoritative survey of the main economic issues, both theoretical and practical, with case studies.)

Michael G. Webb, *Power Sector Planning Manual*, a handbook produced by the ODA, London, June 1979. (Useful on planning, pricing and tariff design.)

World Bank, *Rural Electrification*, a Sector Policy Paper first produced in 1975. (Contains factual data and guidelines on practical issues. The comparative data are interesting, if somewhat dated.)

EDUCATION
HEALTH
HOUSING
WATER SUPPLY
WASTEWATER, SEWAGE AND EFFLUENT

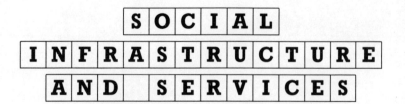

SOCIAL
INFRASTRUCTURE
AND SERVICES

9
Education

Policies and projects

In education, more than in most sectors, national policies circumscribe the tasks left to the planners, appraisers, and financiers of projects. Indeed, it is sometimes hard to separate a 'project' from an educational 'programme'. Is the construction of three primary schools in rural areas a 'project' or part of a sectoral programme? Faced with a 'project', such as a teacher training college, the planner may object to certain basic features, such as the lack of teaching materials in schools or the low level of teachers' salaries, only to be told that these are matters of national policy not to be interfered with. This is true of other sectors, but in the case of education national policies are thought to be sacrosanct because this is such a sensitive subject.

The main task of the planner is to decide which of the features of the project fall within his or her control and influence, and which should be regarded as 'given' by overriding national policy. This is especially true where the planner, consultant, or financier is foreign to the country concerned, since few countries take kindly to 'interference' from abroad in a sensitive area like education. With this limitation firmly in mind, it is useful to review some of the main overriding policy issues which have a bearing on project design.

Some policy issues

The most basic policy question is the **amount of resources** that a country devotes to education, whether through private or public means. Most people regard education as a stepping-stone to higher incomes. In countries with large differentials in personal incomes the economic return to education can be large enough to persuade people to take a chance – by investing in their schooling or by forgoing earnings in a job. But while this habit is rational for the individual or his or her family it may create social and political tensions if there is a widespread disappointment of hopes. In an ideal world governments should match the number of students in the pipeline with prospects for jobs. But social and moral pressures, added to the inexactitude of forecasting and the brevity of many governments, make this a forlorn hope.

There is then the question of **balance between the different levels** of education. On the academic plane, the three stages are primary, secondary and tertiary. Although in developed countries virtually all children pass through to a certain level of secondary education, in developing countries the majority of children never get beyond primary level, and a large proportion drop out before they even complete the primary stage. It is common to find, in both developed and developing countries but especially the latter, a dispropor-tionate concentration of resources on 'tertiary' education, namely universities, colleges and polytechnics. This results from a perfectly reasonable wish to substitute local people for expatriates in running the nation and the economy. But it also arises out of an exaggerated fondness for paper qualifications as the *sine qua non* of advancement in all walks of life (what Dore has called the Diploma Disease – see section on further reading, page 91).

The type of education supplied, and the uses to which it is put, are influenced by attitudes, often unconscious, of rulers towards what education is really used for. The dichotomy of **attitudes to education** has been expressed as 'formation of human capital', on the one hand, and 'screening' on the other. According to the first, education builds up human capital in that it enables its possessors to increase their productive and earning skills. Thus the type of education offered, e.g. the subjects taken, matters, and is related to the sorts of skills required by that country in the future, or else the skills that are in demand abroad. This is particularly true for poor countries.

The second approach views education as a process of selection of the best talents from among all those available to the nation, and what people are actually educated to do is then of secondary importance. Education has even been likened to an endurance test resembling tribal initiation ceremonies (see Andreski in section on further reading).

All this has relevance to the **content of education**, e.g. the choice of subjects for the curricula, and the balance between academic education and the various specialised forms such as vocational, technical and adult education. Andreski has perceptively analysed the balance of subjects in African educational systems:

> The missionaries were primarily concerned with teaching people to read so that they could absorb the lessons of the Bible, while the colonial governments needed only clerks. No large demand for technical skills was envisaged, owing to the conception of the colonies as purveyors of raw materials and foodstuffs produced by uneducated peasants. Adapted to the purpose of forming clerks, ministers of religion and later lawyers and officials, the educational institutions in colonial Africa laid stress on literary and legal studies, and neglected industrial and commercial training, not to speak of the agricultural, shunned by everybody and stigmatized by the notion that anything to do with the cultivation of the soil is fit only for a poor and illiterate rustic. Almost everywhere the lawyers outnumber scientists by at least 20 to 1.

The fear of **illiteracy**, widely sensed as a rebuke to post-colonial governments, accounts for the widespread aim of achieving universal primary education. Of course, illiteracy is often no bar to accumulating a modicum of wealth, nor is it incompatible with a happy and fulfilled life. Moreover, the cynic is entitled to point out that totalitarian governments see greater literacy as a means of spreading propaganda about the regime. But these considerations apart, the desire to bring education to all is a worthy aim, though it can mean that in poor societies the spread of primary schools can become a 'numbers game' which in the absence of sufficient complementary resources (teachers, materials, recurrent funds) can result in a deteriorating quality of education.

Before leaving policy issues, the phenomenon of the **'educated unemployed'** should be acknowledged. This is present to some extent in all countries, but appears at its most grotesque in developing nations where, in the midst of poverty, skill shortages and illiteracy large numbers of graduates are turned out for whom there is no obvious and suitable work. Some of them remain in apparent idleness, some accept jobs that are patently unsuitable, some join government service in positions specially created to mop up idle graduates, while others hold off the labour market until the right job comes up. All these forms of educated unemployment entail waste of scarce national resources, but the last manifestation above – what has been called periods of 'job search' by monosyllabic academics – is less serious than the others. Where there are large earnings differentials between jobs and where the aspirations of graduates are unrealistically inflated, periods of 'job search' can pay off as an alternative to taking the first position offered.

The relevance of the **'brain drain'** to educational planning is also a matter of controversy. Qualified people who emigrate to sell their talents to an international market are not necessarily the same as the educated unemployed. All too often, the latter group do not have marketable skills beyond their own frontiers. Emigrants usually possess skills in great demand in their own country, and frequently are people on whom their country has lavished much time, attention and cash. A common syndrome is the expenditure of scarce educational resources on the production of useful professionals – say, doctors – who cannot be retained locally on account of poor salaries. They leave to work abroad, and in their place expensive expatriates are attracted, often under aid programmes. All over Africa Swedish, Cuban and British doctors are working in locations and in conditions shunned by local doctors.

This clearly has strong implications for the salary levels in a country, if educational outlays are not going to be wasted to the nation. Its implications for educational planning are more debatable. There might not seem much point in a country investing in the education of, for example, a quantity surveyor if he or she is likely to work abroad from the outset. However, working abroad for a spell, and then returning, might be the best way for a professional in a small country to acquire relevant experience which can then be applied locally.

Moreover, the remitted earnings of a professional working abroad can be a useful source of foreign exchange for his native land (Egypt and India are two of the many countries that benefit substantially from the export of their skills). One wonders, though, about the different benefits they would tap if they could use these people productively at home.

Assessing the demand for education and training

In choosing the size and type of projects, planners are entitled to probe the real demand for the output, that is the numbers of pupils and students, and beyond that the jobs they can go into. Education is an investment with a long gestation period. A primary school built today will start releasing pupils into the next stage of education in six or seven years' time, and onto the job market in ten years or more. Moreover, in order to staff new schools teachers have to be trained in advance, which adds three years or more to the planning period. Once created, an educational establishment can expect a long life – unlike in industry the age of a school or college is regarded as an asset – and it takes a period of years for such an institution to become a going concern working at full effectiveness.

All this means that decisions have to be taken now with implications that stretch into the medium- and long-term future. It follows that it is easy for the assumptions about the future demand for education that current investments are founded on to be invalidated. In Britain, for instance, the demand for secondary education was over-estimated when the current establishment of teachers and buildings was planned years ago, consequently excess capacity is emerging.

This points to a close examination of **demographic trends** as being fundamental to planning educational projects. This is especially critical for countries
close to the demographic transition (in which falling death rates, later
marriages, and longer education start to reduce birth rates) and countries,
mainly developed, in which population numbers level out or even decline.
This is less of a problem in most poor developing countries, in which high
birth and mortality rates produce an age distribution ('pyramid') with a
preponderance of school-age children. In such countries educational efforts
are doomed to lag behind potential numbers for a long time, and there is little
danger of creating too much capacity, at least at the primary level.

In all countries, though, it is difficult to predict the **demand for education**
beyond the compulsory minimum laid down by law. In many countries there
is a heavy premium on obtaining paper qualifications, even of a purely
academic kind, in order to get a job, while other countries place more value
on obtaining relevant professional or technical proficiency. Such different
valuations are normally reflected in the different earnings which holders of
the various qualifications can command, and these salary differences are
important pointers to the sort of education and training to create. Another
pointer is the level of vacancies notified for particular trades. But there is no
escaping the difficulty in forecasting, over the relevant period for educational
planning, underlying social and economic trends – the numbers of women
entering the labour force, the customary school-leaving age, preference for
academic over vocational or professional subjects, etc.

Manpower planning, a vogue subject a decade ago, has been somewhat
discredited as a guide to education and training policy. It has come to be
realised that it is only feasible to attempt to forecast the future demand for
labour in a narrow range of occupations and over a short period. At all levels
there is a heavy drop-out rate for students and transfer to other disciplines.
In any case some professions and skills can be learned on the job without the
need for elaborate state provision. Planners are handicapped by the lack of
reliable statistics on the labour market in particular sectors, which is basic
data for manpower planning. To cap it all, fluctuations in economic growth and
changes in the industrial structure make it hard to forecast exactly what skills
are going to be needed. The emigration of unwanted skills, and the importation
of those in scarce supply, are widely resorted to by countries in order to
balance skills required with those available.

Decisions on projects

The above remarks may convey the flavour of the policy setting within which
decisions on projects have to be made. It is clear that at the project level the
scope for decision is marginal, concerning the timing of projects, the balance
at the margin between more primary schools rather than a further technical
college, etc., or how large a teacher training college will have to be. Careful
forecasting, where it is possible, can help to illuminate decisions about the
size and type of resources going into education. Once these policies have
gelled, however, the planner is forced to concentrate on *how* they should be
implemented.

Educationists everywhere complain about the size of a country's **education
budget**, and this is the first constraint in planning educational projects. In the
poorer developing countries budgetary stringency shows itself in myriad

ways. Teachers' salaries are low, and sometimes slow to be paid (there is one Central African country where desperate unpaid teachers steal school-books and even light-bulbs in order to sell them to make a living). Running expenses of schools are skimped, so that when something goes wrong or needs replacing, or the building needs painting, nothing happens. There is often a shortage of materials needed by teachers, such as paper, pencils, and chalk. Sometimes projects are left unfinished because of a shortage of funds (which may be traced to unforeseen inflation or cuts in the budget). These symptoms are aggravated after periods of rapid expansion in the nominal coverage of education, as part of the literacy numbers game.

It follows that **cost-effectiveness** is the most important aspect of project choice in education and training. As Andreski has noted, in any poor country the high quality and comparative splendour of educational buildings stand out in vivid contrast to other structures. The problem is that such buildings can be expensive to maintain, and may need imported materials. This can bring on premature obsolescence. Buildings erected to modest standards and using locally available materials and locally-known techniques are usually more cost-effective as well as easier and cheaper to run and maintain. Some countries have even managed to use their existing buildings more intensively as an alternative to building more schools, e.g. having morning and afternoon shifts at primary level (though this is taxing on the teachers and may be awkward for pupils and their parents).

It is tempting for countries with a shortage of teachers, books, and finance to experiment with new **educational technology**. 'Distance teaching' is the generic term for methods of broadcasting lessons through radio or television, or by correspondence. These methods certainly have a place in schools curricula, but usually as a supplement to conventional methods. They invariably need teachers to interpret and follow up the lessons, and technicians to maintain the receiving equipment, and require special and usually costly programmes. In short, they are not panaceas for the spread of education into remote and poor regions (but Simmons – see section on further reading – shows how radio can have a place in adult education).

Where recurrent finance is scarce it is the duty of project planners to work out and clearly present the **operating cost implications** of what they are proposing. Many projects founder and are wasted through ignorance or over-optimism in this regard. The future availability of teaching materials also needs to be checked. It is very well to get a load of pencils as part of a barter trading deal, but when stocks run out shortages may arise.

Salaries normally make up the largest cost in education. The **numbers of teachers** required at a particular school or college will depend mainly on the number of pupils and the range of subjects being taught. Although staff–student ratios are often laid down as a matter of national educational policy, the extent to which schools conform will depend on local circumstances. In primary schools the ratio varies between 1:30 and 1:40 (though in developing countries much larger classes have been known), in secondary schools 1:15 and 1:25, and at the tertiary level 1:10 and 1:15.

Offering more **subjects** at higher level, for example to sixth formers, is expensive since it requires specialist teachers and sometimes special facilities, and a much larger intake of students at lower levels so as to ensure an adequate ratio at sixth form. As any teacher or lecturer knows, the offer of extra subject options complicates the design of curricula disproportionately.

A well designed curriculum can also lead to space savings and therefore lower building costs, since the maximum use can be obtained from a given number of classrooms.

Another source of savings can arise in **building design** through the flexible use of interior space, such as for different communal activities. Assembly halls can be used as dining-rooms or gymnasia, while dining-halls are more cost-effective when lunch hours are staggered and where there is self-service. There are guidelines for the design and building costs of educational buildings available from UNESCO and Britain's Building Research Establishment.

Some practical points

1 In some poor countries the commendable urge to reduce illiteracy can turn the development of education into a wasteful 'numbers game' unless there are sufficient well trained teachers to support the programme, plus funds in the budget to cover all essential recurrent outlays. Without such complementary resources the race against illiteracy will simply spread resources more thinly and lower educational standards.

2 Students of the labour market should make due allowance for the pheno-menon of 'job search' among apparently unemployed educated people.

3 It is common for the 'brain drain' of educated nationals to coexist with the use of expatriate educators, often provided under aid. At its worst, such aid connives at the preservation of an unattractive salary and career structure for local teachers. However, the positive aspects of this counter-flow are that people joining the 'brain drain' may be acquiring useful skills and experience which they may then use upon their return, and meanwhile are providing foreign exchange remittances to their families and relatives.

4 More than in most projects, in education there is the possibility of dissonance between public and private benefits. On the one hand, society may gain from turning out an excess supply of history teachers, which keeps down wages in this profession and ensures an ample supply to work in schools. On the other hand, turning out more people with strictly unnecessary paper quali-fications who can then get government jobs benefits the students but hardly society. In the latter case, the issue of cost recovery should be explored.

5 In poor countries one of the most frequent and severe problems is the shortage of recurrent budgetary support for projects whose initial funding may have been secured from foreign aid.

Checklist of main questions

1 Country background
Basic data on illiteracy, population, school-age population, current numbers of students at the different levels.
Does the country have an explicit educational policy or target?
How large is the education budget?
What are the main educational institutions, e.g. the ministry of education, universities, colleges, schools? Numbers and location.

Division between the private and public education sectors.

National indices of educational attainment, e.g. number of passes in examinations.

2 Summary of project

Outline of project, and history of its evolution.

Which parties are taking the lead in promoting it?

Is there a feasibility study? If so, give brief details.

How will it be financed? Is there provision in the national budget for all the initial and recurrent costs involved?

3 Demand for education

Forecasts of school-age population in the relevant district or region.

Implication of national literacy or educational targets.

Prospects for students, either in continuing education or in employment.

Is there likely to be a demand for the particular skills and qualifications being turned out by the project? What is the evidence of labour market studies, e.g. trends in relative wages, unfilled vacancies, the 'educated unemployed', etc.? Is emigration likely?

4 Costs and finance

Give details of the construction costs (for a building) or acquisition cost (for equipment). Is there a firm basis for these estimates, e.g. tenders, contracts? What is the breakdown between foreign and local expenses?

Have the recurrent cost implications of the project been fully estimated?

Is the proposed solution cost-effective? How do such indicators as space standards and cost per student compare with those elsewhere?

Is there financial provision for the project? Are the future budgetary implications supportable? Is there a secure source of revenue for supporting services, notably the salaries of teachers and instructors, but also teaching materials (paper, chalk) and services (electric power)?

What cost recovery, if any, is being proposed?

5 Benefits

Is it possible to measure the improvements in the quantity, and the quality, of education that will result?

Will there be cost economies in comparison with present methods?

Will there be tangible benefits to individual students, such as expectations of better pay?

Is the output of educated students likely to be beneficial to society, or will it be destabilising? If the students emigrate, are they likely to remit funds to the benefit of their country or education?

6 Teachers and instructors

What is the overall supply and demand position for teachers?

Are there grounds for thinking that sufficient would be available for the project in question?

Are their pay and conditions of service likely to impair the project?

Do the teachers have a satisfactory career structure?

Is teacher training provided?

Further reading

R. P. Dore, *The Diploma Disease*, Allen & Unwin, London, 1976. (A masterly diagnosis of the malaise in higher education in the Third World.)

Stanislav Andreski, *The African Predicament* (chapter on 'The Shibboleth of

Education'), Michael Joseph, London, 1968. (Very perceptive about the African scene.)

Christopher Colclough, 'Policies for Educational Reform', chapter in Cassen and Wolfson (eds.), *Planning for Growing Populations*, OECD Development Centre, Paris, 1978.

John Simmons, 'Education for Development, Reconsidered', article in *World Development*, November/December 1979. (Pergamon Press Ltd.)

10
Health

Personal health takes up a lot of time, attention and money of people and their governments. Good health has always been regarded as a key to human happiness, and it is recognised as one of the basic needs of life which governments should help their citizens to achieve.

There is a heavy flow of resources into the health sector. In developed countries spending on health by private and public sources combined typically varies from 5% to 7% of national income, while in developing countries it is more likely to be from 2% to 4%. Very rough estimates suggest that in developing countries almost twice as much is spent on health as on education.

The sorts of health projects that come forward in developed and developing countries differ greatly, and this chapter will be addressed largely to the circumstances of developing countries. Where the age structure of the population differs, so will health needs, with the problems of children assuming far greater emphasis in developing countries. The incidence of illness depends on climate and environment, not to mention poverty and malnutrition. Health services in most countries tend to concentrate on the provision of curative urban care rather than on rural preventive facilities. Of course in part this is justified in order to provide a functioning health pyramid (see page 98), but in practice most resources go into expensive curative services – a reflection of the political power structure. Health needs differ from one region to another and therefore the search for international standards of health care is misplaced and dangerous. The search should be for *appropriate* standards.

Factors in improving health

Three important elements in improving health are better nutrition, sanitation and health care facilities. An advance on all three fronts has produced a dramatic drop in the death rate over the last century. Life expectancy is now seventy years or more in most developed countries; in 1850 it was only forty years for males in England and Wales (thirty-five in London). Progress has been even more dramatic in recent times in the developing world; in India life expectancy in 1945 was a little over thirty, whereas in 1977 it was fifty-one, a result that depends heavily on the reduction in infant mortality. Nevertheless, life expectancy in Africa (forty-seven) and South Asia (forty-nine) still has a long way to go to match that in the developed world, and in the poorest regions half of all children who die do so in the first year of life.

Improved **nutrition** is basic to health since it makes people stronger and more immune to disease. This was an important factor in improvements in life expectancy observed in Europe and North America in the nineteenth century before medical advances were made. Of course, nutritional advances are not always regarded as the province of health projects, nor the specific responsibility of a ministry of health. It is true that specific problems of nutrition, like iodine deficiency, goitre and vitamin A deficiency, can be tackled as part of health policy, but general nutrition can only be brought about by overall improvements in social and economic conditions (though school meals, food subsidies and occasionally food aid may help).

In any case specific nutrition projects, apart from those mentioned above, are inherently problematic. Personal nutritional requirements vary according to size, age, type of work, environment, etc., and average figures for calorie intake, for instance, mask these essential differences. It may also be the case that consumers cannot afford what is recommended, or they may not be willing to accept the recommended food – especially if they do not find it palatable. Finally, nutrition projects usually take a lot of administering and recurrent expenditure. They are best started, therefore, on the basis of pilot schemes.

At first sight it is obvious that improved **sanitation** – especially providing clean water, latrines and sewerage – contributes to improved health. But common sense suggests that only when other complementary improvements are also carried out will it be effective. Clean water may be stored in insanitary vessels. People may continue their former unhygienic habits. In short, there are many ways for clean water to become contaminated before it is consumed. What is more certain is that increases in the *volume* of water available to the household will reduce disease inasmuch as it encourages washing and cleaning (though piped water could cause disease to spread rather than reduce it).

In an ideal world, improvements in **health care** services would be closely harmonised with dietary advances and better sanitation in order to produce the complementarity necessary for spectacular gains in health. In practice such programmes are hard to pull off because of administrative complexities. Perhaps the best course is to introduce an improvement in one aspect (e.g. better water supplies) to communities that show signs of awareness of a desire to make progress in related fields (e.g. improved latrines).

Benefits of health projects

If a project has a high probability of increasing average well-being, prolonging life, and reducing the chance of debilitating illness, it could be argued that these reasons are sufficient and should not be weighed in the balance of costs and benefits. The problem is similar to that of valuing airport or road investments that are likely to reduce danger to life and limb. The outlays that individuals make to safeguard their health reflect the value of good health to them, and the size of public spending per head on health services reflects pressures put on government by the public. But spending on health cannot be seen in isolation from other forms of expenditure.

Once decisions are made (e.g. to try and halve infant mortality by a certain date) the main need is to ensure that the most cost-effective solution is chosen. **Cost-effectiveness** is thus the criterion used in appraisal of projects for this sector.

Improved health may have **economic effects** through its impact on people as workers and as users of health services. While common sense suggests this the research evidence has so far been inconclusive. Endemic disease (like hookworm and anaemia in the tropics) can greatly reduce a worker's capacity for physical and mental effort. Periodic illness can cause absences from work which may cause losses for employers as well as the worker. Sickness and malnutrition also impede education and training, and can lead to a waste of national resources as well as the time of the students. People suffering from certain intestinal diseases consume excessive amounts of food, at a cost to themselves and society. Then there is the cost of treatment – doctors, nurses, health workers, drugs, internment – as well as the patient's loss of earnings. A hospital built in Uganda in the 1960s was estimated to cost as much to run per patient per day as the room rate in Kampala's best hotel!

Taking a wider view of the effect of health on economic development, endemic disease can restrict the settlement and exploitation of otherwise promising regions. The eradication of malaria and sleeping sickness, for instance, has opened up large parts of the tropics for settlement. In economies dependent on tourism the outbreak of particular diseases can jeopardise income and foreign exchange earnings.

Health projects can generate some financial returns, since people are often willing to pay something for their treatment. Where charges are made, they can be taken as a minimum (and very unsatisfactory) measure of the benefits received. It is not only in wealthy countries that a private sector in health flourishes. In very poor countries it is common to find people spending relatively large sums on traditional practitioners and simple remedies, including the cost of travel to the nearest service, which also implies a loss of earnings.

For public services it is rarely feasible to recover the full cost of the facilities from poor people. Nevertheless, many governments levy nominal charges to defray part of the expense. Beneficiaries are used to paying for health services and a small charge may even increase the respect they have for these provisions. Some countries impose a small registration fee on patients turning up for the first time, and perhaps a nominal charge for drugs. These levies may be useful in preventing abuse of the service, provided they are not onerous enough to turn away *bona fide* clients. Even in so-called 'free' health services it is common to find employees abusing their position by charging patients. This is frequently the case where public salaries are very low, and/or there is heavy pressure on the service.

There is another form of financial return to public authorities which arises where a new facility is substituted for an inefficient existing one. An improved district hospital might give scope for operating cost savings compared to existing facilities. Likewise, money spent on an effective campaign against a specific disease might save the expense of treating sufferers in hospital.

Planning health services

Ideally, any project in the health sector should be judged against the programme for the sector as a whole to make sure it fulfils national priorities. Planning a system of health services and campaigns should go through at least the following stages:

i. Examine demographic data to find out the distribution of population in the area concerned and its make-up by age and sex. In many countries, however, the size of population may not be known.

ii. Collate data on the incidence of diseases and the causes of death, if possible by region. This would point to diseases that ought to form the main targets of a mass health effort. It would also indicate whether the figures for infant mortality, or for deaths among women in child-bearing age groups, were serious.

iii. Describe the existing pattern of health care, private and public, and the section of the population it reaches. In the majority of countries this will turn out to be biased towards urban centres and the provision of curative facilities. (We refer to modern services. Forms of traditional medicine are usually widespread.)

iv. A comparison of available facilities with national needs should be a pointer to the most urgent projects. Such uncontroversial criteria as population density, mortality rates in different groups and regions, morbidity (proneness to disease), and access to services should give clues as to where the thrust of health policy should be.

v. If the objectives of health policy can be agreed, as in iv, it should be possible to devise the most cost-effective projects to achieve them.

vi. Although a proper cost–benefit analysis will not be possible, an essential part of planning will be to carefully describe, assess and – where possible – quantify the benefits. This should be done in terms of health gains, and the number of people likely to benefit. (One useful check on the cost of the proposals is to work out the annual cost of treating people, or of bed provision. While this is not conclusive, it can help to put the proposals in perspective.)

Planners will be forced to use imperfect statistics, and should be aware of their shortcomings. Health data are normally most complete for urban areas, while evidence on such matters as cause of death and morbidity is least satisfactory for rural areas. Unless allowances are made for such biases, the data could be used to support a further concentration of resources on urban areas, where the problem might appear to be worse. Major health problems in less developed, or more far-flung, regions may be missed. Certainly, better health data would be a good thing, though it has to be said that in most developing countries the major needs of policy are fairly obvious and that better health statistics have a low priority.

One approach which is *not* recommended is to apply desirable overall ratios, say, of doctors to population, or clinics per village, or hospital beds per head, as a means of deciding how much health investment should occur. Such ratios are invariably obtained from countries with different circumstances, or as an average from many different kinds of country. They are not relevant to the real needs of the country in question, nor to the ability of the country to afford the investment and the cost of keeping the facilities and personnel going. As Cassen points out, such ratios ought to arise as the product of careful planning, rather than be plucked from the air at the outset: 'The ratios should arise from a designed health system which on the basis of available resources can provide access to care for the great majority of the people within a reasonably short period of time.' (R. Cassen – see section on further reading, page 102.)

Nevertheless they can be used to check the appropriateness of proposals. For example it is scarcely sensible for a poor country to plan for the same ratio of doctors to patients, or hospital bed space per head, as rich countries.

Types of health service

Mention of 'urban bias' will prepare the reader for discussion of the methods of providing health care. At opposite poles are the **curative** and **preventive** schools of thought. The curatives advocate treatment of patients who already have a diagnosable complaint, in hospitals or clinics under the strict supervision of qualified medical personnel. The preventives urge methods of preventing the emergence of the disease, such as environmental improvements (water supplies, anti-malaria measures, latrines), vaccination and inoculation campaigns, and education of the community in nutrition, hygiene and personal health.

In a properly planned system, as adumbrated earlier, curative and preventive facilities will complement each other. If they do not, strains arise. If 'preventers' do not have sufficiently good curative facilities to refer patients to, the credibility of the whole service will suffer. Or if the 'curers' return their successful cases to an environment where they are prone to a recurrence of the disease, this is a recipe for waste and failure. (The World Bank quotes a South American programme for the care of premature babies that produced survival rates comparable with those in North America, but when the infants were discharged and returned to their homes 70% died within three months.)

Despite the evident need for complementarity, in most countries the *balance* between the preventive and curative sides is not right. There is more to it than 'urban bias', though that is commonly present. The desire to emulate international standards of hospital construction and equipping can lead to over-ambitious plans, which are often abetted by investors keen to leave a prominent landmark. (Mostly the pressure for more elaborate facilities comes from the government – see the case study by Hoadley in Further reading.) The medical profession also has a bias for providing the best curative facilities, since it is then easier to control the type and quality of medical care provided, and doctors have been slow to accept the need for 'para-medical' workers with inferior qualifications to their own.

However, while preventive services will undeniably help more people more cost-effectively the practical results have often been disappointing – if not downright failures. This is because preventive services require a high proportion of appropriately trained staff and a well organised administration. Many such schemes have failed because these were not provided.

The form of measure combining preventive and curative elements is the **vertical campaign** against specific diseases. These campaigns have a single aim and their own personnel, and are only loosely related to the rest of the national health services. Examples are vaccination against smallpox, immunisation against TB, and anti-malarial measures. In the early stages of such campaigns, spectacular progress is often possible. But there normally comes a point where the consolidation of gains, and the final stages of eradication, can only be done by integrating the operation with regular health services. It is one thing to declare an all-out war against a disease – the objective has political appeal and dramatic results are possible in the early stages. But the early gains will be jeopardised, and the disease will recur, unless local health centres are there to diagnose the disease and treat it in its early stages. It is precisely at this point that pitfalls arise, since continued progress depends on adequate budgets and administration.

Family planning is a special case of a vertical campaign, since it is often organised separately from other health services. It has been found that the most effective approach is through programmes of mother and child care. During periods of post-natal care, women are receptive to advice about their own health and that of their existing children. They are often willing to accept contraceptive advice, especially from someone who has earned their confidence through assistance during pregnancy and childbirth. Maternity clinics are among the more successful examples of preventive health care since they meet an obvious need and are easier to plan and maintain than other forms.

In order to achieve the widest possible coverage at low cost, and to make the best use of costly modern curative centres, health services in developing countries should follow a **pyramidal form**. Its broad base will consist of **community health** workers. They will be people working in their own community, or in one they are familiar with, and will have a few months' formal training. Their tasks will be to diagnose and treat simple common illnesses, and to refer cases outside their competence to more highly qualified medical personnel. They will also have a role in educating the community in improved nutrition, hygiene and personal health habits. They will administer simple drugs.

The next layer of the 'pyramid' is a small **district hospital**, the local urban **clinic**, or **rural health centre**. Their task is to provide treatment beyond the range of the community health worker, and a large proportion of their patients will be referred to them. The buildings should have proper facilities for storing a range of drugs, and be staffed by people of the level of medical assistant and midwife with several years of formal training. The third layer, forming the apex of the system, is the **referral hospital**, located in the larger population centres. It would be staffed by fully-qualified doctors, and equipped with an operating theatre, laboratory, X-ray facilities, etc.

Each of the three layers depends on the effective functioning of the other two. The credibility of the community health worker will be impaired if the referral services higher up the pyramid are poor, or lack staff and drugs. The referral hospital will soon become overloaded if too many cases are referred to it, for example because more basic facilities do not exist. The motivation of the personnel, the trust of the community, and the supply of transport, drugs, etc. are essential at all levels.

No outline of health services would be complete without a mention of **mobile services**. These include light aircraft and specially adapted trucks to form mobile clinics. The aim is to increase the access of remote populations to medical care, as well as to enable qualified doctors to visit areas that would otherwise be denied them. Flying doctor services are successfully operated in a number of developed countries (e.g. Australia) and several developing ones (of which Kenya's is the best known). Moreover, they are not confined to evacuating emergency cases from remote areas – most of them provide regular back-up to local health centres.

As a generalisation, though, vehicular services are not as cost-effective as permanently staffed health posts. They can be complementary, e.g. providing professional and logistical support to these posts, and regular visits may be good for the morale of staff working in remote areas.

For all but the greatest distances, land vehicles are cheaper than air.

Transporting staff to meet their patients is costly, and a lot of the time of scarce health care personnel is spent travelling. Organising the service requires efficient administration (e.g. making sure the vehicle arrives in a village on time) and the operation is vulnerable to a shortage of petrol and the breakdown of vehicles.

Hospital and health centre projects

Since the majority of capital projects in the health service concern the supply of buildings and equipment it is as well to focus more sharply on these investments. The structure of the health pyramid has been described above: at the base are local health posts, each serving up to 5,000 people, while at the apex is the large referral hospital at national or regional level. In between are district hospitals, suburban clinics and rural health centres. The first point to be made is that a project should clearly relate to some such national structure, and the services above and below that it depends on should be in place and functioning well. For instance, a district hospital planned for an area without an effective local health network will tend to get swamped with patients who should have been treated at a more basic level.

It is also true that the construction of a large comprehensive hospital cannot make up for the absence of a structure at lower levels. Apart from the points mentioned above, the catchment area of a hospital is usually limited, and does not increase with size. It follows that the best way of extending coverage is by building more modest structures at appropriate local or district levels.

In **planning and designing** hospitals there is a temptation for specialist medical architects and consultants to recommend high standards of facilities, in line with those in wealthy developed countries and catering for the latest advances in health care. Unfortunately, one or two projects of this kind can exhaust a country's health budget, and introduce a bias towards expensive curative care which debilitates the rest of the system. It is important that planners give the right 'steer' to consultants through setting terms of reference and target cost figures.

To be provocative, planning hospitals is too important to be left to doctors. Professional medical opinion is certainly one contribution in the shaping of the final design, but other parties concerned, such as nurses, also have a voice. In some countries strong cultural traditions should be heeded, over such things as the type of building and the latitude allowed to the patient's relatives and friends (e.g. in bringing food). Hospital administrators, too, ought to be consulted. The authors have visited large, brand new and well equipped urban hospitals that had been unused for some years, while over the road the old crowded hospital that was being 'replaced' was still packing in patients. The fundamental reason was that the hospital administration found it impossible to cope with operating the new building, still less pay for its recurrent costs.

One way of reconciling the valid points of view of different interest groups is to appoint a working group or committee to be in charge of planning and design, with consultants reporting to it, and taking evidence from the major parties concerned. The committee should contain spokespeople for the finance ministries or agencies, and the users. It is true that no masterpiece was ever designed by a committee, and that this procedure could be lengthy and cumbersome, but it is more likely to produce a viable and satisfactory answer than entrusting the job to a brilliant individual.

Not all projects involve the creation of new facilities – a common request is for the **rehabilitation** or replacement of existing hospitals that have sunk into dilapidation. In these situations there is some planning data to go on, and the main line of enquiry should be how the facility came to deteriorate in the first place. If other aspects of health provision are so bad, there is not much hope for the survival of the new facility.

In rehabilitation projects the identification of benefits is rather different from that involved for wholly new facilities. It is important to pin down health care staff about what is unacceptable about the situation in question. The benefits might be reduced cross-infection, a lower maintenance bill, reduced loss of drugs and greater longevity of equipment, or the greater ease of attracting and retaining staff.

Once the nature of the required facilities has been decided, the next task is to consider the **scale** of provision. The use of overall ratios, such as beds per head of population, has already been discouraged. It is preferable to relate the size of a unit to its place in the health pyramid, although the size of its catchment area is important.

The hospital's **bed occupancy rate** can be a useful item of data which will depend on the most common cases, and must allow spare capacity for emergencies. It is a useful rule of thumb to expect an 80% bed occupancy rate, though one should remember that the more space there is the more likely it is to be filled, and customs differ between countries on patients' length of stay in hospital. For childbirth, for example, time in hospital varies from two or three days to ten to fourteen days. In many developing countries bed occupancy exceeds 100% since some patients do not even have beds.

Deciding the **number of beds** is the first stage in the calculation of costs. Buildings are clearly the largest element in costs. If medical authorities are able to use a standard cost for building, the crucial factor becomes the **space** required per bed. In developing countries 35 square metres per bed is typical for general hospitals, and less for local hospitals, Bed space includes corridors, services, and medical facilities, so the fewer functions that are provided the less space is needed. The supply of equipment could add 15%–20% to the capital cost.

Finally, the most common problems encountered in running hospitals are shortages of **operating** funds, of qualified staff, and of administrative capacity for handling complex new structures. The planner must be confident that the project can be handled within these constraints.

The problem of **drugs** has received disproportionate attention in the context of hospitals in developing countries. The marketing activities of international pharmaceutical firms have attracted hostile scrutiny. It is alleged that their aggressive selling methods have foisted a large amount of unsuitable expensive drugs on to developing countries, which eat up a large share of health budgets, and reinforce the urban and curative bias in the system.

To an extent the foreign firms are merely responding to the bias already present in national systems. There may be unsavoury aspects to the transaction, the offer of various kinds of bribes by less scrupulous firms or the demand for bribes by some officials in the countries concerned. The demand for pharmaceuticals is endemic and perhaps excessive in health systems, from the poor as well as the rich, and the excessive prescription of drugs is resorted to by medical practitioners everywhere as the line of least resistance. It is facile to expect such attitudes to change with greater education, since the syndrome persists in the wealthiest countries. The planner can try to ensure that drugs bought by the national health system are suitable, are not bought in quantities excessive to needs, and that production and packaging are done locally where possible.

In developing countries the drugs problem is more likely to be shortage than surfeit. While some parts of the system have an excessive supply, other parts, especially rural areas and the more remote networks, run short. This can result from irregular distribution, shortage of funds, over-prescription and/or hoarding by patients, and theft and black-marketing by medical personnel (sometimes in lieu of adequate salaries).

Some practical points

1 The true need for health care services in the poorer rural areas is often not shown up in health statistics. The inadequacy of such data is part of the general syndrome whereby the real extent of poverty in rural areas is hidden to all but the most determined observers. The implication is that planners should not use health statistical data uncritically so as to unwittingly perpetuate the urban bias in the system.

2 Planners are well advised to shun international stipulations such as target ratios of doctors to population, or hospital beds per head. The best can be the enemy of the good.

3 Projects for rehabilitating an old, run-down facility are especially problematic. It is a bad sign if existing facilities have been allowed to deteriorate (just as it is an encouraging sign when staff are coping heroically with antiquated and overcrowded premises). Rehabilitation can be a more cost-effective approach than construction of an entirely new facility, provided the poor state of the premises does not stem from a deeper malaise in the system.

4 The most common problems that arise in running hospitals are a shortage of funds for recurrent operations, a shortage of qualified staff, and the incapacity of administrators to handle complex new structures.

Checklist of main questions

1 Country background
Give details of the size, geographical and age distribution of the population.
What data are there on the state of health of the population?
Outline the present systems of health care, distinguishing moderr from traditional, and private from public.
What is the institutional framework for national health policy?
What has been the size, and allocation, of the national health budget in recent years?

2 Summary of project
What is its purpose? What type of project is it? Does the proposal have a history? Which parties are pressing most strongly for it?
Is there a feasibility study, or preliminary designs? Have the consultants

previously worked in the country? Do they show sympathy with local problems?

What alternatives have been explored? In the case of a big city hospital, is this really a priority use for the health budget?

Show how the project fits into a national or regional system of health care.

3 Need for project

How is the project justified? Is the area to be served especially poor in health provision? Are present services inadequate, or are there no services? What are the main causes of death and morbidity at present? How do inhabitants currently gain access to medical care? What other factors are present that may frustrate the impact of the project on general health? Have any estimates been made of the likely impact of the project on the incidence of disease, infant mortality? Will there be wider benefits, e.g. to agriculture, transport, education?

4 Supporting services and facilities

Will local health staff be available? If they are not currently in place, what plans exist to attract them to the posts?

Are supplies of essential drugs, materials and equipment assured?

What provisions are being made to train all personnel, especially if new equipment or techniques are being introduced?

5 Costs and finance

What are the capital and recurrent costs of the project, divided into local and imported items?

How are these to be met? Specify foreign sources of funds, if any, and whether there is provision for future recurrent costs in the national budget.

Is the solution cost-effective? Compare with costs of alternative solutions where they exist. Do such yardsticks as space per bed, cost per bed, average length of patient stay, etc. compare to those elsewhere in the country? Is the building over-designed, or appropriately designed in the light of local expectations, practice, and materials?

6 Implementation

Are the health authorities fully aware of the possible extra demands on themselves from the new project? Are they likely to be able to cope?

Were they fully consulted over the plans and designs?

Have consultants and contractors been selected? What is their track record? How firm are cost estimates and implementation schedules?

Is there a critical path for the work? Which items are critical?

Will there be disruption to existing medical work during construction? What plans are there to minimise inconvenience?

7 Evaluation

What plans are there to evaluate the completed project?

Further reading

World Bank, *Health: Sector Policy Paper*, Washington DC, 1980. (A very readable guide to the main issues, with a useful statistical annex.)

Robert Cassen, 'Health', a chapter in Cassen and Wolfson (eds.), *Planning for Growing Populations*, OECD Development Centre, Paris, 1978. (A fine review of current issues.)

B. Abel-Smith and A. Leiserson, *Poverty, Development and Health Policy*, World Health Organisation, Geneva, 1978.

J. Bryant, *Health and the Developing World*, Cornell University Press, 1969.

K. W. Newell (ed.), *Health by the People*, World Health Organisation, Geneva, 1975.

Gill Walt and Patrick Vaughan, *An Introduction to the Primary Health Care Approach in Developing Countries*, Ross Institute of Tropical Hygiene Publications, London, 1981. (Contains an invaluable annotated bibliography.)

J. S. Hoadley, *Aid, Politics and Hospitals in Western Samoa*, World Development no. 5/6, 1980.

The 'Health For All' series of publications from the World Health Organisation, Geneva, also contains much important and topical material.

11
Housing

Most people in the world build their own houses. Many others make their own arrangement for building, purchase or rent. Only a minority of households rely on the government for the supply of accommodation. Why is the government called upon to intervene in this, largely private, market?

After food, people spend more on housing than on anything else. In housing studies, occupants have been found to spend between 10% and 30% (or more) of their regular incomes on rent or loan repayments. It is banal to note that housing is a major influence on the way people live. Bad housing depresses welfare. Overcrowded, unsafe, insanitary, unserviced or remote accommodation can make life nasty, brutish and short. Poor housing directly impinges on others. The rapid growth of cities in many parts of the world has made it much more difficult for people to make their own housing in a manner satisfactory to their neighbours and urban authorities.

Thus governments are being prevailed upon to plan, regulate and service housing, especially in urban areas. They also commonly assist private housing development through subsidies to housing loans, favourable tax treatment to house owners, and sometimes help in the supply of building materials. There are many ways in which governments can influence the amount and quality of accommodation short of putting up houses themselves. However, this chapter is concerned with the ultimate form of public housing policy, in which the government undertakes house building or improvement on its own account. For reasons which will become apparent, we will concentrate on housing for the poorer groups.

Policies and projects

The kind of housing projects which governments carry out for the benefit of their poorer citizens has varied over the years in response to changes in public opinion. Until about twenty years ago, governments committed to active housing policies conceived their role as being the construction of good quality finished units for rent or sale to favoured groups. The latter (the 'target group') were often public employees for whom the provision of decent housing was an important part of their remuneration. Later, when publicly built houses were put up in greater numbers, the target group was broadened to include people of more modest means.

Because all countries had limited housing budgets the number of dwellings put up fell far short of those wanting them. The occupants came to form a privileged class among the needy housing claimants, and the standard of housing provided appealed to many outside the target group. So many lower-middle- and middle-class residents occupied units meant for their poorer compatriots.

The provision of **finished public housing** as a solution to the housing problems of lower income groups is widespread only in some developed countries, in city-states like Hong Kong and Singapore, in a few oil-rich countries, and in certain dependencies like Gibraltar.

One form this policy has taken is the construction of new estates to house people dislocated by the **demolition** of inner-city areas. The motives for such action may be a sincere wish to give deprived inner-city denizens a new start, the wish to redevelop central areas for commercial purposes, or to make space for essential services like highways. Whether motives are benign or cynical, it is often the case that demolition runs ahead of rehousing, thus increasing the housing deficit. Alternatively the relocation is in sites far away from the old, destroying informal working links, creating a commuter class, and causing disorientation and alienation among the rehoused people.

Site and service schemes have arisen as a solution to the housing problem. These projects provide land, essential services and (usually) minimal shelter to the residents, who then add to the structure at their own pace and to their own requirements with their own labour or with bought-in skills. It is common for the authorities to help with loans for the purchase of building materials, and to offer technical assistance for plans and building methods. These schemes are clearly an advance on the old policies in that they enable a given housing budget to stretch further, while improving occupants' choice over the accommodation they have. Even these schemes, however, have often been misdirected in that they have been taken up by people outside the strict target group (including many unabashedly middle-class residents). They are also often located away from the main industrial and commercial areas, thus worsening people's access to income and work.

The cycle of opinion now seems to have come to rest in favour of improving people's housing in the places where they happen to be. One approach is to **up-grade inner-city slums** by providing improved public services and assistance to improve structures, as in the celebrated schemes in Calcutta and Jakarta. Another is to recognise illegal occupation of land by squatters, often on the outskirts of cities, and to work towards legalising their tenure, extending the network of services to reach them, and helping with building materials loans (as in Ankara, Turkey). The merit of this approach is twofold. Existing investment in structures is preserved and enhanced, and the network of social and commercial ties is kept in being.

Housing needs

Although some kind of shelter is clearly a 'basic need', in United Nations parlance, it is very difficult to go further and specify the type and standard of housing that is a minimum requirement for life as we know it. In this respect housing differs sharply from water supply or nutrition, where one can describe minimum amounts as being essential for subsistence. Once the most basic protection has been given against the elements, housing needs are socially determined. Many people sleep in shop doorways, drainpipes, caves, tents, and igloos – and survive. Improvements to their accommodation are no doubt desirable, but life can go on without them.

Many of the problems of housing policy arise because needs cannot be objectively defined, and governments come under pressure to satisfy expectations. A housing policy that caters to what people unreasonably expect is soon limited by what the state can afford. This limit is reached more quickly in poor than in wealthy countries. The forces that cause governments to build decent housing come from public opinion, from architects who are often trained abroad in wealthier countries, and from politicians anxious not to be accused of putting up new slums.

Such houses can often not be afforded by people in the target group, unless a public subsidy is applied to the price or the rent. The consequence is either that the housing falls into the hands of families outside the target group (e.g. middle or lower-middle income groups) or else the poorer families require subsidies. Because of a finite housing budget, subsidies use up resources that might otherwise go to benefiting a large number of other poor families.

This is the danger of equating need with expectations. It is equally hazardous to trust in the estimation of housing 'deficits' which rely on a calculation of the number of dwellings falling short of some desirable standard. Fixing such minimum standards is always more or less subjective. The occupants of sub-standard housing may, and often do, resist being moved to better units. Defining sub-standard dwellings is all too often a licence to demolish them, and demolition has frequently proved to be much easier than new construction. Defining a housing deficit may, paradoxically, be a means of increasing it.

Planning in relation to demand

The assumption in what follows is that the government's housing budget is limited and that it wishes to minimise the public subsidy in housing provision. This implies that what is provided must bear a close relationship to what the selected target group can afford to pay.

The type of housing project that the government considers will depend on the position of the target group within the national pyramid of income distribution. Where data on income distribution exists, it is usual to classify households according to their average annual incomes and to accumulate a statistical picture of the share of national income taken by households at different income levels. Households may be arranged into percentiles, or deciles, enabling one to make statements such as 'the poorest 10% of households earn less than x rupees per annum', or 'the third decile of households (those lying between 20% and 30% on the pyramid of income distribution) earn between y and z rupees'.

Although countries, especially in the developing world, vary greatly in their circumstances, as a rule governments can rely on the wealthier half of their population (those households in the fifth decile and upwards) to make their own housing arrangements, with or without the use of official loan agencies. If the poorer groups, the proper target of governmental action, are taken to be the lowest four deciles of households, a layered approach is to be recommended. Site and service schemes, including some built core structures, are suitable for the richer among this group, that is those households with a modicum of economic security, some regular income, and resources to develop the plots. The poorer families may be best helped by slum up-grading, the *de facto* recognition and up-grading of squatter settlements, and the provision of rented accommodation in site and service schemes.

Everywhere, governments find that their greatest problem is designing projects and policies that benefit the very poorest layers of society, say the lowest one or two deciles. Such households tend to have the least prospect of regular incomes to make payments, the fewest financial and personal assets, and the least secure foothold in the modern economy. Governments can try and reach such households directly or indirectly. Direct assistance takes the form of slum up-grading, the recognition and servicing of squatter settlements, or the provision of very rudimentary site and service plots (what in Brazil are called 'urbanised lots' and are simply plots with basic services). Indirect help consists of increasing the supply of rented accommodation, such as in site and service schemes occupied by rather wealthier families. Experience shows that such projects often develop rooms for letting, which the site occupiers use to generate the cash for further building.

A planning sequence

If government policy is to reach a certain population group, then in the normal case where large continued subsidies are not feasible planners need to follow a simple design sequence:

1 Identify the target group

When formulating a national housing strategy, it is helpful to identify needy groups according to their typical household income, and to locate them within the national pyramid of income distribution. This exercise ought to result in figures showing a range of monthly incomes for the households in question. Problems arise where there are no good data on household incomes, where incomes are variable and irregular, and where pay or income is in kind.

Sometimes it is possible to identify the target group directly, as when a settlement is to be relocated, or when the existing population in an area is to be the beneficiary (as in up-grading schemes). Incomes and economic status should then be discovered by household survey.

2 Estimate what they can afford

Estimating what households with a given income can afford to pay on housing can be a very subjective calculation. Some people prefer to have a humble dwelling and to devote most of their income to food or consumer durables. Others value a good house above all else and will spend a high proportion of their income on it. Newcomers to a city may be willing to pay a relatively high sum in order to be well placed for employment. Others may opt for sharing with relatives.

Using as a basis household survey data, planners normally assume that households can afford to spend 20%–25% of their incomes on housing. The need for flexibility suggested above can be met by housing officials exercising judgement about what individual applicants can afford and are willing to pay, against the 20%–25% yardstick. The effect of future inflation on loan repayments should also be allowed for.

3 Derive a design cost

What the target group can afford can be converted into a design cost target once the financial link is specified. If the housing authority intends to sell on credit terms of 10% repayable over twelve years, then a family able to afford 25% from a monthly income of $200 could (in theory) afford a dwelling costing $4,087.

The cost that is to be recovered from the occupant, either through rents or loan repayments, should cover all those elements that are not normally provided by the government and defrayed from general taxation (access roads, schools, etc.) or by public utilities and covered by user charges (power, water, etc.). Thus, land purchase, on-site infrastructure, design and supervision fees, etc. are legitimate charges to make on the occupants of a housing scheme.

4 Provide cost-effective facilities
The target cost figure which is the output of the above planning sequence is, ideally, the ceiling below which the architects and builders have to work. It is pointless to generalise about the standard of accommodation that can be supplied for any particular cost. That depends above all on the local price of land, wage rates and the price of building materials. For a given outlay much more can be achieved in some countries than in others. There are some countries where costs are such that solutions can be considered for the poorest which elsewhere can only be afforded by wealthier groups.

It ought to be a truism that the facilities provided should be designed in consultation with the intended occupants, and should respect local traditions. This is not always so. In some societies families are used to sharing services like cooking units and toilets, while in others privacy and exclusivity are the norm. Many families would prefer an extra bedroom to a separate kitchen. Some occupants would favour a larger plot of land, even at the expense of a larger home, in order to grow food, keep animals or rear poultry. These customs and preferences can be discovered by consulting the target group and observing what currently goes on. They are offended by imported concepts and designs brought from elsewhere without modification. (Industrialised systems building is an extreme case, and has an unhappy experience in both developed and developing countries.)

Self-help is a popular concept in low-income housing since it can simultaneously reduce the initial cost of a project and allow occupants maximum freedom in developing their house as they choose. It is certainly desirable that residents should be able to add on to their core units if and when they want, and in a manner they choose. Some things are done more cheaply and efficiently by a contractor at the beginning, even though they may not be strictly necessary straightaway (on-site roads, wet-cores, mains sewers, etc.). But planners should resist the argument, often heard, that a contractor could finish all the houses more cheaply than the residents themselves could achieve by self-help. This is not necessarily the case, and it might lift the houses beyond the reach of the target group; it would also provide standardised dwellings that could prove unpopular with occupants.

5 Make financial arrangements
Low-income housing schemes often stand or fall by the arrangements made to enable occupants to buy or rent their property. Taking **rents** first, they should be pitched somewhere between the market rent for that type of property and the level necessary for the implementing agency to cover its costs. There should in any case be provision for periodic rent review to allow for inflation.

There are too many examples of public housing schemes where rents are so low that they scarcely even cover recurrent costs of maintenance and repair, with the result that the property rapidly deteriorates and the authority has little cash flow for investment in other schemes. On the other hand, it would be unrealistic to require the authorities to charge rents equal to those prevailing on the open market. Tenants should get some benefit from the economies of scale and the absence of profit that can be expected from public schemes.

Where houses or apartments are sold to occupants it is common for the authorities to include a subsidy in the terms of the loan repayment, as well as in the actual price of the house. (In economic terms the two amount to the same thing, namely a reduction in the discounted value of future repayments.) In most countries house purchasers are given some relief from the onus of fully commercial loan terms, either by interest subsidy or by fiscal offsets. The government may set up a housing bank channelling subsidised credit to house buyers, or it may favour private building societies or loan associations with fiscal privileges to themselves or their clients. Thailand is one country where the spread of private housing finance has done more to improve the housing conditions of lower-income groups than direct action by the government.

Cross-subsidisation within schemes is quite common. The project authorities plan a mixed estate for residents of different incomes and including industrial and commercial properties. The plots, houses and services provided to the better-off occupants can be charged for at an economic rate and any surplus devoted to reducing charges to the poorer occupants. There is much to commend this system, provided it does not become an excuse for building middle-income housing and diverting attention, finance and resources away from the lower-income groups.

If a subsidy is to be provided to occupants of government housing, there is much to be said for applying it to the price of units meant for the poorest groups. It is often valuable for the residents to have a short breathing space before repayments begin. In site and service schemes this releases the plot-holder to do some development, which might result in the creation of space for rent or premises from which a trade can be practised. As every house-buyer knows, the first few years witness serious cash-flow problems. This is particularly true on low-income schemes. This could be recognised by providing, say, a three- or five-year grace period before full repayments begin.

Appraisal and decision rules

The approach outlined so far has employed **cost-effectiveness** as the major decision tool, proceeding from what the target group can afford to the derivation of target costs and the optimal designs within that figure. The existence of some funds for a subsidy does not invalidate this approach since it is likely that subsidies would not stretch very far.

The main issue is the economic treatment of the major cost items: land, labour and materials. **Land** has a value to society, and when it is proposed to use it for a purpose such as housing its 'cost' is the loss from transferring it from its alternative use. If urban land used for low-income housing has a high alternative value for commercial purposes, this is the cost that should be debited to the housing scheme. The fact that the government or housing authority may already own the land is irrelevant to this argument (though it is convenient in other ways). The cost of land should also cover any expenses in removing and relocating existing inhabitants.

Building is normally fairly labour-intensive, and this points to the importance of attaching a 'shadow price' to **wages** that reflects the true cost to society of extra employment. However, housing schemes require a proportionately large amount of skilled labour, which is often in scarce supply. Starting new schemes may cause skilled labour to be drawn from existing projects, to their detriment. Another problem is the valuation of the residents' own time spent in self-help construction, what is sometimes called **'sweat equity'**. It can be measured either by the cost of hired labour or by the value of the residents' time in work, though neither method is wholly satisfactory.

Building materials include many non-traded items. Some components are imported, or have a clear value in trade (glass, sanitary fittings, corrugated iron, metal window frames, door handles, etc.). They should be valued at their import parity price (or export parity, where they have an overseas market). But many materials are not widely traded and are obtained locally or from suppliers a short distance away (concrete blocks, simple bricks, traditional roofing material, sand, etc.). This applies particularly to the simpler kinds of low-income housing in rural areas of developing countries.

There is no categoric rule for valuing these non-tradables, except to try and disregard obvious distortions (e.g. price controls or any monopoly element). Heavy transport costs on bulky materials and the possibility of materials being specific to a locality can make the dividing line between tradable and non-tradable goods difficult to draw. So can government trade policy.

Cost-effectiveness has been used so far because housing is often seen as a service to be laid on by government and its benefits are not always easy to measure. However, it is also possible to use **cost–benefit analysis** as a decision rule. There are two main approaches:

i. The simplest case is to take the (discounted) income from house sales or rental as a proxy for benefits, and to compare these flows with (discounted) costs. Where rents or prices are explicitly subsidised, the subsidy element should be added on to obtain economic rents and prices.

ii. A more sophisticated approach is to allow for consumers' surplus, namely what residents would have had to pay in the absence of the project. Since the object of publicly-mounted schemes is usually to provide housing at lower cost than would otherwise be available, there is always a presumption of consumers' surplus. In most sizeable settlements there is an active market in rented and sold property and the prevailing market level of prices and rents can be taken as the yardstick for estimating consumers' surplus on particular types of houses. Note that consumers' surplus can arise not only on the purchase price but also on the level of repayments, where the latter are subsidised.

Many **externalities** are claimed for house-building, including:

i. Employment. It is apt to question which workers will benefit (family labour, hired labourers, immigrants), whether adequate complementary skilled and supervisory workers are available, and what the indirect effects on employment will be (e.g. the effect on access to jobs from relocation, demolition, provision of *in situ* work places, etc.).

ii. Linkages from the construction industry into the rest of the economy. Several governments (e.g. Colombia, Singapore) have seen housing

110

programmes as a central strategy of development. Chapter 2 contains some cautionary noises about invoking linkages and other externalities.

iii. Multiplier effects on activity and employment in the rest of the economy. The building industry is a favourite instrument for Keynesian reactivation of an idle economy. It certainly played a major part in Britain's economic recovery in the 1930s, for instance. Whether it could play the same role now, in 'stagflationary' conditions, and in a variety of developing countries, is more debatable. If the construction industry ran into bottlenecks its multiplier impetus would be dissipated in imports and/or inflation.

iv. Improvement in the distribution of income and wealth. A low-income housing policy improves the welfare of people earning below-average incomes, and can enhance their productive assets. This should be the result of low-income housing programmes, but there are two main dangers. Firstly, there may be regressive effects on income distribution if subsidies are extensive and greater for middle-income than low-income housing. This is especially true for subsidised housing finance and up-market site and service schemes. Secondly, benefits may be displaced, and result in reduced access by the poorer groups to housing. This is most likely for up-grading schemes where occupants rent the accommodation from landlords who reap the gain from higher property values and are tempted to raise rents.

Important practical points

Experience of implementing low-income housing schemes has emphasised the following points:

1 Prospective residents should be consulted over the essential features of the project, such as the trade-off between plot size, structure, and level of services. Some way should be sought of involving the local community in the planning, implementation and administration of the scheme. Administration should be decentralised.

2 Residents should have a degree of choice over the type, pace of development, and use of the accommodation.

3 Land acquisition can be a source of serious delays. Consequently planners should be absolutely clear about the availability of land, tenurial position, and arrangements for transfer.

4 The rate of progress of housing schemes depends on complementary services being provided on time by other agencies. Dozens of separate agencies can be involved in a housing project. Careful co-ordination is necessary to ensure that the scheme is supplied with requisite infrastructure and services from other local and central government offices and public utilities.

5 The system for allocating public housing should be as objective as possible to prevent units falling into the hands of speculators or families outside the target group.

6 An incremental approach has much to commend it when planning infra-structure services and core structures.

7 Industrialised systems building using prefabricated components has rarely proved a satisfactory solution to low-income housing. Planners are likely to face no shortage of literature describing plausible and ingenious solutions, but the track record of such schemes is not auspicious.

8 Demolition should be used sparingly, and confined to schemes where the land is urgently needed for important non-housing purposes. Ideally, demolition should proceed in step with the provision of new accommodation for those displaced.

9 The self-help principle is a good one but it should not be imposed pedantically on residents. Many occupants prefer to buy in labour for all or part of their building work and this may be perfectly rational. Likewise, mutual help and community involvement in plot development and infrastructure are admirable but there are some tasks that commercial contractors can perform more cheaply and efficiently.

10 The offer of building materials loans usually makes a crucial difference to the rate of housing development in site and service schemes. The loans are usually available in kind, often from government depots.

11 Selling rather than renting minimises the continuing financial liability of government and gives the occupant more choice over development. A long leasehold gives the occupant practically the same benefits as freehold, yet retains some government discretion over future use.

12 Financial arrangements are crucial. Any subsidy is best applied to creating an initial grace period before full repayments fall due, in order to allow some plot development to proceed. But thereafter collection should be rigorous in order to ensure an adequate flow of funds to the authority for future development. Cost recovery is vital to replicability. The collection rate has been shown to depend at least as much on political will and collection mechanisms as on ability to pay.

Checklist of main questions

1 General

i. Population to be served
Has there been a recent population census? What data does it have on geographical distribution, the urban/rural split, number and size of households, and growth in total and urban population?
What is known about house occupancy (proportion of total population sharing, renting and owning dwellings)?

ii. Existing housing
Has there been a housing census? What are the amount and characteristics of the national housing stock? What is the typical mode of housing in different regions and income groups? What are the usual materials? What has been the rate of new construction in the private and public sectors?

iii. Demands and needs
What is the evidence of demand for publicly built or assisted housing? Are there any estimates of a housing deficit, or numbers of homeless? What has been the rate of formation of new households in relation to new house construction? What is the size of the squatting problem? Are there estimates

of sub-standard dwellings, and how are they defined? What data is there on income distribution? Are there figures for income per head or per household nationally and for the various lower-income deciles?

Is there household survey data showing the proportion of income spent on housing in the various social groups? Are there any socio-economic surveys of the area in question?

iv. National housing policy

Is there an explicit housing policy? Is there a specialised housing institution? Which national ministries, departments, or agencies are involved in housing services? How big is the housing budget? How much of the effort and finance is devolved to local authorities? What are the sources of housing finance? How large is the public housing effort relative to private and charitable initiatives? Has foreign aid been used? What is the record of public sector initiatives – e.g. the number of units built, assisted or up-graded relative to overall need? What technical achievements have there been? What has cost recovery been like?

Does the government recognise a particular target group, or region, for its housing policy?

v. Housing resources

Is land available for public housing? Is there a land policy? What are the prevailing forms of tenure? What form of tenure is proposed?

Are basic materials available locally? Which supplies have to be imported? Can local industry supply any of the required fabrications?

Are building skills widespread? Is there an adequate supply of skilled and unskilled building labour? Is self-help or community mutual help common? What is the state of the local building industry? Are there any large contractors?

2 The project

vi. Outline the proposal

Type of project; implementing agency; physical features; criteria for choice of occupant; overall costs; means of finance; time schedule.

vii. Technical features

Are the plans viable, tried and tested? Will training be required in case any features are novel? Who has done the plans? What scope is there for an incremental approach to development? How much of the work is being left to the occupant? What arrangements are being made for assistance to self-help builders, and for supervision? How much is to be done by contractors?

Are building materials loans being provided? Are local materials depots available? Is there a shortage of any of the proposed materials? What are the maintenance requirements and costs? How much will fall respectively on the occupant and on the authorities?

viii. Cost-effectiveness

What is the cost per unit of the houses? How have the costs of land, infrastructure and services been attributed?

Are the proposals a cost-effective solution to what the target group can afford?

ix. Cost recovery

Is there an explicit subsidy, or is one implicit in the price or the credit terms? What financial arrangements are planned, e.g. rent or sale, loan repayment terms? Are the terms fixed for all time, or are there provisions for rent reviews, changes in financial terms, etc.?

What are the arrangements for collection of loan repayments? What is the authority's policy on defaulting clients?

What is the likely effect of the project on the finances of the housing agency? How much of the total national housing budget will this project account for?

x. Cost–benefit analysis

What are the benefits from the project, either as direct income to the housing authority or as the consumers' surplus of the occupants?

Have the costs been adjusted to arrive at economic values?

Is there an internal rate of return?

What is the effect of the project on employment, both direct and indirect?

What other externalities are claimed? Are they plausible?

Further reading

Discussion of the issues

Patrick Crooke, 'Housing and Settlement', a chapter in R. Cassen and M. Wolfson (eds.), *Planning for Growing Populations*, OECD Development Centre, Paris, 1978. (A fine survey of the main issues in low-income housing.)

J. T. Winpenny, 'Housing the Poor', a chapter in P. J. Richards and M. D. Leonor (eds.), *Target Setting for Basic Needs*, International Labour Office, Geneva, 1982.

J. T. Winpenny, *Housing and Jobs for the Poor*, a monograph issued by the Development Planning Unit, University College, London, 1977.

Orville F. Grimes, Jr, *Housing for Low-Income Urban Families*, published for the World Bank by Johns Hopkins University Press, 1976. (A concise survey of the main issues, heavily based on the experience of Singapore and Hong Kong.)

Peter M. Ward (ed.), *Self-Help Housing. A Critique*, Mansell Publishing Ltd, London, 1982. (A lively and varied discussion of self-help housing efforts in a number of developing countries.)

Practical guides and manuals

Shankland Cox Partnership, *Third World Urban Housing*, a Report for the Building Research Establishment, Watford, UK, 1977.

Clifford Culpin and Partners, in conjunction with Ove Arup and Partners and Roger Tym and Partners, *Urban Projects Manual*, prepared for ODA, London, 1981.

News

The Urban Edge, a monthly newsletter published for the World Bank by the Council for International Urban Liaison, 818 18th Street, NW, Washington DC. (A good source of news about policy, research, and training opportunities in housing and other aspects of urban development.)

12
Water supply

Water is essential to human life. The search for water supplies is a problem as old as mankind, and many communities that have failed to solve this problem simply perished. Though commonplace, the problem is far from being overcome. In 1975 the World Health Organisation estimated that at least 1,500 million people lacked access to adequate supplies of safe water and adequate facilities for waste-disposal. The 1980s have been designated the International Drinking Water Supply and Sanitation Decade, with the aim of ensuring adequate water supply and sanitation for all.

This chapter will review the main sources of water, methods of treatment, its distribution to the consumers and the main problems faced in providing better supplies. (The associated problems of disposing of wastewater and sewage are dealt with in a separate chapter.) It also covers assessing demand, judging the benefits, and recovering the financial costs.

For the purposes of exposition, urban supply will be taken as the general case, and a separate section is included on the special issues arising in rural areas. This does not imply that urban supplies are more important or more urgent; indeed, frequently the number of people in rural areas with inadequate supplies is greatly in excess of those in towns.

Water sources

Rain-water can be collected directly by households and stored in barrels or tanks. This method is used in many parts of the world where rainfall permits. In general, though used in some areas, this source can only supplement water supplies and provide a modest reserve. Moreover, the rain collects impurities, particularly from containers and birds, and some form of treatment is desirable before it is safe for drinking.

Large-scale regular water supplies must come from groundwater, surface water, or the sea (or a combination of these). **Groundwater** depends on the existence of an aquifer, a saturated layer of ground resting on an impermeable stratum preventing the seepage of water. Where the aquifer is confined between two impermeable layers, wells may produce water rising under its own pressure (artesian wells), otherwise the water must be pumped up or lifted. Depending on the nature of the rock and any slope in the land, the area tapped by the well may naturally recharge with water. However, where the well's offtake exceeds the natural recharge, the water table in the vicinity of the well falls.

Groundwater exploration and drilling can be an expensive business. It does have the advantage, however, that the water is relatively clean and normally does not need treatment. Costs of groundwater development vary enormously – from hand-dug wells using manual or animal power, to the use of drilling rigs and pumping machinery. Pumping is normally required (except where natural springs occur that can be piped by gravity) and where power or fuel are in intermittent supply there will not be a constant supply of water. However, where groundwater has been located and mapped and wells set up, this is a source that is relatively cheap and easy to work. Cities tend to rapidly exhaust groundwater sources since the rate of use soon exceeds the rate of natural recharge.

Surface water is a more obvious source, especially for cities located on or near a river. London, for example, has for a long time drawn most of its supply from the river Thames. River water can be drawn off in 'run of the river' schemes by building a diversion weir. However, where the flow varies between seasons storage will be necessary to maintain an even flow to consumers. Treatment will usually be necessary and control will need to be exercised over the upstream discharge of wastewater, sewage and industrial effluent.

Lakes and reservoirs obviously combine supply with storage; where they are at a higher altitude than the area of consumption it will also be possible to economise on pumping when piping the water down. With the advances in dam technology it has been possible to build larger and larger artificial reservoirs, in some cases as part of hydroelectric schemes.

Reservoirs formed by damming have a high capital cost. (Where they have a joint function of providing electric power and/or flood control as well as water storage for drinking there should be an appropriate allocation of the capital costs between the various functions.) To this should be added the cost of constructing large-capacity pipelines, often over long distances. Then there is the (much lower) recurrent cost of maintaining the surrounds of the water and, frequently, pumping. Evaporation loss is also a factor, according to temperature and the relationship between the volume of the water body and the size of its exposed surface.

Salt water is increasingly being treated for human consumption in prosperous communities lacking other alternatives. Sea-water has an average salt content of $3\frac{1}{2}\%$, while brackish water occurring inland contains less, say 0.5%. There are now a number of technologies available for desalination. Whether or not they are commercially viable depends partly on the capital cost and above all on the source of energy for the process. Although some processes use fuel oil, it is more economically attractive to tap free energy that comes as a by-product of power stations, waste heat from smelters, exhaust steam from nuclear power stations, burning refuse, etc.

A common technique is distillation, where the salt solution is heated, vapour or steam is led off and it then condenses as pure water. Solar distillation is a possibility for small isolated communities – the technique is simple, and running costs are minimal though capital costs can be high. For solutions with a salt content – such as brackish water – lower than about 1%, electrodialysis is normally the most economic process (an electro-chemical method in which ion transfer separates the salt from the water). Reverse osmosis and freezing salt water are other possible methods.

In general, desalination by any of these techniques is more expensive than conventional sources, both on account of the capital cost of the equipment and the need for energy in the process. Technology is being developed rapidly and it is important to ask whether a particular technique is proven, and whether it is in commercial production anywhere in the world at the scale being proposed. The cost and source of energy are usually the critical factors.

Treatment

Most people in the world probably drink untreated water. While societies develop immunity from many water-borne diseases it is obviously undesirable that any community should have to put up with unhygienic water supplies. It should be stressed, however, that medical benefits of improved water supplies, particularly in rural areas, are far from being proven. (See section on Benefits, page 124.)

Protected sources of supply and systems for allowing users to separate drinking water from washing water are desirable. Invariably education in environmental health matters is essential. While improved water supplies are a precondition for better health they will achieve little unless other measures are taken. This is more important the more concentrated a population becomes.

The overwhelmingly important priority in treating water is **sterilisation** via chlorination. This is a relatively simple and inexpensive operation which should eliminate the most significant health hazards associated with water supplies.

Water treatment proceeds through various phases of increasing technical sophistication and cost.

Large-scale **open storage** is actually an elementary form of treatment since it stimulates the natural conditions in which water purifies itself. For example, sunlight can kill bacteria present in shallow water. Thereafter, the main treatment processes include screening and straining, coagulation and floc-culation, sedimentation, filtration, aeration, and sterilisation.

Screening and **straining** are done at the intake from the river, lake or reservoir. Bars spaced from 6 cm to 10 cm apart remove floating or suspended debris, fish, etc. Finer screening is possible by using rotating drums of perforated material, while the finest screening occurs with a micro-strainer, a drum of fine steel wire mesh.

Treatment plants usually contain large shallow basins in which suspended solids gradually sink to the bottom by the process of natural **sedimentation**. However, the really fine particles have to be settled differently, with chemicals being added to make the particles form clusters. This is **flocculation**, normally done by adding aluminium sulphate or hydroxide.

Sand filtration relies on the percolation of water through beds of sand, when organisms in the sand oxidise and purify the water during its passage. The sand needs cleaning every few months, when the water is drained off and the top few centimetres of sand scraped away. Slow sand filters are costly to build and maintain, and since filtration is very slow, they have to be large. Hence the rapid sand filter, which can move twenty times more water than the slow version, is more common. It is cheaper to install and operate, and uses up less ground space per unit output. It uses flocculated water. Daily cleaning is necessary.

Aeration, the exposure of water to air, enables the oxygen in the atmosphere to purify the water. The cascade is a simple form of aerator, and the natural cascade effect of waterfalls can be reproduced in weirs.

A water treatment plant does not, of course, need all these components. However, a typical plant, treating between 9,000 and 18,000 cubic metres per day, might involve the following. Water is taken from a river intake, screened, and pumped to a sedimentation tank. Flocculant is added, together with a softening and alkali regulating agent. (Sludge is meanwhile drawn off into a sludge lagoon, the liquid from which is recycled.) The water is then put into rapid-gravity filters, and activated carbon may be added to improve colour, smell and taste. Finally the water is sterilised using chlorine (or in some countries ozone) before being pumped into the mains.

Recycling of wastewater and industrial effluent is on the increase, and not just by eco-freaks and trendy architects. It already provides large volumes of drinking water for some countries. Windhoek, the capital of Namibia, now gets most of its household water from recycled wastewater. A shortage of high-volume supplies is forcing industry to recycle its own effluent, neutralising its impurities by de-mineralisation processes (see next chapter).

Storage and distribution

There is a clear distinction between bulk storage, e.g. in reservoirs, prior to treatment and distribution, and storage of much smaller bodies of water after treatment as part of the distribution system. The purpose of the former is to provide an even flow of water to consumers, allowing for seasonal variations in the natural water source, while the purpose of the latter is to maintain constant daily pressure during reticulation (see below).

Deep, narrow valleys form natural settings for creating capacious **reservoirs** by damming rivers. However, it is usually cheaper to build shallow ('bunded') reservoirs enclosed by low embankments, which can be built almost anywhere on flat land, do not silt up as quickly as valley reservoirs, and do not require flood control spillways, etc. The large area of West London given over to bunded reservoirs of Thames water, clearly visible to passengers taking off from Heathrow airport, is a good example. Depleted aquifers are increasingly being used as natural storage basins. Water is pumped back in the ground into aquifer formations and can be recovered when required by pumping. This method obviously has a very low capital cost, but it incurs some pumping expense.

The large-scale transference of water, e.g. from mains to service storage reservoirs, can be achieved in either open or closed channels, and is commonly done by gravity. Where the gradient is unsuitable, a pressure tunnel is used to regulate the flow by control valves. Prefabricated large-bore concrete pipes are the usual material for aqueducts, and these have a long life. An electric booster pump may be installed in the main to increase natural flow in a gravity system. Tunnels are usually lined with concrete.

Service reservoirs, normally carrying about one day's supply of water, are distributed throughout the distribution system. This is part of the **reticulation** system (literally, the creation of networks) under which urban systems are divided into pressure zones which take account of local physical circumstances in order to deliver water at a suitable pressure to consumers. Service reservoirs are, where possible, located at a height sufficient to provide pressure throughout the area they serve. They can be mounted on concrete stilts, and are normally covered concrete tanks. Where gravity pressure is insufficient, pressure can be increased by electric pressure-booster pumps.

Water is taken from the mains pipes to consumers either by piped connections to individual households or to public standpipes. The choice, or the combination, depends on the income levels of the consumers, the budget of the water board, customary practice, the size of the low-income settlements relative to the middle-class area, etc. For cities in developing countries with rapidly growing peripheral slum and shanty town developments, the provision of water through public standpipes may be the only way of bringing about anything near universal coverage. To rely on the extension of individual connections would take too long, and supply would never catch up with demand. Individual connections can of course be metered and direct charges made on consumers, whereas no satisfactory system has been devised for charging for water delivered from standpipes.

There are many districts in poor towns and cities where even standpipes are absent, and water is carried from the public mains to households in water carts or in water skins carried by oxen. This is often done by private enterprise, and the unit charges are high.

Rural water supply

Densely populated areas with industry and commerce have no alternative to a centralised piped system. The risks to public health from bad water or insanitary methods of distribution are much greater in such areas and justify a centrally controlled system under close supervision.

Rural areas have more choice in the matter. Population is scattered, the risk of epidemics is low, and there are seldom industrial users. The economics of providing rural water also tell against centralising supplies. The alternatives in rural areas are: the habitual methods (rain-water, rivers and lakes, wells); drilling new wells; deeper wells (which may be lined, sealed or covered); or providing mechanical means for lifting the water out of the ground. Once the supply is improved, it may then be moved to the centres of population by pipe (helped along by gravity or pumping). There may be rudimentary storage, treatment and reticulation. Only the wealthier users are likely to get individual connections.

On the basis of experience in designing rural water systems in developing countries, Cairncross (see section on further reading, page 129) has pointed out that water treatment facilities are unlikely to be reliably operated. Such plant usually requires operational care and skill which is very rare. It follows that it is usually preferable to find a source of good quality water and to protect it from pollution, rather than to take some more doubtful water and attempt to treat it. Since pumps also often break down and become inoperative in rural areas, it is safer to select a source of water such that supply can be gravity-fed, or, where motorised pumping is inevitable, to make satisfactory arrangements to finance their running costs and maintenance. There is a lot to be said, in the rural setting, for technology to be cheap and simple, and require little maintenance.

Springs are obvious sources for community water. No pumping is required, since the water is forced out under natural pressure, and it is only necessary to protect it from possible pollution by building some simple structure, of brick, stone or concrete, around the spring in order to channel the water directly into a pipe.

There are various ways of sinking **wells**. Digging by hand is still the most common, but it can be dangerous and requires skill. The advantage of this method is its low cost and the use of simple tools. Tube wells can be sunk either by driving in a well-point (a specially designed tube), by hand boring with an auger, or by using a tube in association with water to loosen the ground. Bore holes can also be made with special drilling rigs which can be mounted on trucks.

One of the most important considerations in designing wells is the need to avoid pollution. This may arise from locating the wells too close to pit latrines or refuse dumps, from the vessels used to draw the water, from rubbish thrown down the well, from surface water, or from water which spills back into the well from the people collecting it (having made contact with their feet). Open hand-dug wells are the most exposed to pollution. Infection from guinea worm is rife in certain hot, dry climates and can easily be spread from water spilled back into the wells. This can be prevented by building a wall around the top of the well and a drainage apron to take spilt water off to a soak-away.

Of the various ways of raising the water to the surface, an elementary decision is whether to use hand power or some kind of motor. The simplest form of hand power is a bucket on a rope, though the shaduf using a weighted pole is also common. Either method is suitable where the users can draw the water themselves. Next in order of lowest cost and complexity is a hand-pump, which can be used for deep hand-dug wells or tube wells. These are notoriously prone to breakdown. Then there is the choice of motorised pump, which is either diesel or electric. Where power is available, electric motors are preferable since they need less maintenance and tend to be more reliable.

Storage of water for village supplies can be done quite satisfactorily in tanks made from local building materials. They should be covered in order to prevent them being used as breeding grounds for mosquitoes. Since water treatment is a complex business, it is desirable to minimise it at village level by the choice of a safe water source, which can be improved by storage, or by constructing small sedimentation tanks to allow settlement. A simple pot chlorinator may, however, be used for hand-dug wells, consisting of a pot of sand and bleaching powder suspended in the well.

Maintenance of pumps in rural areas is a major problem. Remoteness and poverty make purchase of spares and acquisition of skills difficult. Responsibility for constant maintenance is a real problem in small communities. Voluntary responsibility cannot be relied upon and payment by the community encounters administrative and collection problems. Lack of maintenance capacity is the most serious, and is a widespread problem of pumped water supplied in village communities. In some countries, particularly francophone ones in Africa, the expensive, but effective, solution has been to set up government-financed institutions to maintain wells in working order.

A survey of 200 village wells and boreholes was carried out by the European

Development Fund (EDF) (see section on further reading) in villages in francophone Africa. It showed that the extent to which wells were used depended upon the ease with which water could be obtained, determined by depth, distance and flow. Hygienic quality had little or no influence on usage, in fact frequently villagers chose traditional wells whose taste they preferred to new better quality sources. Improved access only affected consumption where the savings in travel were considerable, for example one or two kilometres. The survey concluded that it was higher incomes which increased water consumption rather than its availability. It was found that water supply had no obvious direct effect on development, in that it did not lead to more agricultural or industrial activity. This is hardly surprising.

Assessing demand

The accurate forecasting of the effective demand for water is difficult. The EDF review of water supply projects discovered that an overestimation of the growth in demand for water was the most common weakness. This was largely due to the exaggerated estimate of consumption per capita, often put at 50 or even 70 litres per capita per day (1/cap/d) when the true figure normally lay between 10 and 20 1/cap/d.

Any assessment of the future demand for water has to be based on the growth of population in the area to be served, and its likely consumption of water per head. It should also include an estimate of frustrated demand, namely households that do not have satisfactory access to water and whose consumption is therefore exceptionally low. An improvement in the supply network will result in a rapid jump in consumption as it brings these households up to the consumption levels of the rest of the population.

Consumption per head varies widely according to climate, custom, tariffs, wealth and available facilities. Convenience is obviously a major factor, since consumption is likely to be greater where water is piped right through to the household, or where the public source is brought closer to the home. Wealth is a major determinant of the facilities possessed by the household: homes with kitchens, bathrooms and flushing toilets obviously have a higher usage than homes with more rudimentary facilities. The most dramatic increases in consumption per head are likely to arise at the point when individual household connections replace communal sources. In many cities gardens and swimming-pools use up a tremendous amount of water while in hot climates more water is used for bathing.

Average consumption per head depends directly on the source of water and the method of distribution. Minimum consumption is about 20 litres, when water has to be obtained from sources such as wells or public standpipes that are reasonably accessible to the home. Household connections, coupled with simple indoor plumbing, can raise consumption to 100 litres per day per person. In developed countries and in the middle-class areas of cities in developing countries an average daily consumption of 200 to 400 litres is common. For example, European cities have an average consumption of 160 litres, North American cities around 250 litres, Kumasi (Ghana) about 180 litres, São Paulo (Brazil) 200 litres, Lima (Peru) 380 litres, etc.

A survey carried out by a consultancy firm in a West African capital city suggested the following rule of thumb for consumption forecasts:

	litres per head per day	
Standpipes	40	Unmetered
Single yard tap	70 ⎫	
Plumbed houses	120 ⎬	Metered
Luxury houses	400 ⎭	

Accurate measurement of consumption is fraught with difficulties. Meters are often not maintained, and wastage is very high, while industrial and commercial usage is often difficult to separate from domestic uses.

Although much of the discussion here is about household consumption, it must be remembered that most towns and cities have industry and commerce, which tends to take up between 30% and 60% of all water consumption in those areas. The precise amount of consumption clearly depends on the type of industrial process.

Since consumption will be influenced by incomes and by the system of water pricing (if it works) assumptions need to be made about the income- and price-elasticity of demand for water (the response of consumption to changes in income and water charges respectively).

Assumptions have to be made about future charges. It is helpful to estimate the place of water charges within the household budget of the target population group (they should not normally exceed 5%), and the elasticity of demand for water in respect of price changes. If a deficit-ridden water authority has announced that it is moving towards financial self-sufficiency some increase in the real level of tariffs should be expected. Some water tariffs are levied at a flat rate, e.g. according to the value of property, and thus exercise no restraint on marginal consumption.

In practice the most sensible approach is to ensure that past data are as accurate as possible, project these trends into the future making adjustments for probable increases in demand (such as population increases and industrial expansion), and use that as a basic estimate of demand. Alternative forecasts can be made showing increasing demands arising from income increases adjusted for possible tariff changes.

What is important is to avoid embarking on detailed, sophisticated demand forecasts where the range of options on the supply side makes forecasting of little relevance. Just as important, of course, is to avoid embarking on investment proposals without checking, and collaborating, with those responsible for demand analysis.

Water losses

In matching water systems to expected demand, a distinction should be made between the volume of water to be produced at source (often called water requirements) and the volume reaching the end user (consumption). The difference is accounted for by various water losses. (For the purpose of financial analysis, there is also a distinction between water consumed, as shown by mains meters, the amounts that consumers are billed for, and the revenue they actually pay.)

Perhaps the lowest system losses one can expect are of the order of 10%, but they can be as high as 50%. They are likely to be between 25% and 50% in countries without careful control. There are many possible causes of system losses, but the most important are leaks resulting from badly connected pipes, from disturbances occurring when building is taking place and from unauthorised tapping of the supply system. Most leakage appears to occur in the distribution system rather than in service reservoirs or trunk mains.

In appraising water supply projects, it is necessary therefore to make a substantial allowance for system losses in making consumption forecasts and making sure that efforts are made to reduce system losses by better maintenance and rehabilitation. It should be borne in mind, however, that prevention of further losses becomes increasingly costly as losses are reduced, so there will come a point at which further expense is not justified.

Designing a cost-effective system

It will be clear from the above outline of the elements of the water supply system that there are many different circumstances and that it is impossible to generalise about the technical features of a desirable system. Fortunately, there are many reputable firms of civil engineers who can do this. There is one yardstick, however, that should be applied to systems in all circumstances, and that is that the water supply solution that is proposed should lie within the financial capacity of the authorities installing it and of the household and other users. This often means installing a relatively modest system at first, but with scope for adding to it as demand and financial resources grow.

The World Bank has produced some indicative total capital costs per head of different systems in urban and rural areas. Individual house connections may cost $120 in urban areas and $150 in rural areas. The provision of public standpipes might cost about $40 in both urban and rural areas, while the provision of systems relying on hand-pumps can be achieved at about $25 per head in rural areas. These figures are clearly derived from an average of data from a large number of countries, and cannot be used uncritically to indicate likely costs for any one country. Nevertheless, they do indicate the relative costs of different types of system, and the savings that can be achieved by choosing the simpler solutions. They also underline the need to ensure that capital expenditure should bear some relationship to personal and national incomes.

The ideal, an individual water supply to every dwelling from a centrally controlled and treated source, is some way off for the majority of poorer countries. For a start the capital cost is very high, and frequently the growth of the city is such that it is not physically possible to service the increment of consumption by this method. Many potential users are too poor to pay for the cost of house connections and the necessary plumbing work inside their dwellings, even where their dwellings are suitably constructed for this purpose. There is also the high cost of disposing of the wastewater produced by households with individual connections. Consequently, public standpipes should be regarded as the least-cost solution to the mass coverage of an urban population in poorer countries.

Water systems lend themselves to incremental development, as demand and resources expand. The costs of distribution relate more to the length of an underground pipe than to its diameter, hence it makes sense to design the system for its eventual capacity rather than the present need. Public standpipes can be widely spaced to begin with, and then the network can be gradually filled in, culminating in house connections. Householders who need and can afford individual connections are enabled to have them, while the majority of people whose need is for a lower-level service can be catered for without serious backlogs developing.

Benefits

It is important to distinguish real from financial benefits. The supply of improved water to a community entails benefits (health, amenity, convenience, etc.) not all of which are measurable, and not all of which can be charged for. Water users are normally prepared to make some contribution towards the cost of improved supply and this determines the financial return to the project. However, it is clearly an error to add the financial return to the (measurable) real benefits, since the one is simply what people are prepared to pay for the other. Normally the financial returns will be less than the real benefits, leaving users with a consumers' surplus (the difference between what they would have been willing to pay and what they are called upon to pay). However, it should be stressed that there is no known method of measuring benefits. The only practicable solution is to try and assess what consumers would be prepared to pay for water as a proxy for benefits. The willingness to pay may be undermined by low income, but it is impossible to come up with any measurable alternative.

The real benefits of an improved water supply are of three main types:

i. Convenience
A reliable supply delivered either into the home or to a public source nearer than the existing one is a major benefit. One of the marks of an over-loaded and antiquated water system is frequent reductions in pressure or supply cuts, which disrupt washing and cooking and can spread disease. Reliability saves the need for storage or forward planning. Providing a proper public standpipe is a more certain, convenient and reliable means of getting water than buying it from visiting wagons. The installation of individual house connections is an improvement on the use of public standpipes.

Time saving is a special case of the same factor. It is especially important where the improved supply means that water does not have to be carried such a great distance from the well or standpipe to the home. In the rural areas of poor countries women may have to walk a few miles, several times a day, to fetch water from the well. This is good for the posture, but wastes a lot of time. Hard-nosed critics have pointed out that time saved by the provision of a nearer source is rarely used for productive activities and therefore cannot receive a money value. This may be true, but increased leisure has a subjective value that the beneficiaries might be willing to pay something for.

ii. Health
It might seem axiomatic that greater quantities of improved water is good for personal and public health. So many of the serious diseases in the tropics (and not a few in temperate zones too) are transmitted by contaminated water (typhoid, cholera, bacillary dysentery) or passed on by washing (skin and eye infections). In other cases, the quantity of water is at least as important as the quality, and its absence inhibits personal hygiene and the cleanliness of clothes and utensils.

Nevertheless studies of villages with and without improved water show little or no effects on health from the improved supply. It is even possible that the availability of more water could spread water-borne diseases more rapidly, compared to the situation where users consume less from their own private sources. The reality is that there are so many ways in which clean water can be contaminated on its way to the hands (or face) of the final user that the expected health benefits are all too often frustrated. In particular, pipes, storage vessels, and eating and drinking utensils can be dirty.

One can only be confident of two propositions. Improved water supplies can lead to improvements in public and private health when they are introduced into a situation which is favourable in other respects (where there is a level of awareness about public and private hygiene, where homes are reasonably sanitary, and where personal health is otherwise good). This underlines the need for health education to accompany water projects. Secondly, in urban settings adequate supplies of clean water can prevent epidemics (again with the proviso that other factors conduce to the same end).

iii. Productivity
Certain industries rely on large amounts of water, e.g. manufacture of beverages, and processing and freezing of fruit, vegetables and fish. Thus the provision of water can result in increased value-added in these occupations. In so far as water improves health, it can raise the productivity of workers, but as we have seen the link is tenuous. Another link is via a reduction in the time and effort expended in carrying water from the source to the home. One estimate is that in Africa up to one-quarter of a person's daily energy intake could be spent fetching water. The savings in time and energy could be, and usually are, devoted to leisure activities rather than work, which makes such benefits difficult to quantify.

Recovering costs
Improvements to water supplies confer benefits which can form the basis for charges. However, there are several problems in recovering costs in full. First, if health and amenity benefits are to accrue from increased consumption of improved water, people should not be discouraged from using the new sources. In many cases, especially in rural areas, the new system has to compete with traditional sources which, in the eyes of the users, may be more convenient. A number of studies of existing schemes conclude that many users do not value cleaner water enough to persuade them to go further to expend more effort in getting it (e.g. waiting at a well, or pumping it up, rather than taking it from a local contaminated pond). Clearly, charges are best imposed where the new water source brings undisputed benefits of convenience, as well as quality.

Secondly, whatever benefits flow from the new supply, they are rarely directly converted into productive activity. It has been shown by several studies that any savings in time that result from a new source in rural areas are invariably taken out in the form of extra leisure. People may be willing to pay something for the time saved, but their ability to do so is not altered by the project (and the immediate benefits are to women who may not have a cash income).

Thirdly, there is no easy answer to the problem of charging for communal outlets, like wells or street hydrants. The charges would need to be made by officials permanently present at the well or standpipe. Their pay might exceed takings, and they would be subject to strong social pressures to relax their vigilance. Some type of communal funding seems called for.

The national water authority should aim to break even overall. This eliminates reliance on an erratic government subsidy, and generates cash flow from which maintenance, repairs and additions to capacity can be made. Raising revenue in urban areas should be no problem, and there are arguments for cross-subsidising rural schemes from the proceeds. At the same time, rural schemes should generate some revenue in order to finance the upkeep of the system.

Urban revenues may be raised from individual household connections, either by metering or by a property tax. The sanction on non-payment is to turn off the water. Installing water supplies to communal outlets cannot be charged for directly, but some contributions can be expected from general property taxes or forms of community levies. For instance, urban up-grading schemes in Colombian cities, which include providing water, are financed by a 'valorisation' levy, which is a betterment tax specifically related to the improvements taking place.

At the rural level, the proportion of communal to individual outlets is likely to be higher than in cities, and the level of incomes lower. Nevertheless, it is desirable that users pay something towards costs, and if possible contribute in kind to construction and maintenance. This will help to identify users with the improvements, as well as provide some cash flow. The principle of payment for services, even if at a modest level, will become important if at some future date a more elaborate level of provision is made. If some users prefer to contribute in kind, e.g. by working on periodic maintenance, this should, in principle, be encouraged.

Cost recovery should be implemented flexibly, especially in rural areas. It is unreasonable to expect rural users to meet the full cost of their systems. The costs per head of installing improved water supplies can vary enormously, depending on the nature of the water-bearing rocks and position as well as the size of the settlement served. The only safe generalisation is that in rural areas the charges made on each system should at least cover its operating and maintenance costs.

Important practical points

1 Forecasts of future demand could turn out to be wide of the mark unless these are based on painstaking estimates of **current** consumption.

2 In many systems water losses are high (possibly up to 50% of water entering distribution). The reduction of losses can thus be a cost-effective way of increasing supply to consumers, and is one of the alternatives that should be investigated at an early stage.

3 The costs of a system should bear some relation to the resources of the water authority and the public budget, which ultimately means the income per head of the country. A method of incremental addition to the system should always be considered, as both incomes and resources grow and expectations rise.

4 Desalination is an expensive solution that should only be entertained when

conventional systems are shown to be not feasible. Technology is developing rapidly in this area, and for most risk-averse authorities it is relevant to ask whether the technology has a proven track record. The type of energy to be used, and its cost, are likely to be critical factors.

5 Improved water supplies as such are unlikely to lead to direct benefits to public health without concomitant improvements in other spheres.

6 In rural areas of developing countries water treatment units are unlikely to be well maintained. It is therefore wiser to discover a water source of good quality and protect it instead of relying on the treatment of an inferior source.

7 Village pumps in developing countries are prone to failure because of mechanical breakdown, a shortage of spares, fuel scarcity, the lack of clear responsibility for maintenance, or a shortage of recurrent funds. The choice of cheap and simple technology can avoid some of these problems, while if pumps are absolutely necessary, electric ones tend to be more reliable than other kinds.

8 In such villages new wells are not necessarily going to be used just because they provide 'better' water. Traditional wells in the vicinity may be preferred for a variety of reasons. Potential users should be consulted.

9 It is useful to establish the principle that an improved water supply is a service that should be paid for. This applies even if the full cost is not recovered. In rural schemes, where some cross-subsidisation from urban users may be expected, a useful yardstick is that revenue from charges should at least cover the costs of operation and maintenance.

Checklist of main questions

1 Consumption

i. What is the present consumption of water in litres per day?
   What are the main features of consumers in the area to be served? (Population, consumption per head, the breakdown between household, industrial, commercial and institutional consumers, etc.)
   What proportion of the total population is served by individual household connections, as opposed to public standpipes, and how many consumers are unprovided for?
   How many consumers are metered, and what is the basis of the water charge?
   Are there any special factors accounting for the observed consumption (e.g. climate, high waste factor, presence of gardens, swimming-pools, etc.)?
ii. Are there any signs of unsatisfied demand at present (e.g. are any consumers totally unserviced, is there a backlog of requests for individual connections, how frequent are cuts and water rationing)?
iii. What estimates have been made of future demand for water in this area? (What assumptions have been made about population and city growth, the growth in incomes per head, the enlargement of the serviced area compared to the total area, etc.?)
   How do these projects relate to past trends? (If they are radically different, what are the reasons?)

2 Existing supply network

i. What are the main features of the present system, including sources, treatment, storage, and distribution?
ii. What is the capacity of the system in cubic metres per day? What is the capacity of each major component of the system (i.e. are there obvious bottlenecks)?
iii. How soon is demand expected to overtake the supply capability?

3 Adjusting the system to likely demand

i. Is there any scope for reducing waste in the system?
ii. Is there any scope for discouraging unnecessary consumption, e.g. by raising water charges where they are clearly inadequate, by levying higher charges on non-essential uses or the more affluent consumers?
iii. What will be the effects of the investment proposals on the capacity of the system?

4 Cost-effectiveness

i. What alternatives have been examined?
ii. What are the capital and operating costs of the different alternatives, discounted to the present?
iii. What is the capital cost per head of the proposed system?
iv. Have different levels of service been examined (e.g. the mix of public standpipes and household connections, the density of public standpipes, etc.)?
v. Has the possibility been examined of phasing the project so that demand is catered for through incremental development of the system?
vi. Will the proposal enable all urban consumers to be covered by *some* kind of service?
vii. How appropriate is the technology to the area?

5 Management

i. Does the authority that will be in charge of the project inspire confidence? (Its past record in catering for the expansion of demand, in balancing its books, in avoiding cuts and rationing, may be relevant.)
ii. Will the proposed project strain the ability of the authority to implement the new system?
Are there going to be drastic changes in technology that might pose novel problems?
iii. Are measures being taken to attract and train the necessary managers and technicians?
iv. What is the authority's record on maintenance?
Is there any assurance that it will have the necessary manpower and financial resources to operate and maintain the new system?
v. Is there likely to be an adequate supply of essential complementary inputs, such as fuel, chemicals, etc.?

6 Financial aspects

i. What will be the effect of the project on the financial position of the water authority?
ii. Are any changes in water charges or the spread of meters being proposed, and are such desirable?
Is the water rate adequate? Are the arrangements for collection satisfactory? What proportion of typical household income is accounted for by water charges?
iii. Will installation and connection costs be recovered by once-and-for-all charges on consumers?

iv. Are continuing subsidies from the local or national budget likely to be required, and are they likely to be forthcoming?

7 Benefits
 i. Who will be the principal beneficiaries?
 ii. Are the benefits claimed mainly on the grounds of public health, the convenience of the consumers, or the needs of industry and commerce?

8 Rural water supplies (for which the following additional questions have to be asked)
 i. What criteria have been used for the selection of these particular villages and schemes?
 ii. Is the proposed technology appropriate to available local skills, tools, and financial resources?
 iii. How accessible is the new source to the body of users?
 iv. Is there any policy of cross-subsidy from urban schemes to loss-making rural schemes?
 v. In the case of pumps, what specific arrangements have been made for maintenance, repairs, finance, and the supply of fuel?
 vi. Are there to be any complementary measures for health education and community welfare such as to maximise the public health benefits from the scheme?

Further reading

General
Michael Overman, *Water: Solutions to a Problem of Supply and Demand*, Open University Press, Milton Keynes, UK, 1976. (An Open University textbook, especially interesting on methods of water treatment.)

World Bank, *Water Supply and Waste Disposal*, a booklet in the Poverty and Basic Needs series, Washington DC, September 1980.

Tropical conditions
R. G. Feachem, M. G. McGarry and D. D. Mara, *Water, Wastes and Health in Hot Climates*, John Wiley and Sons Ltd, 1977.

Commission of the European Communities, *Sectoral Evaluation of Urban and Village Water Supplies*, EEC, Directorate-General VIII, Brussels, 1978. (A good evaluation of the experience of installing water supplies in Africa.)

R. G. Feachem, *Water, Health and Development*, Tri-Med Books Ltd, London. (Based on a study of water supply in Lesotho, with particular reference to health benefits.)

Village schemes
World Bank, *Village Water Supply*, Washington DC, 1976.

A. M. Cairncross, *Village Water Supplies*, an Overseas Building Note issued by the Overseas Division of the Building Research Establishment, Garston, Watford, UK, 1978. (A simple illustrated description of the alternatives for village water supply with sound practical advice.)

S. Cairncross, I. Carruthers, D. Curtis, R. Feachem, D. Bradley and G. Baldwin, *Evaluation for Village Water Supply Planning*, John Wiley and Sons Ltd, 1980.

R. S. Porter and M. R. Walsh, 'Cost-Effectiveness Analysis in Practice: A Case Study of Domestic Water Supplies in an African Country', article in *World Development*, Pergamon Press Ltd, 1978.

Bernard J. Dangerfield (ed.), *Water Practice Manuals 3. Water Supply and Sanitation in Developing Countries*, The Institution of Water Engineers and Scientists, 1983.

13
Wastewater, sewage and effluent

Communities discharge various kinds of liquid waste. Storm-water and rain-water run-off is a fairly innocuous kind. Of the two types of discharge from households, used kitchen and bath-water ('sullage') is less noxious than toilet waste, though the two types are normally collected and treated together. Finally, industrial wastewater, or effluent, varies greatly in its toxicity and nuisance value, and may be treated either in-plant or through the public system.

The collection and treatment of wastewater is the least glamorous of public services. Little of it can be seen, heard, or (normally) smelt by the public, and it only receives attention when it goes wrong, becomes overstretched or causes gross pollution. It is not a popular undertaking, and caters to a need rather than a demand. Yet one man's waste is another man's poison and the consequences for health and amenity of inadequate provision are drastic.

This chapter will concentrate on water-borne sewage systems, since this is the hard core of the investment problem and effluent can be considered as a special case of this general issue. As in the chapter on water, the exposition will focus on urban systems, with appropriate digressions on the needs of smaller and rural communities. This does not imply any judgement about the size or severity of the needs of rural as opposed to urban dwellers. One should not ignore the importance of non-water-borne systems which in the form of pit latrines, etc. are likely to continue for many years – even in major urban areas. These systems are relatively simple and while they should never be overlooked in planning a sewage system they do not require significant amounts of capital investment.

As usual, we begin with a simple description of the main features of a wastewater collection and treatment system, before proceeding to a discussion of planning, economic, and financial aspects.

Storm-water and rain-water

Formerly storm-water and rain-water were collected in the same underground sewers that were used for household sewage. Nowadays the usual practice is to collect the run-off in separate underground storm-water sewers, or even in surface channels.

The change has occurred because of the realisation that the volume of rain-water run-off can vary enormously, especially in countries with a marked seasonal rainfall. Thus the capacity of the sewers cannot be tailored to an average flow, and in dry periods flow could be inadequate to prevent the deposition of solids. On the other hand, at periods of peak rainfall there might be flooding and overflow of the combined material, with obvious hazards for public health. A combined system would also require the treatment works to be designed to a much larger scale than average requirements.

Storm-water sewers have to be large, and, at the same time, storm-water needs little, if any, treatment. This suggests that for poorer communities priority should be given to the construction of separate sanitary sewers. Storm-water can be led off, in some cases, by surface channels.

Sanitary systems

Sewerage and water systems need to be planned in harmony. A high proportion (70%–90%) of water used up in an urban household may be assumed to emerge as wastewater. Thus an increase in urban water supply has obvious and urgent implications for the design of sewerage systems. The capacity of a sewerage system, normally measured in cubic metres or litres per day, should be designed in relation to population, the number of households connected to mains water, the pace of expansion of the sewered area to the entire urban population, as well as the average consumption of water per household.

The interdependence of water and sewerage systems can be expressed in the opposite way. The installation of a modern water-borne sewage scheme requires large throughputs of water to stay viable. Water-borne sewage requires larger volumes of water than is available from public standpipes. Toilets flushing from cisterns use 50–100 litres of water per head per day, and account for most of the water consumption of the average modern urban household.

The installation of a sewerage system is a major undertaking. It is likely to be expensive and capital-intensive. The benefits of sewerage are not always realiseable until the majority of houses are connected, which may occur years after the start of the system. As noted, it requires large volumes of water to function properly. It is permanent, and it is not easy to adjust the system to the rapid growth and changing land use patterns of modern cities. Repairs and alterations are quite costly and entail disruption to street life. (In practice traffic disruption can be kept to a minimum by the gradual planned closure of streets.)

Even if street sewers are installed, it does not follow that residents will wish to connect their houses to them. The cost of in-house plumbing may be high, the cost of house connections has to be taken into account, there may be sewerage charges, and there is an associated need and therefore cost for increased water. Many households may therefore prefer to continue existing practices for the disposal of excreta. It may not in any event be within the financial capacity of municipalities to extend modern water-borne sewerage systems to all city dwellers. In laying down a system it is important to install a skeleton mains structure to allow for subsequent connections.

Poor sanitation and bad waste management are particularly serious in poorer communities like squatter settlements. The rapid growth of cities frequently exceeds the ability of municipalities to build and finance modern sewerage systems, while households may be too poor to afford normal water closets. But inexpensive latrines are available for use in urban areas, and poverty as such is not a reason for having unsatisfactory systems. A wide range of sanitation methods is available for households, many of which do not rely upon being connected to modern sewers.

Thus the choice of sanitary methods, as between water-borne sewers and others, is largely a question of the availability of water and the financial resources of the municipality on the one hand and of households on the other. However, the other important factor is the availability of skilled workers and professionally qualified engineers, both of whom are required to install water-borne sewerage. The simpler techniques of household sanitation can be put in by householders themselves. (See Household sanitation, following section.)

The collection and disposal of solid dry refuse (garbage) is a separate undertaking, and is not discussed here. However, refuse collection can have implications for sewerage. Where there is no satisfactory system for collecting refuse, residents may resort to emptying it into drains or toilets, leading to blockages in sewers. This is a common event in badly-serviced poor urban areas. The clear moral is that the expansion of sewerage and garbage disposal systems should proceed roughly in balance.

Household sanitation

The water-closet toilet flushing into conventional main sewers requires a financial outlay and a high throughput of water. Though this is the norm throughout cities in the developed world and in middle-class areas of developing countries, it is not yet feasible for mass adoption in poorer parts. The only practicable approach to universal provision in poor countries is to start with something simpler and to progressively up-grade the facilities. The World Bank has estimated that the cost per household of installing conventional sewerage is about $1,500 (in 1978 prices) compared to only $125 for a pit latrine and $205 for a low-cost septic tank.

There are many types of toilet (succinctly described, with diagrams, in the World Bank's booklet *Water Supply and Waste Disposal*). The simplest are the dry latrines that rely on material settling and soaking away into the ground via pits or trenches. Improved varieties are available, from which solid matter can be extracted. Then there are various kinds of 'wet' systems, though still relying largely on on-site disposal. These include pour-flush latrines, aqua-privies or low-volume WCs discharging into a soakaway or septic tank from which solids can be extracted periodically. As water supplies increase and sewers become available these can be up-graded and connected. Finally there are the dry latrines requiring solid collection and disposal off-site. They include vaults, vacuum tanks, buckets and mechanical buckets.

It must not be thought that these alternatives to conventional sewer sanitation dispense with the need for public services. Most of the alternatives, other than the simple pit latrine, need to be periodically emptied, and this is normally done by the public authority.

The environment is a further element in the choice of system. Latrines relying on waste fluid soaking away into the ground are not recommended for densely populated areas (where the sub-soil could become over-saturated) nor in the vicinity of fresh-water wells (where the risk of contamination arises). Accordingly, densely-populated low-income housing settlements are often planned with conventional sewerage from the outset, although the capital cost per household can be reduced by providing communal toilets.

Sanitation planning for poorer settlements now favours an incremental approach whereby facilities are up-graded as resources and water supplies increase. One sequence is to start by assuming water supply through public hydrants, and providing households with a ventilated improved pit latrine (called, with some irony, the VIP toilet). This toilet has a concrete block and superstructure, and a screened venting pipe to reduce smell and insects. Alternatively a Reed odourless earth closet (ROEC) could be used. Both would need emptying at infrequent periods (between five and twenty years, or when up-graded).

These toilets would serve until the water supply was improved from public standpipes (or wells) to yard hydrants. With the consequent increase in water consumption, disposal of sullage becomes a problem – and also an opportunity. At this point, the dry latrine can be converted into a pour-flush toilet, using sullage water, and connected to a septic tank with soakaway or alternatively to a cesspit.

The third stage would be the connection of individual households to the water mains, when consumption per head would tend to rise from below 100 litres per day to over 200. Disposal of sullage would become even more serious, and at this point a new lined pit would be dug and the existing bowl connected to it. An overflow pipe would connect this pit to a small-diameter sewer system, paving the way for the introduction of cistern-flushing toilets.

The World Bank estimate that the discounted cost (including recurrent expenses) of this three-stage incremental approach over a thirty-year period would be little more than one-tenth that of introducing a full conventional sewerage scheme from the outset.

Sewage collection

The conveyance of sewage and wastewater to the treatment works involves a number of stages: household plumbing, household connections to the public sewers, the sewers themselves, and pumping stations.

Household plumbing in private dwellings is normally left to the builder and residents, subject to conformity to local by-laws. The system should be watertight, and the material flows by gravity at atmospheric pressure. Pipes should be accessible for maintenance, and there should be no possibility of back-pressure that might lead to contamination of the water supply.

Connection to the public sewer is by means of the **'house sewer'** or lateral connection, a small-bore pipe (4–6 in.) laid in a shallow trench and with a gentle slope. The pipe can be of cast iron, vitrified clay, concrete, asbestos cement or even plastic. Because house sewers are often left to the householder there is a risk of incorrect construction. Apart from setting strict building codes, the authorities can reduce this risk by having house sewers put in by the same organisation that lays sewer extensions, and levying a charge on the householder.

In designing a sewerage system a basic criterion is whether the 'self cleaning' velocity is achieved. At a speed of one metre per second the wastewater flow will be sufficient to prevent solid matter blocking the sewer. It is also desirable that the flow down to the treatment works should rely on gravity as much as possible. However, there can be a trade-off between the excess design costs of using gravity and the cost of installing lifting and pumping stations. In countries where labour is cheap relative to the costs of pumping equipment it may be sensible to use longer sewers or deeper excavation to obviate pumping. This also by-passes the risk of pump failure.

The depth of the **sewer** below the street should be influenced by two main factors: the need to avoid damage from traffic (which dictates a depth of at least one metre); and the necessity of being below the (sloping) house sewers. Excavation of sewers is usually the most expensive part of installing the system. The possibility of local manufacture depends partly on what material is chosen. Unreinforced concrete is economical and effective for small- and medium-bore pipes (say, up to 24 in. in diameter). They can be made at or near the site, using local labour and materials. For larger pipes, the concrete needs to be reinforced; this is a slightly more elaborate process but still one within the capability of many countries.

Cast iron is a good material, but too costly for all but specialised uses (e.g. in pressure – 'force' – mains, sewers above the ground or in wet terrain). Wooden pipes, bamboo poles, etc. are sometimes used where other materials are not available, but they are unsuitable for permanent general use. Vitrified clay produces an excellent sewer pipe but it requires skilful manufacture to high quality standards. Asbestos cement is another possibility. Finally, plastic is gaining ground. It is light, easy to handle and assemble, and has good technical characteristics. Its main disadvantage – an uncertain lifespan – may not be so important in developing countries where the cost of excavation to replace pipes may not be prohibitive.

An important element of cost is the installation of **manholes**, essential for inspection, cleaning and unblocking the sewers. They are normally spaced at intervals of 100 metres, and wherever there is a change in direction, pipe size, or branching. The manhole walls are most commonly made of concrete, though brick can be used, and the covers are either cast iron or reinforced concrete in order to withstand traffic and discourage unauthorised entry.

Where the contours of a settlement do not permit sewerage to rely entirely on gravity, or where such a system would be unduly circuitous and expensive, pumping stations are required. Of the two main types, the **lift station** raises the sewage to a higher level, from which it can flow by gravity thereafter. The second type pumps the sewage under pressure into **force mains** which carry the material to the point of discharge. Pumping stations thus have several functions: transferring sewage from one zone to another; raising the sewage so as to avoid more excavation; enabling the treatment plant to be more conveniently located; and providing the necessary head of pressure for the treatment process.

In designing the pumping station it is advisable to plan the structure with an eye to the peak flow at some future date when the community is fully developed and discharging maximum sewage. It is possible to install pumps (at least two, to provide cover for servicing and breakdown) that are smaller than ultimately required, and to add more, or larger ones, as the flow builds up. It is less easy to alter the structural features of the station.

Treatment

The degree of treatment required of wastewater varies according to its degree of pollution, what use the receiving waters are put to, and – in the case of recycling – what the treated water is to be used for.

The quality of the wastewater prior to treatment may be measured by its BOD (biochemical oxygen demand) factor. The higher the BOD, the greater the organic matter present, and – other things being equal – the greater the need for treatment.

The second factor is the use that is made of the water body into which the wastes are discharged. Such water bodies may be classified according to their 'best use', and this determines how much treatment is necessary. For instance, the need for treatment increases according to whether the best use is for wastewater disposal, agricultural and industrial uses, fishing, bathing, and finally water supply. The volume of waste discharge relative to the volume of the receiving water body is obviously relevant, as well as seasonal variations in the latter.

The types and degrees of treatment can be summarised.

Preliminary treatment simply removes coarse solids, and this is sometimes sufficient for wastes discharged into the open sea. It embraces screening, comminution (cutting solids up), grit removal and flotation (scum-removal). Where the waste goes on for further treatment, this stage prevents subsequent machinery from becoming blocked or damaged.

Primary treatment comprises sedimentation, and can remove 35% of BOD and 60% of suspended solids. In developed countries it is becoming the minimum treatment for wastes emptied into inland water or estuaries. Sedimentation ponds can either have deep 'hopper' shaped bottoms from which the accumulating sludge is piped off, or can be shallower and have sludge removed mechanically (e.g. by rotating underwater scrapers).

Intermediate treatment can provide BOD removal up to 60% by adding coagulant chemicals to the wastewater prior to sedimentation. Chemicals can add flexibility to the treatment works where the volume or quality of waste varies annually. On the other hand, in developing countries the supply of chemicals poses problems of cost and logistics, and the increased volume of settled solids that results from this process may be hard to dispose of.

Secondary treatment uses biological methods to achieve BOD removal up to 95%. Trickling filters are large open tanks containing layers of stones, inert media with a large surface area on which micro-organisms can flourish. A rotating distribution arm sprays the wastewater continuously into these stone beds. The activated sludge process, which requires less land, relies on mixing the wastewater with oxygen (e.g. by bubbling air through a tank) to stimulate the growth of benign micro-organisms. Stabilisation ponds are shallow basins in which wastewater remains long enough for the sludge to stabilise at the bottom, and oxidisation occurs by virtue of the large surface area. These ponds take up a lot of land, but are especially useful for small communities where land is no problem.

Tertiary treatment further refines the quality of effluent, and is normal where the wastewater is to be recycled. A number of processes are possible, such as microstraining, rapid sand filtration, carbon adsorption, ammonia stripping, coagulation and flocculation, ion exchange, electrodialysis, etc. Chlorination is common where water is recycled for drinking.

Sludge drying and disposal completes the treatment. Sludge is the unlovely term for solids that have been removed from the wastewater, together with the water that it has not been possible to separate from them. Sludge builds up at a number of points during treatment, e.g. in settling, activated-sludge, trickling-filter, coagulation or digestion tanks. It is bulky and noxious. It is common to dispose of sludge by any or all of the following means: concentration, digestion, dewatering, drying, lagooning, land-fill and incineration. Treatment can form a high proportion of total cost in a sewage plant. In practice, air drying on sludge drying beds is the most common process in poorer countries, especially those with an arid climate.

This is clearly a case where the specification of the end-product, namely the purity of the treated water, determines the technology required, and the cost of treatment. It is difficult to generalise about treatment costs, except to make three observations. Firstly, all the methods described exhibit marked economies of scale, and a process that is expensive for a population of 10,000 may be feasible for one of 100,000. Secondly, for most processes operating and maintenance costs are substantial, and can approach annualised capital costs. This depends on the cost of labour, chemicals, etc. Third, treatment plants take up a lot of land in or on the edge of cities and, however this is measured (acquisition cost, rent, opportunity cost), it can be a major consideration. (A new treatment works planned for Cairo had to be relocated some way distant because the authorities were unwilling to see prime agricultural land used in this way.)

Treatment in developing countries

Mara (see section on further reading, page 145) adduces three reasons why the typical Western urban processes summarised above are unlikely to be suitable for tropical developing countries. There is first the question of cost – conventional methods are more expensive per head than the simpler processes to be mentioned below, and involve costly imported equipment. Secondly, they depend on good maintenance of the electrical machinery used in most of the processes. Maintenance skills are rare, while malfunctioning sewage plants are common. Thirdly, the treatment process itself may be inappropriate. In hot climates the destruction of faecal pathogens is more important than the removal of organic matter (BOD). Sludge treatment is difficult and expensive, accounting for up to 40% of the total cost of sewage treatment. Finally, in hot countries smell can be a serious problem from trickling filters and other units and they may also attract flies.

Waste stabilisation ponds are being promoted as an appropriate solution to the above problems. These are large shallow reservoirs in which the raw sewage is treated by entirely natural processes involving algae and bacteria. There are three types: anaerobic ponds do preliminary treatment of strong wastes; facultative ponds remove BOD; and maturation ponds destroy faecal pathogens. A system should always involve a facultative pond followed by several maturation ponds, and a preliminary anaerobic pond is an optional extra.

Ponds are easy to build and cheap to maintain (surrounding grass needs cutting, scum should be removed from the surface, and sludge removed every few years). Little equipment is needed, and there are no significant economies of scale. At the same time, the ponds are effective in removing faecal bacteria.

Land is a basic factor in the choice between ponds and the two other obvious processes – aerated lagoons and oxidation ditches. The aerated lagoon is basically an activated sludge method, bringing air into contact with the wastewater. Compared to the pond, it economises on land. Least land of all is needed by the oxidation ditch, which achieves aeration by rotors. However, this method makes heavy demand on operating and maintenance skills and entails the use of chemical disinfection of the effluent, if bacteria removal is to be comparable with that of the stabilisation pond.

Recycling treated water and sludge

The amount of treatment that wastewater needs to undergo depends on what it is going to be re-used for. If it is intended to be used for public drinking water, the most thorough treatment is necessary. Although there are successful examples, experts recommend against the use of recycled wastewater for drinking where there are viable alternatives, on the grounds that a technical failure could have serious consequences.

However, recycled wastewater can indirectly increase the supply of water for drinking by releasing water for that purpose and substituting in uses that do not require water of the highest purity, such as watering of gardens and parks, industrial processes or cooling, fire-fighting, recreation, and even toilet flushing where there is a dual water supply.

Treated wastewater used for agricultural irrigation should normally undergo at least primary treatment and where feasible secondary treatment as well. Disinfection is an additional safeguard. Untreated wastewater should not be used indiscriminately for irrigating farm crops, least of all where food crops are produced that are eaten raw. There is less difficulty with grains, tree crops, cotton, and forests.

Treated wastewater has also been successfully and widely used for fishponds and recreational lakes. The amount of treatment required varies according to local circumstances, and disinfection is often necessary. The other possibility is to use the water for recharging groundwater aquifers or to prevent the intrusion of salt water into soils. Where the aquifer is used as a source of fresh water, tertiary treatment of wastewater may be necessary.

The handling and disposal of sludge is normally the most difficult part of sewage treatment. Two obvious and feasible uses are for land fill and fertilisation of soil. Sludge can be used to raise the level of low-lying areas. Dried sludge from drying beds is most suitable for this purpose. Sludge can also help soil building, by improving its capacity to hold moisture, its structure, organic content, etc. It also has value as a filler for chemical fertilisers and as compost. Depending on the precise balance of chemical elements in the sludge, it can compare favourably with commercial fertiliser. Where the sludge is to be applied to soil used for growing edible crops eaten raw, disinfection by chlorine is necessary. Sludge tipped in depth can cause a nuisance if it catches fire due to spontaneous combustion.

Industrial effluent

Industrial wastewater can be dealt with either by changes in the industrial process itself, on-site treatment to deal with specific contaminants, or discharge to municipal treatment systems. In this connection, many of the techniques appropriate for treating industrial effluent are similar to those used for treating household waste, or are adapted from these techniques.

Changes in the industrial process could reduce the **volume** of wastewater, though possibly at the expense of seeing more waste being retained in the final product or substituting dry waste for wastewater. Likewise the **toxicity** of waste can be reduced, e.g. by substituting a chemical or material with reduced contamination effects. Another possibility is to **neutralise** the waste by adding either acid or alkali to balance its properties. Or the waste could be held back, or mixed with other types of waste in order to produce a more regular and homogeneous mixture for the convenience of municipal treatment.

An alternative is to have the industrial effluent delivered to the municipal treatment system. The advantages of joint handling and treatment of industrial and municipal wastewater spring from economies of scale and land use. Okun and Ponghis (see section on further reading, page 145) suggest as a rule of thumb that a 50% increase in treatment capacity raises costs by only 25%, and a 100% increase in capacity raises costs by 50%. The cost can be recovered by charging the industrial producers a sewer rental, or some other such levy.

In developing countries, or in communities where the industrial plant produces a large volume of waste relative to households, it may be more attractive to require the industry to carry out some treatment of its effluent. If need be this can be subsidised. The in-plant treatment of 'specialised' or particularly toxic effluent may be more economical than adapting an ordinary municipal system for this. Moreover, where the municipality lacks finance or necessary skills and know-how, this would seem a sensible division of the burden. Unless there was a subsidy to the industrial plant, this would in effect be making the consumers of the product pay for the cost of treatment. In terms of welfare economics this is entirely defensible.

Assessing the effective demand

The most important data required in planning wastewater disposal are the consumption of water per head and in total. A related issue is the quantity of water supply enjoyed by different kinds of water users, and the appropriate standards of sanitary systems that they can reasonably expect.

Normally between 70% and 90% of water consumed by urban households emerges as wastewater. The lower figure applies where there is a high proportion of use for watering gardens and parks. Thus the scale of the wastewater system to be installed needs to be commensurate with that of water supply. Moreover, the expansion of sewerage needs to keep closely in step with changes in the volume of water supply. Households served by public hydrants are not normally provided with a sewered system, and such a system would not be viable at low levels of flow. But once households get their own water connections and the associated sanitary appliances, volumes may be such that connections to a sewer system become justified.

It follows that estimates of water consumption and wastewater discharge, per head and in total, need to be complemented by a description of the different standards of service, present and planned, enjoyed by different parts of the community. The expected rate of urban population growth needs estimating, with the caveat that in developing countries this is normally greatly above, and in many developed countries below, overall population growth. The physical expansion of the city is obviously relevant to the scale of the system and its costs, as is the expected growth in the unserviced area (especially slums and shanty towns on the outskirts).

Since treatment makes up a significant proportion of investment, and even more so of recurrent costs, it is fruitful to try and project future treatment needs. This is one of the more difficult parts of planning. For a small community it might be acceptable to discharge sewage after only preliminary treatment into neighbouring rivers or seas because the volume of the waste would be small relative to that of receiving water bodies. At high levels of discharge, this would cease to be so. Moreover, as a community grows it is likely to exercise an increasing demand for recycled water and solids. Thus, other things being equal, a growing community will probably require increasing standards of treatment over time.

Planning a cost-effective solution

There might appear to be a tension between the engineer's natural instinct to build a system that will last and cater for likely demand for years ahead, and the economist's inclination to build a system incrementally as demand requires. There is room for both approaches in planning wastewater systems.

Building a sewerage system and treatment works is a heavy investment, and for some components it is sensible to plan well ahead of demand, that is to have a long design period. For instance, the new Cairo system incorporates a deep central collecting tunnel. After testing alternatives on a discounted cost basis, it has been decided to build a collector capable of handling expected flows in the year 2050. This is because the heavy outlay involved in excavating a deep tunnel outweighs the relatively small extra cost of having a conduit larger than is currently necessary, allowing for the cost of repeating the excavation in the future. Likewise, it is sensible to design a pumping station with an eye to maximum future demand, since the number of pumps can gradually be increased.

More generally, in poor countries where labour is cheap relative to capital equipment it is commonly more economical to replace and extend facilities than to try and cater now for future generations.

The incremental approach to providing a wastewater system is even more important in poor communities where neither the authorities nor the house-holders are currently able to afford a full sewered system. A staged approach to sewerage provision, when discounted, can cost a small fraction of that involving installation of sewerage right away, yet can be just as satisfactory from the public health viewpoint.

Benefits

The benefits from improved wastewater disposal are of three kinds:

i. Public health
In densely populated urban areas inadequate wastewater disposal tends to spread gastro-intestinal diseases. The failure to properly dispose of faeces is especially dangerous. Disease can also be spread by flies, the contamination of fresh water supplies, the discharge of insufficiently treated sewage into

waters used for swimming, washing, fishing, etc., and the use of effluent as irrigation water for food crops.

Studies done for many badly-sewered cities illustrate the sorts of health hazards that arise. Existing systems, designed for a much smaller population of one million, become grossly extended coping with the current exploding population. Sewers are not able to handle flows at peak periods, leading to regular flooding. Treatment plants likewise have inadequate capacity even for regular flows, and untreated sewage is discharged into open drains and, eventually, into rivers and lakes. Where street flooding occurs, children are directly exposed (hence the high incidence of infantile gastro-enteritis) and there is a danger of seepage into fresh water supplies. The people not served by the sewers use either unsatisfactory private sewerage schemes without proper treatment, earth closets which dump their night soil in the streets, or septic tanks that discharge into ditches flowing through densely populated areas. In economic terms, sewerage improvements confer important 'externalities'.

As in the case of water supply, it is not always easy to prove a direct link between improved wastewater disposal and better public health. Other practices and habits will frustrate the expected gains to health, in the absence of improved education and living standards. However, the link between wastewater disposal and health is probably stronger than that between water supplies and health, at least in urban areas, since faecal contamination is very potent.

In smaller communities or rural areas the public health benefits are more tenuous. It is easier for the waste material to be harmlessly disposed of by traditional methods and the risk of epidemics is reduced by the lower population density. In such circumstances it is even possible for the installation of a modern sewerage system to *increase* the risks to public health; the resistance that the population builds up under the old methods may be undermined, and if the new system breaks down disease can spread rapidly.

Many of the public health benefits can, in any case, be obtained from installing or up-grading simpler unsewered latrines. The strongest public health case for a sewered system is in large and densely populated cities, or where the water table is high.

ii. Amenity
There are gains to public and private amenity if wastes can be disposed of in a less conspicuous and unpleasant manner. One way in which these benefits are captured is in gains to property values in the zones affected. In one scheme in a Brazilian city open sewers were replaced by piped sewers, and benefits were measured by estimating the likely increase in the value of adjacent property (by reference to the value of property elsewhere that was similar in all respects but its proximity to the sewage canal).

iii. Financial savings
A sewered system might operate more cheaply than the various methods it replaces. This is especially true of individual households. The cost of running a septic tank is normally greater than the charge for being connected to a public sewer. Moreover, the cost to a group of households of installing and operating a private sewer will normally exceed the cost to them of a public connection. As for the public authorities, once the demand exists there are

compelling cost savings to be had from economies of scale from building and working a unified system of collection and treatment.

Cost recovery

It is desirable for the municipal sewerage authority to have its own source of cash flow, not just to repay any funds borrowed to expand the system but also to meet the recurrent costs of operating the collection and treatment works. This is all the more important if this authority is a separate institution from the water board and not able to count on the latter's cash flow.

One of the constraints on full cost charging is the need to encourage people to use the sewerage facilities in the interests of public health. If they are charged too much they will revert to old methods. Householders are more reluctant to lay out money on improved sewerage services than on a better water supply.

However, this influences the form of the charge rather than the case for making the charge. One possibility is to pay for sewerage out of general taxation, since all members of the community benefit from an improved service, and not just the people who are being connected. However, the people who benefit most are those who already have water supply connections, since as we have seen most water consumed emerges as wastewater. Furthermore, improved sewerage increases property values; thus the benefits to house-holders are roughly in proportion to the size of their property.

Part of the system can reasonably be financed by direct charges on householders. When a street sewer has been laid, it is feasible to charge householders a once-and-for-all amount for connecting them to the sewer.

This apart, it is most common to recover the costs of sewerage from some combination of a supplement to the water rate and a levy on local property taxation. It is important that neither charge should be seen as optional, otherwise there is a possibility of householders choosing not to pay. The supplement to the water rate is probably the simplest method.

In the case of large industrial producers of wastewater, a more sophisticated method of charging can be followed which tries to relate the charge more faithfully to the actual cost incurred by the municipality. For example, a number of developed countries use a formula for charging industrial users, which allows for both the quantity of industrial wastewater discharged into public sewers, and the quality of such waste measured in terms of BOD content, or suspended solids content, etc.

Important practical points

1 It will be difficult to discover the population distribution unless census returns are available.

2 The initial response of the client is likely to be that anything less than full water-borne sewerage is not good enough, even if it only services 10% of the population.

3 Who is to maintain and clean communal facilities?

4 Is there sufficient wastewater from the household to flush a water-borne system?

5 Is local management able to maintain pumping stations, pit-latrine emptying vehicles and dumping stations?

6 Is a health education programme being organised in parallel with the public health engineering work?

7 There could be communication problems during the study period. The commissioning authority may agree with procedures during the study but reject them at the report stage.

8 It is good practice to construct sewer laterals (outlets) to boundary lines at community cost during the laying of the main sewer. This reduces piecemeal reinstatement costs and actively encourages connections.

9 Road work disruption can be dealt with by closing roads and constructing sewers in short lengths.

10 For low-cost solutions such as pit latrines it is recommended that implementation proceeds via a standardised construction programme, a supply of components by the authority for sale to householders, and a demonstration programme.

11 In hot climates the formation of hydrogen sulphide and sulphuric acid will lead to sulphate attack of cement products in a sewer. This is a maintenance problem which can be overcome by the use of other materials.

Checklist of main questions

1 **Present situation**
   i. What are the main features of the present system for disposing of wastewater?
   ii. What are the capacities of the present network (cubic metres or litres per day) in each trunk sewer, its average throughput, and its condition?
   What is the pattern of peak and minimum flows, both daily and annually?
   iii. How many households are served in one form or another by the wastewater authority?
   What proportion is sewered?
   How many households have individual connections to public sewerage?
   What proportion of flow is accounted for by industrial, commercial and institutional users?
   Do they have local treatment plants?
   iv. How does the wastewater collection system relate to that for water supply?
   Are the two compatible, e.g. in respect of the standard of service?
   v. What evidence is there of unsatisfied demand, backlogs for connections, public health hazards, in the present system?
   vi. What information is there on geological and topographical aspects?
   Are there maps and records?

2 **Future requirements**
   i. What is the expected growth in the population in the area to be served?
   What is the expected growth in city area?

ii. What trends are expected in the consumption of water both per head and in total?

iii. What plans are there to expand or up-grade water supply? Are there any plans to enlarge the service to presently unserviced areas, and if so what standard is proposed?

iv. Are any large industrial or commercial investments foreseen that might have implications for waste disposal?

v. Are any changes in treatment requirements foreseen in future, e.g. are the usual receiving areas becoming polluted, are there any proposed changes in land or water use that would require higher standards of treatment?

3 The cost-effective solution

i. What solution is proposed?
How far ahead is the system being designed for?
What are the design lives of different components of the system?

ii. What are the costs and the costs per head of the proposed solution?
What is the breakdown of these costs between imported, local, labour items?

iii. What alternatives have been explored (e.g. the possibility of a more modest investment now and incremental expansion of the system)?

iv. Do the specifications take account of the local availability of materials, equipment, labour and skills?

v. Is the degree of treatment appropriate to environmental requirements?

4 Management

i. What agency will be responsible for installing and operating the system?
How does it relate to other local and central government agencies?

ii. Is the agency well funded? What are its sources of finance?

iii. Are its management and senior staff capable of implementing the proposed works?
What is its record in recent years (e.g. whether it has been carrying out regular maintenance, replacement and enlargements)?

iv. Does it have access to enough labour and skills to install and run the system?

v. Is the technology proposed, especially in the treatment plant, familiar, and if not what technical assistance is being sought?

5 Finances

i. How does the sewerage authority propose to obtain funds for the project? Would it be required to repay, and if so on what terms?

ii. Does the authority have adequate revenue for regular operation and maintenance of the total new system?

iii. How are costs to be recovered from users?
What proportion of the average household's income will go on sewerage charges?
Will households have any choice over payment of these charges?

iv. How are the larger industrial users to be treated?
Is a separate, and more complex, tariff proposed?

Further reading

World Bank, *Water Supply and Waste Disposal*, Washington DC, September 1980. (A brief overview, especially interesting on alternative household sanitation systems.)

D. A. Okun and G. Ponghis, *Community Wastewater Collection and Disposal*, World Health Organisation, Geneva, 1975. (A full-length, authoritative and comprehensive textbook.)

Arnold Pacey (ed.), *Sanitation in Developing Countries*, J. Wiley and Sons, 1978.

R. G. Feachem, M. G. McGarry and D. D. Mara, *Water, Wastes and Health in Hot Climates*, J. Wiley and Sons, 1977.

Duncan Mara, *Sewage Treatment in Hot Climates*, an Overseas Building Note published in June 1977 by the Overseas Division of the Building Research Establishment, Garston, Watford, UK. (A short, illustrated practical guide to appropriate techniques.)

World Bank, *Environmental Considerations for the Industrial Development Sector*, Washington DC, August 1978.

W. Rybcynski, C. Polprasent and M. McGarry, *Low-cost Technology Options for Sanitation*, International Development Research Center, Ottawa, Canada, 1980. (A review of the many possible intermediate sanitation systems.)

J. M. Kalbermatten, D. S. Julius and C. G. Gunnerson, *Appropriate Technology for Water Supply and Sanitation*, World Bank, Washington DC, 1980. (A wide-ranging review of cheaper sanitation options.)

INDUSTRY
AGRICULTURE
LIVESTOCK
TOURISM

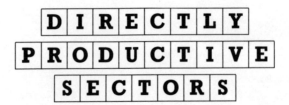

14
Industry

Of all sectors of the economy, industry shows the greatest variety and complexity. One might reasonably ask what there is in common between a petrochemicals plant and a textiles weaving shed, or between a modern automobile assembly plant and a tea drying and packing factory. All one can say is that all four activities are normally defined as belonging to the 'secondary' economic sector, as opposed to the 'primary' (production of food and raw materials) or the 'tertiary' (production of services) sectors.

Given the immensity of the subject, this chapter could either be very long, a book in itself, or disarmingly short. We have preferred the latter. Even more so than the other chapters, this one is only a preface, suggesting a common approach. Before starting an industrial plant (and this is as true of tea packing as of petrochemicals) planners need to call on advisers with a working knowledge of that particular industrial branch. There is no such thing as a general industrial expert, whether economist or engineer. Specific expertise is eventually indispensable.

A bad industrial project is capable of causing more damage to the economy than a bad project of comparable size in any other sector. It can simultaneously reduce the real incomes of consumers, linked industries, taxpayers, competing firms, and all users of foreign exchange. Since a factory is highly visible and often a political symbol it tends to be operated long after the original mistake becomes evident. By then vested interests gather momentum and keep the project going. Good money disappears after bad. Some factories, especially highly protected import-substituting industries using imported raw materials, actually reduce national income.

The bargain

The technology of industry is more complex than that of most other sectors discussed in this book, and is changing more rapidly. Much of the know-how rests in the hands of parties having a vested interest in how it is used, such as machinery suppliers, patent-holders, multinational firms with manufacturing bases elsewhere, consultants with a financial interest in implementing the project, etc. Truly impartial advice is hard to come by, and not always easy to recognise. Some international agencies and aid donors can provide disinterested advice to developing countries in their dealings with foreign suppliers, partners, consultants and owners of proprietary technology.

Many countries can obtain benefits from developing their industries in partnership with foreign investors, either through joint ventures or through the supply of management and technical expertise. Foreign investment as such is not inherently good or bad, but it provides an opportunity for mutual benefit, subject to factors raised below.

Mounting industrial projects entails a process of bargaining. Often the foreign supplier (or investor) has the stronger hand, especially if he has a stranglehold on the technology and little interest in the local market. However, even a poor country can have important cards to play if, for example, there is a buyers' market for the equipment due to a world recession, there is a potentially large market for the product and the prospect of further sales of equipment, parts or kits, or the country can offer a manufacturing base for export to other countries.

It is impossible to offer advice to cater for all the potential bargaining situations, except to point out that there are many permutations between a full turnkey deal, on the one hand, and an independent local operation, on the other. Many projects have taken longer to bring to fruition, and some have failed, because parties in the host country dispensed with, or shed too soon, the props offered (at a price) by their foreign partners. Equally, of course, many countries have burdened themselves with a range of equipment and services they did not really need, at excessive cost, because they failed to realise the alternatives, shop around and drive a harder bargain.

Part and parcel of the decision about the *type* of industrial project is the extent and nature of foreign involvement. Even in the simplest case, where an autonomous local company buys equipment from a foreign supplier, there is the decision about the amount of foreign supervision during implementation and the early years of operation. Should the supplier be retained to give training to local workers, should a management team be kept on for the first year of the project, should a performance guarantee be written in, etc.? These features, if desired, may raise the cost of the project.

In more complex cases the degree of foreign involvement can be a major issue. In the case of a large steel or petrochemicals plant, the host country may be tempted to accept a **turnkey** contract under which the leading foreign supplier undertakes all aspects of supply and installation, together with financial arrangements. Although this would remove a large headache from a weak and unsophisticated buyer, the arrangement would deprive a more mature and experienced buyer of the opportunity to split up the contract, shop around and retain responsibility for the design of the project and the pace of implementation.

Foreign ownership of the industrial project is the ultimate degree of outside involvement. This is not the place to discuss the appropriate degree of foreign investment for each circumstance. The main point of raising it here is to note that a foreign equity holding is a two-edged weapon. The host country can insist on a minority equity holding by the supplier as a way of ensuring the latter's continuing interest in the fate of the project.

Types of industry

Private entrepreneurs or state corporations have a large measure of choice over the activities they select to pursue. In agriculture natural climatic and soil conditions limit the choice of crops. There is no such natural limit in industry and the constraint is the relative one of efficiency. According to elementary theory the best industries to select are those in which the country has a 'comparative advantage' ('comparative' because the choice should be relative to other activities in the same country, rather than in respect of international competitors).

The most likely reasons why an industry may conform to the principle of

comparative advantage are that it is well located in relation to its inputs of natural resources, is close to its market, or finds a suitable labour force in the vicinity. There are many other reasons, of course, but these are the 'classic' determinants of the location of industry.

The attraction of siting near raw materials is greatest for those industries in which a lot of material is shed during processing, such as in mineral refining, timber products, the preparation, canning and processing of perishable crops and the first stages in the processing of cotton, tea, palm oil, etc. Where the cost of the raw material features heavily in total costs, there is a *prima facie* case for considering locating near materials to minimise transport costs.

A location near the market is attractive for industries that *add* weight (e.g. drinks) or bulk (e.g. furniture). It is also important for industries with perishable goods, such as bakeries, or where close liaison with customers is vital (e.g. fashion garments, specialised machinery). Since markets (e.g. urban or industrial concentrations) often contain sizeable labour forces and sources of materials and components it is easy to see how, for some industries, all three of the main location determinants coincide.

Labour can influence location where wages are a high component of costs or where skill is vital; in short, where an industry is labour- or skill-intensive. Labour-intensity can be a case of circular causation; an industry can develop in a labour-intensive way precisely because there is abundant labour in the vicinity, at low wages. In a different context, or at a different time, the same industry can develop in a capital-intensive way if labour becomes scarcer relative to capital. One sees this type of variation in car assembly and in coal-mining.

The same is true of skilled labour. Where there is a heavy skill requirement, and where it is not feasible to persuade such labour to migrate, a concentration of skills (or aptitudes) can be a powerful magnet for industry. This is especially true of assembly industries, mechanical engineering and high technology occupations. A special case is the 'finishing touch' industries using local labour (that normally needs to be dextrous and quick to learn) to put imported components together (notably in electronics).

In many countries industry has tended to become less intensive of labour; this is the result partly of increases in the cost of labour relative to capital, and partly of technical changes that economise on labour. In an attempt to combat this trend a movement has recently grown up to make industry more labour-intensive in order to create more jobs. This involves the encouragement of 'appropriate technology'. It is also often associated with the promotion of small-scale industry.

It is, of course, too simple to view industry as being governed solely by access to raw materials, markets and labour. For instance, industries needing a lot of energy or power may locate close to cheap hydroelectric power, oil or coal, even if materials and labour have to move some distance. Other industries are 'footloose' and could thrive almost anywhere. Many of them settle in countries or regions where their operations can maximise official incentives (or minimise their taxes).

149

How industries develop

There have been statistical studies which show that the size and structure of a country's industrial sector are closely related to that country's size (population) and wealth (income per head). Allowing for aberrations, the growth of industry is fairly predictable. The growth, and increasing complexity, of the domestic market would appear to be the main determinant of the pattern of industry.

At low levels of development industry consists of activities closely tied to the local market (utensils, tools, food preparation) or elementary processing to locally-available raw materials prior to export. Cotton can be cleaned, ginned and baled prior to export. As local know-how and capital increase, local industry can perform more processing functions, capturing increasing amounts of the value that is added to the raw materials in the process of manufacture. The cotton can be spun into yarn, then the yarn can be woven into fabric, and finally can be made up into garments. This can be regarded as a 'natural' evolution of industry. We do not imply that there is no scope for purposeful government promotion, but simply that there is a sequence and pace to this evolution which makes for efficient use of resources.

The sequence just described is of increasing local value-added on exported materials. There is an opposite sequence, consisting of the gradual replacement of imported items. This might start with the growth of industries concerned with handling and servicing imported products – e.g. workshops to repair vehicles. As local skills develop, and as the market widens, warehouses set up to hold and distribute spare parts might become the nuclei of assembly units, transforming imported kits into fully-assembled vehicles. These rudimentary assembly operations, starting with a small amount of value-added, may gradually develop into fully-fledged manufacturing units as an increasing number of the imported components are made locally.

This process of **'import replacement'** describes the growth of manufacturing and assembly industry in many countries that we now regard as semi-industrial. In the automobile industry, which is the model for this process, governments often force the pace of development by requiring (foreign) motor firms to follow a schedule for replacing imported parts by locally-purchased items, pushing local value-added up to 80% or 90% of the value of the finished item.

Both sequences described, whether through exports or imports, are natural, to an extent inevitable, and quite consistent with the principle of comparative advantage. It is also clear that there is scope for 'artificial' interference in the process with the aim of forcing the pace of development. A government can ban the export of unworked raw materials, tax the export of crude materials at a higher rate than the processed form, or offer cheap power or energy to processing units. The replacement of imports can be hastened by outright bans, tariffs, exchange control, a bias in government procurement towards local items, cheap capital and credit to local firms, etc.

It is clear that we cannot draw a clear distinction between 'natural' and 'artificial' industrialisation. Most industrialisation, like most development, is affected by the state in various degrees. Nevertheless, if pressed too far and too fast industrialisation can waste resources and fail to achieve its objectives. This is especially true of **import substitution**.

Industries are set up to save (or earn) foreign exchange, create employment, reduce dependency on foreign companies, increase local value-added and profits, stimulate the development of linked industries or encourage techno-logical change. These are common ostensible reasons. The ultimate reasons may be to create a monument to a particular leader or regime, to create an industrial labour force that can become a political constituency, or, most cynically of all, to cash in on a bribe or commission from an equipment supplier or promoter. The fact is that much industrialisation in developing countries does not fulfil the objectives that are claimed for it.

Protection given to local industrial output reduces the incentives to efficiency. In combination with generous subsidies to investment, privileged access to foreign exchange for imported equipment, and the effect of an over-valued exchange rate in lowering the cost of imported supplies, this can lead to the choice of inappropriate, capital-intensive techniques of production with a high foreign exchange requirement. Costs and prices settle at above international levels, penalising domestic consumers and other industrial users. Even with protection and (sometimes) a local monopoly, corporations may have trouble breaking even financially, and depend on continuing public subsidies of various kinds.

Economic appraisal

This common syndrome increases the importance of properly calculating the real benefits from an industrial project. We have seen, for instance, that the price of the product is usually allowed to settle at above that of imports; this is due to the effect of tariffs or import controls. Domestic competition may bring down the price level, but this is unusual. For the purpose of appraisal the price to take is the delivered price of the imported equivalent to the country (its main port, or in the case of the landlocked countries, the main market). If this procedure is not followed, almost any highly protected industry could be justified.

We should not pretend that the concept of the **international price** is free of ambiguity or practical difficulties. In the case of an investment with a long gestation period, such as a steel mill, it is necessary to estimate international prices that will prevail starting some years in the future, and extending over the economic life of the investment. This requires predictive skills of a high order. The task is complicated by the fact that for many products, of which steel is again a good example, world prices fluctuate widely since producers use exports to dispose of residual production.

It is also important to value imported supplies correctly. The actual money outlay by an industrial firm on imported equipment, spares, materials and know-how may seriously understate their true value if the exchange rate is heavily over-valued or foreign equipment is available at specially favourable exchange rates. Some correction to reflect the true exchange rate is desirable.

Local raw materials should also be correctly valued. In the effort to promote processing industries raw materials may be offered cheaply, in the sense of less than the price at which they could be exported. This is common in the case of cotton textiles, for instance. Nevertheless, these raw materials have an opportunity cost equal to the foreign exchange that could have been earned from their export, and this is the real value of the resources that the factory uses up. The provision of cheap electric power is another hidden subsidy which has a cost to the rest of the economy. In principle, the full economic cost of inputs should be entered when appraising a project, irrespective of prices that are actually charged to the enterprise.

There may be a case for considering the opposite sort of adjustment in the case of workers' wages. Because of the 'showpiece' nature of many industrial ventures, and the protected environment in which they operate, firms tend to offer wages that are higher than are strictly necessary to attract labour. Minimum wage legislation and trade union pressures may produce the same result, namely wages exceeding the 'supply price' of labour. This is the case for **shadow pricing** labour, as discussed in chapter 2, within reason.

It should be apparent that in the artificial conditions that we have sketched here it is possible for an industrial enterprise to record a financial surplus, while a proper economic cost–benefit analysis would show a loss. If a high proportion of costs consists of imported inputs, and if these are converted wastefully, it is conceivable that the industrial venture would reduce national income, since the value of resources used up exceeds the value of output, when both are correctly valued at international prices.

In any case, the effect of the project on the balance of payments needs to be set out. An 'import substituting' industry is quite capable of *increasing* imports for a number of years through its appetite for foreign equipment, spares, materials, and management services. At the same time the local materials it uses, which could have been exported, subtract from export income. Other industries, compelled to use its costly, and possibly inferior, products, may have their export competitiveness impaired. Because of the macro-economic effects of import-substituting industry, tending to make the exchange rate over-valued, such industrialisation makes life much harder for export-oriented industries.

The fiscal effects on the government's budget may also be negative. Since the purpose of industry is often to reduce imports, and since in most countries import duties are an important source of revenue, there will be a direct loss to the budget. In addition, imports of equipment are frequently allowed free of duty as a promotional device, tax holidays and accelerated depreciation are built in, and subsidised capital and credit often made available. Recurrent subsidies and cancellation of debt are common where the venture is less successful than expected.

Advocates of industrial projects may concede some of these snags yet invoke the **infant industry** argument in favour of limited protection and unlimited patience. They argue that promoting any kind of development tends to involve some subsidy, or an initial period during which the full rigour of the market is suspended. To cite the metaphor often used in this context, plants reared in a hothouse need time before they can be transplanted outside to face all weathers.

In principle, subsidies and protection should be offered at a level which tapers over time, disappearing after a few years. In practice, industries that demand high protection or support from the outset are rarely able to dispense with these crutches within a reasonable time span. Planners should certainly allow an industry a period of time (which will vary according to the industrial branch) to build up to full capacity working and to get costs down to competitive levels. During that period, it may need help with its cash flow. The longer this period goes on, however, the greater is the burden on government, consumers, and other industrial users.

Some practical points

Experience shows the value of attending to the following points in appraising an industrial project:

1 Many feasibility studies should be treated with reserve since they are often written by interested parties. Some 'consultants' have links with equipment suppliers which compromise their objectivity.

2 Where the project will replace imports by domestically-produced items the market study should make full allowance for initial differences in quality between goods from the two sources. Some market surveys imply that the entire existing market is up for grabs, and that, with import restrictions, the new project will be able to capture the entire existing demand. However, what usually happens is that for some time after the project comes into operation the imported goods continue to be smuggled in. Thus, if local production is calibrated to serve the entire existing demand, some part of output will remain unsold. One of the worst examples we have seen of a market survey that ignored quality factors was one that calculated the annual consumption of shoes in an African country in kilograms per head!

3 Estimates of the time necessary to build up to full capacity working are normally optimistic. This is especially true of large projects in heavy industry. What often happens is that the period of build up (sometimes hopefully referred to as the 'learning curve') takes longer than expected, and the rate of capacity utilisation that the plant settles down at is less than hoped for. This eventuality should be allowed for in the sensitivity tests of the rate of return.

4 Sensitivity tests, where they are included in the economic and financial analyses, normally take too narrow a range of the values of the main variables. The range rarely exceeds plus or minus 20%. In practice, the values of variables such as output price, raw materials price, total output (in which capacity utilisation is subsumed), proportion of output exported, etc., are likely to vary more widely around the expected value of the outcome. In short, sensitivity tests should err on the side of boldness in order to highlight the sorts of events that will make or break the project.

5 In estimating the correct economic prices to apply to output, the calculation of future international prices can be very speculative. Such products of heavy industry as steel, fertilisers, and chemicals move cyclically back and forth into shortage and surplus, with disproportionately violent effects on the price of the relatively small part of their output that is exported. It is a nightmare trying to project the price of these residual traded amounts for the 10–15-year future period relevant to appraising a project in heavy industry. What is sometimes more useful is to identify the most efficient international producer and project the future price of that product on its own domestic market.

6 A large new factory or plant will normally require the construction of some social infrastructure for its management and labour force. (Certainly isolated projects that have not properly catered for their employees have suffered

poor morale and high staff turnover.) If such housing, schooling, and medical services would have been built anyway to serve an expanding population, the appraiser should not attribute all its cost to the project. Where the new infrastructure clearly duplicates what is available elsewhere, most or all of its cost should be attributed to the project it serves.

7 Competition among industrial equipment suppliers, supported by their governments, often takes the form of the offer of project financing at well below the market rate, but only for the project in question. If it is beyond doubt that the aid or officially-backed export credit at subsidised rates would only be available for the project and no other, the convention is to disregard the initial cost of equipment financed in this way and to enter it as a cost to the project only as and when it is repaid. These circumstances are unusual, and this procedure should be employed sparingly.

Checklist of main questions

i. Does the project involve the creation of **new capacity**? If so, is it in competition with other firms or will it supersede them? In the case of a rehabilitation of, or extension to, existing capacity, what has been the operating performance of the present firm?

ii. Will the **market** for the output be local or foreign? In either case, has there been a proper market survey? Will imports be protected?

iii. Is projected **capacity** reasonable in relation to demand? How long will it take the firm to build up production to near full capacity working?

iv. Is the **managerial structure** appropriate? How will the owners (especially if government) influence policy? Will there be enough managers of the right calibre? What will their delegated authority be?

v. Is the **technology** suitable for the country's level of development? Have alternatives been explored, including the use of second-hand plant? Will the suppliers supervise installation and oversee the first months or years of operation? Have local managers and foremen been trained on such equipment and is its upkeep within their capability?

vi. Where a **foreign partner** is involved, what are the terms of its involvement (equity, management contract, royalties, etc.)? Are there any restrictive conditions, e.g. over exports, sources of new technology, supply of materials and components?

vii. What **official incentives**, subsidies and protection are being offered? How much is really necessary? How long will it be before costs become competitive?

viii. What is the source of **raw materials**? Are they likely to be available in the required amounts, price and regularity? What arrangements are being made for their transport and storage?

ix. What are the prospects of attracting a **labour** force at the wages envisaged? Does the factory or locality have a good record of labour relations? How much new employment is being created, and at what cost

154

per job? Is shift working planned? Is it intended to employ many women, and if so are there any social barriers, or particular customs to respect?

x. What are the net direct **balance of payments** implications?

xi. What are the net effects on the government's **budget**, allowing for any loss of customs duty on imports, the cost of fiscal incentives and allowances, any initial equity participation, and recurrent subsidy?

xii. What is the expected **cash flow** of the enterprise? For an established firm, is it consistent with recent performance?

xiii. In the **economic analysis**, have international prices been used in valuing output and inputs?

xiv. Has the **land** been acquired? If not, what steps are being taken? Is the project compatible with local by-laws, planning regulations, and environmental legislation?

Further reading

There is a vast literature on industrial development. In keeping with the brevity of this chapter, the following list is kept short.

Industrial policy
I. M. D. Little, T. Scitovsky and M. Scott, *Industry and Trade in Some Developing Countries*, Oxford University Press for the OECD Development Centre, Paris, 1970. (A classic contemporary statement of the case for 'liberal' economic policies and the use of market forces in industrial development.)

R. B. Sutcliffe, *Industry and Under-Development*, Addison-Wesley Publishing Co., 1971. (A comprehensive review of the main policy issues from an ideological standpoint opposite to that of the authors above.)

J. Cody, H. Hughes and D. Wall (eds.), *Policies for Industrial Progress in Developing Countries*, Oxford University Press for the United Nations Industrial Development Organisation and the World Bank, 1980.

Industrial appraisal
Two of the path-breaking works on project appraisal, already quoted in chapter 2, were written principally with industrial projects in view.

I. M. D. Little and J. A. Mirrlees, *Manual of Industrial Project Analysis in Developing Countries*, Vol. II, *Social Cost–Benefit Analysis*, OECD Development Centre, Paris, 1969.

A. K. Sen, S. Marglin and P. Dasgupta, *Guidelines for Project Evaluation*, published for the United Nations Industrial Development Organisation, UN, New York, 1972.

There is a wide-ranging discussion of appraisal methodology, including a comparison of the above two books and the problems of calculating world prices, in a special edition of the *Bulletin of the Oxford University Institute of Economics and Statistics*, February 1972.

15
Agriculture

Since agricultural projects come in so many shapes and sizes, and all contain elements common to each other, the most effective approach to a generalised appraisal is to isolate their constituent parts and to analyse them separately. Those designing agricultural projects can thus put together component parts in whatever shape and size is appropriate.

The principal components of an agricultural project are the natural resources base, the economic and social structure, agricultural inputs, and the institutions which will hold it together. These component parts will interact. None of them in practice is wholly changeable, but all can be modified and improved. The degree to which this can be achieved will depend upon a fifth factor, the policies pursued by the responsible authorities. The extent to which policies will achieve their ends will depend upon their realism in relation to these components.

1 Natural resources

Significant variations in natural land qualities are to be expected within a development site and must be anticipated over time. In agricultural development, natural land qualities are major factors in the decision on which production objectives are economically feasible. They decide the level of inputs and expertise necessary to attain the required level of productive return. Land qualities have an important bearing on the risk of an enterprise. Land differs in its versatility and a false step on land that is not versatile can cause irreversible damage. The speed of change in land qualities, even under the influence of unsophisticated development, can be very rapid. Land is a complex dynamic factor, not a constant.

2 Economic and social structures

Clearly no project is likely to succeed in the face of opposition from central or local government authorities, or farmers themselves. In many, perhaps most, cases authorities may take a lukewarm attitude and judgement then needs to be made as to whether the proposal is likely to succeed. A very strong case for going ahead will be required if there is not a strong government commitment.

Many governments try to ensure that the rural sector provides resources for investment elsewhere while trying to prevent this acting as a disincentive to agricultural growth. At the same time, the need to placate the urban consumer often means that food prices are kept at artificially low levels, which either seriously reduces agricultural output or leads to black market distortions. Many governments compensate for low farm prices by subsidising farm inputs. If there is an efficient administration capable of perceiving the real needs of farmers this can be justified, but this is all too often not the case. Governments tend towards **urban bias** as it enables them to mollify consumers and to control farmers.

It is, however, not only food production which is penalised but also export crops. Their production can be seriously jeopardised by high levels of taxation required to finance either a subsidised industrial sector or high levels of consumption of imported goods for the towns. Investments in the agricultural sector may thus be used to support economic and political policies which will nullify their positive effects.

At a national level the patterns of land ownership and the industrial structure could undermine attempts to promote rural development. Industrialists may have an interest in obtaining cheap agricultural materials, or preventing competition in the provision of imported agricultural equipment.

Farmers, like any other group, will respond to **price incentives**. It has been argued in the past that traditional farmers have certain 'target incomes' and if these are achieved they will not respond to price incentives. In this respect, however, they are not different from any other social group. While it is true that price incentives which are insufficient for them to reach a particular target may not lead to a positive production response, it is not unreasonable to assume that, over time, farmers do raise their targets as economic and social aspirations change. As with most social groups there is not always a linear response to price incentives. Response can proceed on the basis of a series of jumps to new levels of satisfaction – much will depend upon the availability and cost of services and goods which farmers want.

A major difference between farming and industry is the very large number of producers engaged in the agricultural sector. This often means that farmers responding in a uniform way to external factors such as prices can produce a massive over- or under-supply of produce. This is particularly obvious where supply can rapidly be altered, as with annual fruit and vegetable crops.

The large number of producers in agriculture makes it far more difficult to plan changes as there are so many differences between one farm and another. It is particularly hard to assess what changes farmers will be prepared to accept and how quickly they will do so, yet forecasts of these reactions are essential in agricultural planning. It is also more difficult to regiment farmers than industrial workers. As many governments have discovered to their cost, disgruntled farmers can be very unproductive.

Farms and villages
There is no evidence that in the longer run farmers within traditional rural societies are any less interested in improving economic welfare than their compatriots. However, they do operate in a very different environment and the problems of change are normally greater.

In developing countries rural poverty is widespread, and the narrow margin between survival and starvation is such that few farmers are going to take risks with subsistence crops. The amount of ill-considered and ill-researched technical advice which has descended on farmers more than justifies this caution. No sensible farmer is likely to respond very readily to advice which entails transforming an age-old technology. At best, after having seen the measure of success on the part of farmers who he thinks he can emulate, he will embark upon change. Schemes which depend upon results under the privileged conditions of government research stations make them untested as far as farmers are concerned, and are unlikely to be accepted. Much research is of this sort. On the other hand, research which has been applied on a demonstration basis by large or small commercial farmers is likely to be accepted much more readily. **Risk avoidance** is therefore a more important consideration among poor farmers than among those who are fully commercialised with resources sufficient to carry them over a bad season. Plans envisaging rapid rural transformation must be regarded as suspect.

Another important factor is the amalgamation of home and work places in agriculture. In industrial activities the home is seldom the work place and it is therefore much easier to introduce changes, and indeed to supervise them. The farmer has to live with changes not just during his working hours but in his spare time. His family, who almost always have a vital role to play on the farm, will be affected and may resist changes which do not benefit them. Supervision is also more difficult and costly than it is in industry.

Hallowed techniques of production create work allocations and rewards between members of the family which are difficult to change. The roles of men, women and children in carrying out different types of agricultural activity are well established and the rewards arising from these efforts well recognised.

Technologies which benefit one member of the family at the expense of others are not likely to be enthusiastically embraced by the family as a whole, unless compensating benefits are likely to emerge. The role of women (and indeed of children) is all too often insufficiently recognised.

The nature of traditional society often makes it invidious for members to innovate, and they are expected to share their success with the extended family. It is frequently the outsider, the nonconformist (either as an individual or a group), who is responsible for change. An understanding of the social hierarchy, structure and kinship patterns is essential in contemplating change in the rural sector.

On the other hand, it is important not to exaggerate the social problems which will emerge in agricultural improvement as these are common to any form of economic change. Economic development can never be an egalitarian process as areas have different resource endowments and individuals potentially different skills and motivations. The important thing is to try and ensure that those who benefit should do so with a minimum of disadvantage to others (e.g. via compensation), and that in the end the increases in efficiency which result will eventually bring benefits to society as a whole.

3 Improvements in inputs

Agricultural inputs can be divided into those physical resources available to the farmer – land, water and labour – and various purchased inputs, primarily seeds, fertilisers, chemicals for pest control, machinery, implements and items of fixed capital investment. Technological innovation which, for example, leads to high yields per hectare may not be a suitable solution if land is not short and labour in ample supply. Equally it would be better not to embark on development if physical constraints are such that sustained increases in production can only be achieved at a level of technical input that is too sophisticated for the community.

Land settlement
Opening up new lands for settlement (as opposed to intensifying production on existing farms) is a diminishing, but by no means defunct, option. Even

within existing farming systems there is often scope for expanding the amount of land which can be cultivated.

Intensification of farming is usually seen as the only solution. Professional education tends to concentrate on intensive systems of agriculture, and mistaken proposals for agricultural improvement are frequently made. Emphasis on increased use of fertilisers, soil conservation, pesticides and water is often not the right solution. It is important to assess whether farmers are likely to be able to extend the area under cultivation. This would be inadvisable if it entailed moving into areas that were environmentally fragile (subject to soil erosion, excessive depletion of fertility, drought, etc.) or better suited to some other purpose (forestry, plantation crops, irrigation, etc.). It is important to see the farming system as a whole.

Land settlement schemes entail a process of migration in which governments play a role. Generally speaking, a major government participation in those countries where there is little freedom has seldom led to successful land settlement schemes. This is not a doctrinaire issue, but arises from the very complexity of planning a comprehensive settlement scheme from the centre.

No person or committee can plan for all the problems likely to be encountered by new settlers. Only in a totalitarian society can centrally directed schemes work, but this is at great economic, social and human cost.

The major criteria for successful land settlement schemes include:

i. Choice of farmers who, due to population or other pressures, are prepared to move into new areas and who thus have a strong motivation to succeed, and who can expect a sufficient income increase to justify this move

ii. The availability of an acceptably high proportion of well distributed land suitable for growing a sufficient quantity of saleable crops to provide an income greater than that obtainable elsewhere. This income to be obtained after essential inputs and transport costs have been met and using management methods within the compass of the settlement community

iii. Provision of demarcated plots, with a prospect of title and access to roads and water

iv. Provision on credit of certain basic equipment for clearing and preparing land, and for house building materials

v. Possible clearing of some land for first-year crops and provision of foodstuffs and seeds for the first season. However, it is vital that settlers make a significant physical or financial contribution in order to have a stake in success

vi. Technical knowledge of a suitable agronomic 'package' and guidance from agricultural extension services directly relevant to land conditions

vii. An adequate marketing system

viii. Basic housing provision

ix. Social facilities, such as a health post, a school, and possibly shops, bank, religious centre, central meeting-place

x. Good management of the settlement.

To be successful a settlement scheme must depend on the determination of the settlers to succeed. The more public assistance is available the less will be the will of farmers to establish themselves. The capital investment per farmer should be as low as possible in order to promote dissemination, and the loans advanced should not be so excessive as to become a psychological burden. Loans which exceed in total two or three times gross earnings per annum are likely to be counter-productive.

Irrigation

The application of water to land is as old as the history of settled agriculture. Most developments have been the result of gradual technical and social improvements at very low cost by using farm labour. Large-scale systems of irrigation with highly centralised forms of social control characterised many early civilisations. The success of these systems was, however, heavily dependent upon a despotic system of government which was able to ensure that the technically complex nature of water control was adhered to. It also depended on annual self-fertilising floods which maintained yields and kept salinity levels low. In recent years the technical capacity to build immense dams for hydroelectric purposes has encouraged the development of large-scale irrigation systems. Integrated river basin development has become popular but has proved to be far less successful than planned.

i. Large-scale river basin schemes

The most common fault is attempting to emulate the success of individual irrigation schemes on a very large scale without appreciating that individual on-farm irrigation has advantages denied to a large-scale public sector scheme. These include:

a. Farmers using off-peak labour, usually over years, can develop schemes at very low costs

b. Control and management of water supplies is easy on individual farms

c. The small-scale nature of these schemes enables farmers to produce high-value crops for sale without encountering the marketing problems which large schemes encounter

d. High overhead costs are avoided.

The ability of small-scale schemes to minimise costs may enable them to successfully produce two crops a year, from water for supplementary irrigation. Large-scale irrigation schemes, however, are so costly per hectare that they are seldom, if ever, justified on the basis of providing merely one extra crop per year (supplementary irrigation). Large-scale public sector irrigation projects are only likely to be justified in dry areas of the world where average rainfall does not allow annual crop production at all or makes it very risky.

The success of large-scale public irrigation schemes will therefore depend largely upon:

a. the technical, social, and economic prospects of producing crops which will find a large enough market without depressing prices to an uneconomic level. This usually means cotton, sugar or rice as the economic mainstay of the project. A scheme dependent on intensive crops (e.g. horticulture) yielding potentially high incomes will almost certainly encounter serious marketing problems

b. The existence of a social system, or modes of social control, which will make it possible to introduce and enforce the management systems and disciplines which ensure that water is used efficiently. Payment for water used will be essential for success, but difficult to implement

c. The absence of natural conditions which enable annual crops to be grown on any scale without irrigation. Otherwise the additional investment is only justified for a limited period of the year for growing one additional crop. This is unlikely to justify heavy capital investment, which will require the growing of at least two additional crops per year

d. Land conditions, particularly those relating to topographical features, soil and water quality, which will not result in salinity, water-logging, excessive water use or an excessive need for other inputs

e. A willingness to accept that the technical and social problems of adaptation are likely to be formidable and will at best take many years to resolve in societies unaccustomed to the required discipline.

While large river basin development schemes stir the imagination, their success rate has been low. They need to be appraised with the greatest caution by fully experienced interdisciplinary teams in which social and managerial problems are analysed at the earliest stage.

ii. Small-scale schemes

Widespread success has been achieved by individual farmers in improving their own farming systems with irrigation. Water can be applied from rivers in the age-old fashion by building canals which use gravity to spread the water, or by lifting water from rivers with human or animal effort or simple low lift pumps. On-farm storage of water has also been important.

The introduction of pumps enables water to be applied with greater speed and ease, and of course in greater quantities. The introduction of pumps has, however, not always been successful for technical, social and economic reasons. The most common problems are:

a. Failure to ensure that there is a system of administration responsible for servicing and maintaining the pumping equipment

b. Failure to ensure sufficient high-value crops to justify the investment

c. Failure to control the number of groundwater pumps, which will lower the water table, or to control grazing in cattle areas, which will have disastrous ecological effects.

Successful pump irrigation will therefore depend upon a community able and willing to maintain the pump. Individuals and large social groups may be able to do this. Unfortunately in small communities it will be difficult to find trained staff and to finance them. The social pressures on anyone seeking to ensure that water usage is controlled are likely to be such as to render the task impossible. In grazing areas the introduction of pumps has created deserts where no satisfactory system of control has been socially or politically feasible.

The amount of water needed for a given crop will depend on water quality, the nature of the soils and the climate. The cost of pumping depends on the height to which this amount of water must be raised. These factors determine the type of crops which it will be economical to produce. In the vicinity of large urban markets deep wells applying water to intensive crops are more likely to be justified. Further from markets, annual extensive crops might be justified with low lift pumps. In distant, drier areas only capable of producing cattle, pumped water supplies are not likely to be economic.

Irrigation development has often been proffered as the solution for rural areas in drier parts of the world. These hopes have frequently been disappointed. Many schemes have failed as a result of inadequate maintenance or water and pasture depletion.

Labour and training
Labour is the critical input into all projects, but possibly the one least understood and analysed. Both labour motivation and labour availability need to be carefully considered.

Motivation may be lacking. In areas dependent on rainfall or endowed with perennial crops, the average amount of adult work in agriculture can be as low as three of four hours per day. There will, however, be peak planting and harvesting periods which could be severely jeopardised by withdrawal of labour. In those areas of the world where rainfall is higher, and/or irrigation possible, average hours worked could be double. Harsh environments, hunger and sickness will act as a brake on greater human effort unless significant economic rewards are thought certain. Social structures which allocate different forms of work to men and to women can inhibit change if all the benefits accrue to one sex and the costs accrue to another. The sharing of surpluses throughout the community can also discourage above-average individual effort.

Over the last two or three decades it has been all too commonly assumed that there is a vast pool of unemployed labour in rural areas which can be used in other economic activities at no economic cost to the community. This is very seldom so, since families can rarely afford to subsidise non-productive members capable of working. The true picture is that the marked seasonality of rural work enforces long periods of idleness during the year, but labour is usually short, and valuable, at planting and harvesting time.

While labour productivity in rural areas is generally low, it is usually positive, except in some exceptional areas of the world. Projects planned in other sectors must therefore assume that in most cases labour has a significant cost to the rural sector, though it may be less than the annual market wage. Labour moving out of the rural areas temporarily during the off season does have a very low, possibly zero, opportunity cost, but it is not feasible to plan on any scale for economic activities based on seasonal labour, although when organisation is good, or compulsion possible, seasonal labour can be used for public works programmes.

The introduction of new technologies and crops often fails because of a lack of appreciation of labour implications. Crop planting machinery which increases output will create labour problems during harvesting. Technologies which, through better pest control, increase yields will require more labour, possibly more experienced labour. It is surprising how rapidly successful peasant farmers turn to hiring labour. Many attempts at bettering the conditions of farmers through technological change have failed because of a lack of understanding of their labour implications. There is vast scope for increasing labour productivity in rural areas in developing countries, but only if it is appreciated that labour motivation and availability must be analysed.

Training labour, either informally or through educational institutions, is important but all too often a failure. Apart from the frequent irrelevance of the training courses, other common factors are poorly trained teachers, lack of central government support for recurrent costs, and the high cost of teaching per student. Equally important is the lack of effective demand for the output of training institutions. For this reason trainees need access to the means to implement their newly acquired skills – for example, land, credit and seeds.

The main issues in establishing training systems and institutions are:

i. The likelihood of an effective demand for the numbers of people it is proposed to train

ii. Availability of relevant material with which to train students

iii. Suitably trained staff

iv. Suitable numbers of potential candidates of the right calibre

v. Minimal cost per student trained in comparison with other forms of training

vi. A willingness of government to accept the recurrent budgetary burden which training entails

vii. Provision for re-training.

Seeds
The introduction of new and improved varieties of seeds has been possibly the most successful of all technological changes which have occurred in the history of agriculture. New methods of cross breeding carried out in research stations do, however, need to be adapted to local environments to ensure their technical, social and economic compatibility. Research needs to be carefully planned if maximum results are to be achieved. Apart from concentrating on crops which are most likely to be of greatest benefit to the largest possible number of people, research should, in the first instance, concentrate on varieties likely to produce the most cost-effective results. Technologies requiring improved husbandry practices and locally available inputs should take precedence over research requiring purchased inputs, capital investment and complex managerial control.

Continual consultation with farmers in formulating and implementing research is critical to success, as well as with extension agents and other commercial organisations likely to be the beneficiaries of research.

Building up certified seeds through a multiplication process needs a series of reliable producers. These are not easy to find. Further, new seeds often require complementary inputs which may require considerable managerial skill and sizeable financial outlays and credit.

Normally, yield increases in agriculture are of the order of 1%–2% per year as gradual improvements take place. With improved varieties, startling increases can be obtained on an individual basis – 5%–15% is not uncommon for short periods of time. However, it is not possible to rapidly obtain widespread increases of this order, even with massive technical assistance and subsidies. With an efficient organisation it might be possible to achieve average increases, over a large number of farmers, of 4%–5% per year. To expect much more, other than in special circumstances, would be rash.

Seed improvement schemes need to ensure that:

i. There is likely to be a market for the seeds

ii. A reliable system of production and distribution exists or is built up

iii. The quality of technical staff is high

iv. Research has been good enough to justify embarking on the creation of seed farms

v. Farmers are fully acquainted with complementary requirements to maximise best use of seeds and have the prospect of obtaining them.

Fertiliser
Fertilisers are normally important complementary inputs in rural development projects. Few inputs have had such a successful impact on farm output. However, there have been many failures resulting from the belief that they are a panacea.

Failure can usually be traced to lack of research to justify the programme. Research results, if carried out competently, will always be far better than farmer results. More detailed and skilled management, lack of financial restrictions on investments and the small-scale nature of research plots can lead to quite unrealistic expectations. On-farm trials are essential before fertiliser recommendations are applied. These should be carried out for a minimum of three years, and longer in areas with very variable conditions, since field trials are likely to achieve yields little better than 25%–40% of those achieved on research plots.

The risk of applying fertiliser is often ignored. In the first place, without irrigation outlays on fertiliser could be a total write-off if rains do not fall at the right time. Secondly, fertilisers simply may not be economic. In areas where land availability and tenure allow rotations that will maintain soil fertility, there is little need for fertiliser. Fertiliser must be available to farmers at the right time. This is often prevented by the failure of delivery systems. Finally, farmers need training in how and when to apply fertilisers.

Farm machinery
While a vast range of equipment is available we propose to restrict the discussion to tractors and their equipment, as they account for most of the purchases of farm machinery.

Tractors increase the speed with which land preparation and cultivation are carried out, thus allowing scope for an expansion of production. They can also, because of their speed of operation, ensure much more timely planting. Their strength gives them the power to cultivate soils which animal traction cannot, and they are useful transporters and prime movers for threshing machines, etc. They can improve the quality of operations, and reduce land required to feed animals.

Tractors can be labour-displacing. The degree to which this happens will vary with the availability of labour and the efficiency with which tractors are used. Efficient use can generate considerable demand for labour through increased output. In fact they may create labour shortages during harvest.

The effective use of tractors requires skilled and centralised management, with a personal interest in maximising usage together with a workforce able to maintain machinery. Tractors have, however, often been introduced into communities where there is no one with these skills, no back-up services to maintain them, and no labour available to cultivate and harvest the larger areas which have been tractor-planted.

When considering proposals for the introduction of tractors, the following conditions are desirable:

  i. Circumstances which allow tractors to be used for 800–2,000 hours per year (depending on costs of operation and the value of extra output)

 ii. A social system favourable to the use of machinery on a joint basis (although not via state-controlled bodies, all of which have required vast subsidies)

iii. A cultural system where timeliness of planting is important

 iv. Farmers who can repair and service machines (or who can be trained to do so)

  v. A back-up system for providing major repairs and spares

 vi. Adequate labour willing to carry out extra work generated by tractor plantings.

Storage
Crop storage is carried out for two very different purposes. One is to prevent crop losses. The other is to influence seasonal price fluctuations. The benefits from this latter activity will accrue to whoever controls the storage facilities. They could be farmers, middlemen, consumers or government.

Crop losses are extremely difficult to assess and little or no credence can be given to general claims about 25%–50% of crops being lost in storage. In part this is because a national figure for losses can never be anything moie than a guess. But more to the point, it is very difficult to measure economic losses of stored crops. It is hard to relate physical losses to economic losses since the first are gradual while price changes are frequent.

It needs constant monitoring to assess farm level crop losses. The few detailed studies which have been carried out suggest 5% 'on farm' storage losses. This seems plausible, otherwise farmers would have acted to reduce them. Under the circumstances expensive farm storage is unlikely to be justified.

The provision of storage (and possibly credit) to farmers to enable them to hold back supplies does not generate benefits to society as a whole, as the reduction of crop losses would. It entails transferring income from one group, such as traders, to another, such as producers.

Central storage systems can be controlled by the state, by traders or by farmers. Whoever controls the storage wields great political and economic power, and an assessment is needed of how this power is likely to be used.

Strategic (as opposed to seasonal) reserves are often built up at an unjustifiably high cost. Keeping stocks ties up scarce capital. It is important, therefore, to ensure that stocks are kept at as low a level as possible consistent with food security. The cost and speed of obtaining imported stocks in an emergency should be the main criteria for determining how many months of supplies are required to maintain food stocks.

An appraisal of crop storage proposals should thus:

i. First determine what purpose storage facilities are to serve. Will it be reduction of losses or a transfer of benefits from one group to another?

ii. In the case of storage losses, ensure as far as possible that claims made for economic losses have been substantiated. The claims made for crop losses are related to economic, not physical, data

iii. Ensure that since on-farm losses are likely to be low, the remedies are simple and cheap

iv. Check that when central storage systems are appraised, it is appreciated that new production is not being created and that central systems of storage will give great political and economic power to those who control them. These powers will not necessarily be used in the interests of producers, and sometimes not even in the interest of consumers

v. Be clear that central storage systems require local funds for the purchase of products to be stored. The recurrent financial cost of this may turn out to be unacceptably high to the local financing agency

vi. Make certain that central storage systems will have methods of financial control and management so as to maximise financial benefits, and that there are staff properly trained in the physical management of crops to be stored

vii. Ensure that ancillary handling systems are available and a system for arranging orderly stock flows is set up.

Credit
Credit is not an agricultural input, but is merely a business transaction which enables a borrower to bridge the time gap between present spending and future income. Not all farmers need access to credit, but it has been found that when it is made available it provides some additional inducement to farmers to apply new technologies or to purchase improved inputs.

When appraising credit proposals, either under a separate programme or as part of a project involving a package of inputs, it is important to ensure that:

i. The most suitable form of credit will be available, which will be determined by the purpose for which the credit is to be applied. Production may need to be financed by short-term seasonal credit. Capital investments in livestock, mechanisation, irrigation schemes or other farm improvements may need long- or medium-term loans

ii. The target group of borrowers can be identified. Better-off farmers can usually obtain their credit from banks or other commercial sources. Most credit schemes, therefore, are provided for small farmers, and the target group should be clearly defined. It has been found difficult to ensure that only members of an identified group gain access to the credit or that loans be used for the purpose intended

iii. The borrowers will benefit from the use of credit. Income generated from the use of credit should not only cover its cost to the borrowers but also bring them a net incremental gain. Inducements and opportunities should be provided to encourage the borrowers to save part of their gain and thereby build up their own capital

iv. Local funds are mobilised. The financing of agricultural credit depends largely upon funds provided by governments. It has been found that the use of locally raised funds within a credit scheme provides some additional incentive to the borrowers to repay their loans. Where part of the capital at risk has been contributed by the borrowers themselves, they are likely to exert more effort to ensure that the objectives of a project are achieved

v. The credit scheme is administered by the most suitable lending institution. Various institutions, including development banks, commercial banks and co-operatives, are involved in channelling loan funds to farmers. The institution responsible for administering credit should:

    a. Have corporate existence (informal associations are best for doing informal things)

    b. Have the ability and the capacity to reach the target group of borrowers; and

    c. Be operated efficiently.

vi. Interest rates are realistic. To borrowers, especially of production credit, the rate of interest is usually less important than the timely availability of loans. However, cheap credit is sometimes made available by government as a form of indirect subsidy, to offset the effects of high input prices or low produce prices. Where there is no government intervention rates of interest need to be set to cover the high cost of administering agricultural credit and to attract lenders by offering positive real returns on their investments. Interest rates also need to cover the cost of defaulters

vii. Security requirements are reasonable. Crop liens, mortgages of land, charges on movable property, and the provision of guarantors are among the types of security which may be available from the borrowers. But when there arc defaults in repayments it is often difficult to realise securities or obtain payment from guarantors. Whenever possible, credit should be advanced after an assessment has been made of the viability of the project to be financed, or of the capacity of the borrower to repay, rather than on the basis of the security available

viii. Adequate supporting services and supervision are available. The provision of credit should not be considered in isolation, but should be linked with input supply storage, transport and the other factors contributing to agricultural production. Advisory and supervisory services need to be available to help ensure that the best use is being made of these factors and that loan funds are being controlled

ix. Marketing is co-ordinated with credit. Marketing outlets should be available for the increased produce obtained from the use of credit. Wherever possible, arrangements should be made for loan repayments to be collected by deduction from the proceeds of the sale of produce

x. The credit offered relates to farmers' perceived abilities. Often farmers are mistakenly encouraged to accept credit many times larger than their current incomes on the assumption that many technical changes will enable them to increase incomes rapidly and repay their loans. Apart from the often misplaced optimism which this policy depends on, there is the psychological burden on farmers of a debt which is likely to discourage them rather than the opposite. Loans should bear some relationship to a farmer's current income and his realisable ambitions. Loans several times his current annual income should be avoided.

4 Agricultural organisation and institutions

The effective management of agricultural activities is one of the critical components of rural change. An understanding of existing systems of decision-making and the power structure and vested interests which they depend upon is critical. Attempts to alter organisations always meet resistance from existing systems and will not be successful unless strong and continued political and economic support will be available for new institutions.

The managerial efficiency of an institution will largely be determined by the following:

i. Clearly defined objectives

ii. Limited number of objectives and responsibilities

iii. Clearly established freedom of management to be responsible for day-to-day decisions

iv. Stability of staffing so as to allow for experience to be acquired

v. Reasonably well-paid staff and especially a well-paid manager, accountant and secretary, all with well defined job descriptions and terms of service

vi. The use of effective accounting and control systems for the timely payments and production of information

vii. Freedom to obtain and use funds according to clearly laid down conditions

viii. An effective link between marketing of produce and production.

Organisations burdened with a multiplicity of responsibilities, dealing, for example, with a wide range of crops, or with a large number of farmers' needs, are far less likely to be managed efficiently than the organisation which deals exclusively with one commodity or one function. The commodity boards, for example, which are responsible for the marketing of single crops, can be very efficient provided the basic criteria for good management are observed and they are not obliged by government policies to embark on uneconomic activities.

Ministries of agriculture
Agriculture necessarily contains a spectrum of public and private activities. At one end a ministry of agriculture has to be responsible at least for policy issues while at the other end the individual farmer is basically an entrepreneur. Central government must have an organisation for policy formulation but normally also assumes a wide range of executive functions through ministries of agriculture, including research and extension. Ministries may also be responsible for marketing, credit and development projects.

The efficiency of ministries of agriculture is seriously weakened by their great diversity of responsibilities and usually through their lack of experience in marketing. Lack of management by objectives, the sheer lack of physical oversight of field staff in distant areas, combined with frequent political involvement in management, ensure that few ministries are effective executors of government policies. In order to solve these problems, quasi-governmental bodies are frequently set up whose function it is to ensure that efficient, co-ordinated staff can get on with project implementation. Some countries have divested ministries of agriculture of almost all direct executive authority and left them only with responsibility for policy.

Regional development institutions
Regional bodies have become common in the last few decades, partly as a result of the integrated river valley approach and later through the desire to ensure integrated rural development projects in dryland areas.

Their advantage should lie in:

i. A greater knowledge of the area they work in compared with a national body

ii. Freedom from central day-to-day interference, and

iii. Greater ability to control and co-ordinate staff and work in the field.

However, regional development institutions have seldom proved successful when they have sought to spread their responsibilities over a range of activities. The two main problems which they encounter are:

i. Political and/or bureaucratic resistance from existing institutions. Political resistance will arise from the centre as the delegated responsibility establishes new focuses of power and patronage. The central bureaucracy will also tend to resent or envy these new centres of power. Lack of financial control can be a genuine concern of central government since it is they who, in the last resort, are financially responsible

ii. Those working in these regional bodies may also feel that they are isolated in remote unattractive areas far from promotion and power. Staff will find that in a small regional body the promotion ladder is too short or non-existent.

Nevertheless, regional bodies are set up from time to time as a result of extreme pressures but few outlive the loss of external support. Some survive only where they have developed some specialist expertise, such as the production of hydroelectric power.

Commodity boards

Commodity boards normally have the advantage of being responsible for marketing single crops, and frequently too for processing, research and extension. This has the great advantage of ensuring that market forces are not ignored and that considerable experience is built up by staff about one commodity. This assists such boards to ensure that a properly oriented research and extension programme is carried out. For these reasons they have a high success rate.

These are two main sources of problems:

i. Some governments have used these boards to siphon off resources from farmers to such an extent that they have led to diminished production. The Ghana Cocoa Marketing Board is a classic instance

ii. Commodity boards may deal with a multiplicity of crops and sometimes with farm inputs. The problems, as set out earlier, which this creates for management are formidable and they seldom operate successfully. Difficulties mount as government bodies move into the production, processing and marketing of perishable crops. These require both rapid decision-making and specialised knowledge which large organisations cannot easily provide.

Co-operatives

Co-operatives are voluntary associations which farmers can form and use to gain some economic benefit. Most of the activities which are carried on within the agricultural sector can be undertaken on a co-operative basis. Co-operatives have been established, for example, to mobilise savings and provide credit, to supply inputs, to undertake production and to market produce. The basic requirements for their successful development are the same as for any other type of business – clear objectives, access to capital, trained staff and competent management free from outside interference.

Co-operatives provide their members with the opportunity to become involved in the management of their own development. In many countries a registrar of co-operatives heads a government department established to administer the laws under which co-operatives are registered. Officers of these departments assist in the promotion of co-operatives and provide advisory and supervisory services.

Agricultural production co-operatives have been a disappointment in many developing countries. They have proved to be extremely difficult to operate and there have been many failures. It has been found that the complex technical, economic, social and psychological issues involved in agricultural production decisions do not easily lend themselves to this form of co-operation.

Mutual help is, of course, common in most farming communities, but this is quite different from co-operative farming, or communal farming where coercion has been used.

Other types of co-operatives have met with some success where their members have been made fully aware of what co-operatives can do and what they as members are expected to contribute. In too many cases, however, co-operatives have been formed under government fiat, rather than from farmers' conviction that they need them and are prepared to participate in their operation. Failures can be attributed to interference, social pressures to favour family or region, inexperience in business, corruption by those financially responsible, and all obligations that conflict with the basic tenets of successful management.

Despite frequent failures, co-operatives have often contributed to the development of the agricultural sector. The most successful co-operatives are those engaged in marketing. Once a successful marketing operation has been established, it has been found that cost savings can be achieved and further benefits obtained for members by venturing into other related activities. This has led to the development in some areas of multi-purpose co-operatives which can provide a wide range of services including the provision of credit, the supply of inputs and the marketing of produce.

Research and extension
It is often thought to be axiomatic that investment and effort dedicated to research and extension must have a positive effect on rural change. While both these activities are keys to the success of changes in agriculture, it is becoming increasingly obvious that much of the effort has been misdirected and that bureaucratic structures have been established which are highly inefficient, and which paradoxically have served to retard rural projects.

In research, major problems arise from the shortage of experienced natural research personnel at all levels, inadequate research facilities, shortage of funds, lack of appreciation of the social and economic constraints facing farmers, and the understandable desire of researchers to seek status and promotion by the publication of scientific research.

Research is likely to be most successful when:

i. The location of the research resembles conditions in areas where advice is needed

ii. The crops chosen (or the subjects chosen which apply to crops) have a large potential market

iii. The proposed research has been tested against the social and economic requirements of farmers so that there is a reasonable chance that it will be implemented. The research should be periodically evaluated to ensure it remains relevant

iv. The results have been tested at farm level, by farmers themselves

v. The organisation responsible for research is composed of researchers, farmers or (if they are not educated enough to deal with researchers) effective substitutes such as extension workers, who should meet at least annually

171

vi. Where long-term research (e.g. plant breeding) is essential, management, funds and recording systems should be available for matching periods

vii. There is an adequate supply of competent research workers and technicians, with administrative structures to ensure that good staff can be recruited and retained

viii. Adequate laboratories and experimental stations exist with funds to maintain them

ix. Interdisciplinary co-operation occurs between scientists of different disciplines

x. A proper balance of research is struck between local and national levels.

Extension work has often been promoted to a level which experience suggests has been unjustified. Over the last few years there has been a proliferation of government extension workers, few of them properly directed, few of them supervised carefully to ensure that they visit farms regularly, and often lacking research back-up to make their visits worthwhile. Their backgrounds and attitudes often hamper their impact on farmers and they may become a massive recurrent cost burden to governments.

The successful extension agents and institutions tend to be the ones which are carefully supervised by farmers, by commercial organisations or commodity boards. Where there is a direct link with the marketing process, and financial responsibility, excellent extension work can be carried out. This applies especially if the extension agent concentrates on one or two commercially viable crops or one or two technical improvements at a time. Good results have been obtained by extension and research funded by commodity or farmers' organisations. On the other hand, ministry of agriculture extension work suffers too much from a lack of direction and direct financial and marketing responsibility.

Successful extension schemes will flourish when:

i. There is a direct feedback between research, extension and marketing. Extension workers should always have a major say in research priorities and be conscious of or directed by marketing opportunities

ii. For reasons of good management the extension work is directed to concentrate on a very limited number of technical improvements at one time which make economic and social sense to the farmer. Seldom will extension workers have the knowledge or education to cope with all problems at the farmer level. The first objective should be to gain farmers' confidence with unambitious, guaranteed effective techniques

iii. There is a concentration on a restricted number of crops – possibly only one

iv. The farmers, or anyone with something to gain or lose financially, have an important say in directing the proposed extension advice

v. There is a system of research capable of providing extension workers with advice, and career prospects exist for extension workers.

Generally speaking farmer co-operatives and crop commodity boards which decide to spend money on extension workers are those which benefit most from research and extension efforts.

The private sector
The farmer is the natural entrepreneur. The complex of family and social responsibilities and the intricate nature of farm production has made it difficult for outsiders to plan comprehensively for an ideal production unit. State control of farming systems has always been difficult and usually unsuccessful.

Only when there has been a limited number of farm operations, e.g. wheat, rubber, tea or beef production, has large-scale planning been fruitful. Only in irrigated cultures, with a long tradition of despotic control, has central direction been effective. Large-scale company farming has been successful where appropriate products are being grown (e.g. wheat, tropical export crops, beef), but for mixed farming something akin to the family farm has proved most appropriate.

The private sector has been most vulnerable to criticism in its role as intermediary, providing inputs and selling outputs. In most cases there is a degree of competition but there are many cases of traders making large monopoly profits. The state has often taken over some of the key strategic roles in trade in order to eliminate middlemen's profits. Unfortunately, in many cases the state has exploited the rural sector to an even greater extent than the private sector – and provided an inferior service.

Crop technology should be a critical factor determining the degree of state participation. In the marketing of perishable crops such as fruit and vegetables, state intervention has seldom been successful. These crops need a rapid decision-making system and a knowledge of sources of supply and demand in order to market produce successfully. A large bureaucratic organisation simply cannot cope with these problems. On the other hand, the state has much better prospects in marketing non-perishable export crops, such as coffee, cocoa, and palm oil.

Between these two poles lies a range of crops which could be marketed by state or private organisations. Which would perform better depends upon what objectives are established, who is supposed to benefit most, and how the management structure is organised.

Marketing
An efficient marketing system and a high level of demand for crops are essential to the success of any new scheme and these should be examined at the earliest stage. As far as market prospects are concerned, it is necessary to differentiate between an international and a domestic market.

As far as the **international market** is concerned, it is likely that the scale of output that is proposed is not going to affect international prices. However, an examination of international price forecasts frequently shows that the prospects are not particularly good.

It is necessary to treat these forecasts with caution:

i. The forecasts are seldom for more than five years, whereas the investment which is under consideration is likely to be for twenty years or more

ii. The record of price forecasting is so dismal that, had forecasts been acted upon, agricultural export earnings would barely have risen over the last few decades

iii. Those countries which have concentrated on agricultural exports have been more successful in the longer run than those which have turned their backs on international trade.

The important issue is not whether the price forecasts are favourable but whether the costs of production in the region or country are likely to be competitive with those of other areas in the longer run. In the history of any export crop there are certain to be violent price fluctuations and what is important is to ensure that the crop is grown in an area which has a comparative advantage and can ensure its survival in the periods of depressed prices which are bound to occur.

The **domestic market** is somewhat different. Output is likely to be a much greater share of the domestic market than it would be in international trade, and therefore it will have a direct effect on domestic prices. The extra supplies could lead to a dramatic fall in prices and market analysis is thus crucial.

Perishable crops are subject to more violent price fluctuations, partly because they normally serve the domestic market and frequently because there are a larger number of producers all reacting in the same way to price changes. In addition, the demand for these products is less sensitive to price changes. The market for fruit and vegetables requires a rapid and appropriate system for distributing produce to consumers. This is why traditional fruit and vegetable marketing is left to small-scale entrepreneurs who are able to adapt rapidly and efficiently to changes in supply and demand. Large organisations, particularly those in the public sector, are generally unsuited to marketing this type of produce since they seldom possess the required flexibility.

Many misconceived projects for central or municipal markets have been set up to provide cleaner and better marketing facilities in town centres. Attempts to charge users a fee in order to recover the costs have seldom been successful, since traders frequently move to adjoining areas where they can sell just as much produce without paying any fee at all. Central marketing systems will only be economically successful if traders have not the space to set up selling points in areas adjoining the market, or where the public administrative system is sufficiently effective to curtail this competition. A more hygienic central market may have social benefits which outweigh financial losses, though this is hard to prove. These facilities are easiest to justify in densely populated urban areas, and even then they need to be assessed with some care.

Further reading

General guides

Theodore Schultz, *Transforming Traditional Agriculture*, first published by Yale University Press, 1964. (A classic argument that rural producers are economically rational.)

Guy Hunter, A. H. Bunting and A. Bottrall (eds.), *Policy and Practice in Rural*

Development, Overseas Development Institute, Croom Helm, London, 1976. (The proceedings of an international seminar.)

Guy Hunter (ed.), *Agricultural Development and the Rural Poor*, Overseas Development Institute, London, 1978. (A useful brief guide to the wide-ranging problems met in agricultural change.)

J. C. De Wilde, *Agricultural Development in Tropical Africa*, Johns Hopkins University Press, 1967. (Experiences of African development problems.)

Michael Lipton, *Why Poor People Stay Poor: A Study of Urban Bias in World Development*, Temple Smith, London, 1977. (A classic and wide-ranging indictment of developing countries' policies towards agriculture.)

K. R. M. Anthony, B. F. Johnston, V. O. Jones and U. C. Uchendu, *Agricultural Change in Tropical Africa*, Cornell University Press, London, 1979.

Case studies in rural change
Polly Hill, *Studies in Rural Change in West Africa*, Cambridge University Press, 1970.

Arthur Gaitskill, *Gezira*, Faber & Faber, 1959.

A. Wood, *The Groundnut Affair*, The Bodley Head, 1950.

W. McEwan, *Changing Rural Society – Case Studies of Communities in Bolivia*, Oxford University Press, 1975.

Project identification and preparation
J. Price Gittinger, *Economic Analysis of Agricultural Projects*, Johns Hopkins University Press for the World Bank, 1982. (A popular text used on training courses.)

Uma Lele, *The Design of Rural Development: Lessons From Africa*, Johns Hopkins University Press for the World Bank, 1975.

Overseas Development Administration, *Rural Project Identification and Preparation*. Limited numbers are available from the Library, ODA, Eland House, Stag Place, London SW1E 5DH. (A series of brief guidelines on the identification, preparation and appraisal of a range of agricultural projects.)

Crop storage
National Academy of Sciences, *Post-Harvest Food Losses in Developing Countries*, Washington DC, 1978.

D. W. Hall, *Handling and Storage of Food Grains in Tropical and Sub-Tropical Lands*, FAO Development Paper No. 90, Rome, 1970.

Boxall, Greeley, *et al.*, *Prevention of Farm Level Food Grain Losses in India*, Institute of Development Studies, Sussex, UK, 1979.

The Tropical Products Institute, now a department of the Tropical Development and Research Institute, has produced a number of reports on this subject.

Co-operatives and credit
FAO, *Operational Efficiency of Agricultural Co-operatives in Developing Countries*, Rome, reprinted 1977.

Marketing
The Food and Agriculture Organisation in Rome has produced a series of useful guides to the marketing problems of agricultural produce. Readers should contact the Marketing Branch, FAO, Via delle Terme di Caracalla, 00100, Rome.

The TPI, now a department of the Tropical Development and Research Institute, has likewise produced a large number of reports on marketing for particular tropical crops.

Education
M. Ahmed and H. Coombs, *Education for Rural Development*, Praeger, New York, 1975.

Administration
Guy Hunter, *The Administration of Agricultural Development*, Oxford University Press, 1970.

Land settlement schemes
G. Bridger, *Planning Land Settlement Schemes*, Agricultural Economics Bulletin for Africa, No. 1, 1963 and republished in *Rural Project Identification and Preparation*, by ODA. (Guidelines for successful schemes.)

M. Nelson, *The Settlement of Tropical Lands*, Johns Hopkins University Press, 1973.

R. Chambers, *Settlement Schemes in Tropical Africa*, Routledge, London, 1969.

Irrigation projects
I. Carruthers and C. Clark, *Economics of Irrigation*, Liverpool University Press, 1980.

G. Bridger, 'Appraising Irrigation Feasibility Studies', in the ODA booklet *Rural Project Identification and Preparation*.

Seeds
J. R. Thomson, *An Introduction to Seed Technology*, Leonard Hill, London, 1979. (Provides valuable technical background.)

FAO, *Report of Afghanistan Seeds Industry Project*, Report No. 3, DDC AFG10, FAO, Rome, 1976. (A useful case study.)

Village level problems
Marshall Sahlins, *Stone Age Economics*, Aldine/Atherton, Chicago, 1972. (A sociological insight into life in traditional societies.)

Robert Chambers, Richard Longhurst and Arnold Pacey, *Seasonal Dimensions to Rural Poverty*, Frances Pinter, 1981. (A vivid description and analysis of the real problems of village producers.)

Extension
D. Benor and J. Q. Harrison, *Agricultural Extension: The Training and Visits System*, a World Bank publication, Washington DC, 1977. (An excellent brief account of common problems and guidelines for reform, based on successful work in India.)

16
Livestock

Livestock systems

Although there is great international diversity in the types of livestock reared for sale, subsistence and drawing-power, this chapter concentrates on the most universal forms, beef and dairy cattle, pigs and poultry. The rationale for treating these together is that certain problems are common to these various types. In fact, a more fundamental distinction even than the type of animal is the nature of the system, and this means principally whether it is extensive or intensive.

Extensive and intensive livestock systems do sometimes overlap, for example where extensive systems supply stock for fattening and improvement on intensive systems. Moreover, it would be idle to look for a sharp dividing line between the two, even though at the extremes they are quite distinct. Beef is produced under both systems, while dairy cattle, pigs and poultry are usually produced under intensive regimes.

The main characteristics of the systems are:

Extensive systems, which have, by definition, a low ratio of livestock to land. They require very little labour and management per unit of land and are entirely dependent on natural pastures. This means that animal growth is a long process – for cattle around four to eight years (though it can be as low as three in a few exceptionally favoured areas). Capital investment in livestock is high in relation to other investments and the social systems that have been influenced by the production process tend to have changed little over generations. The whole system – physical, social and economic – is fragile and a traditional conservatism may be the only way to survive.

Intensive systems, which by contrast are intensive of skill and management and require a great deal of feed for the animals. They depend on a rapid turnover to maximise returns to fixed investment in equipment, buildings and livestock. Efficient management is also essential to deal with fluctuations in feed supply, availability of stock, and disease control measures. In some countries considerable investment is needed to obtain a satisfactory return, while elsewhere it can be done on a small scale on peasant-type farms.

Between these two extremes are a range of semi-intensive systems. Improvements in livestock production can start with improved grazing management and ultimately extend to a highly intensive system of feeding. The extent to which improvements can take place will be limited by the natural resources of the area. In some unusual cases intensive systems can be developed in areas of poor natural endowments (e.g. the Gulf States) if capital and management are not in short supply. A process which attempts to jump one or more stages in development must be matched by radical improvements in associated activities. In practice, it is difficult to ensure that a radical change can be maintained efficiently for long if too many new practices are introduced at the same time.

The most effective projects will be those seeking to up-grade rather than to transform extensive systems. Good and sustained management is a critical agent of change.

The demand for livestock products

As incomes increase people tend to spend a higher proportion of their incomes on meat consumption. This does not imply that consumption will increase steadily, since consumer incomes do not increase at a steady pace, nor will supplies always be stable.

Beef prices fluctuate less than those of other livestock products, mainly because changes in supply are slow to take effect, though at the level of the world market there are long-term cycles of about five years. The supply of smaller livestock, like pigs and poultry, can change more rapidly, leading to violent price fluctuations.

Price forecasts tend to be pessimistic since they usually assume that supplies will not be subject to unforeseen interruptions. This is seldom the case. It is important to differentiate, however, between international and domestic markets for livestock products. The latter tend to be far more restricted than the former and prone to generate surpluses. It may be easier to forecast domestic demand but surpluses occur much more frequently.

As with most primary agricultural products the most appropriate criterion for determining future investment is whether or not the area or crop has, or is likely to have, a sufficient comparative advantage in production. This boils down to low unit costs. When the inevitable occurs, and prices fall, producers should then be able to survive until prices recover.

Extensive systems

These systems can be divided into pastoral and ranching systems. Pastoral systems are to be found in drier areas where cattle have to adjust to seasonal changes by moving long distances to obtain adequate supplies of water and pasture. Under these circumstances land is generally regarded as belonging to the community though the cattle are owned individually.

The numbers of cattle owned by farmers vary widely, with large herds co-existing with very small ones. This does not, however, necessarily indicate an inequality of wealth among pastoralists. Larger herd owners frequently support more household members and other dependants than their poorer neighbours, and sometimes lend out cows for indefinite periods to others. Thus the availability of cattle looked at on a per-head basis is frequently more even than appearances suggest.

Ranching systems are those in which both land and cattle are in private ownership and are normally to be found in areas where there is sufficient grazing for it to be economically enclosed and provide an adequate income for the owners. There is a vested interest on the part of the owners of land to ensure that it is not over-grazed. This distinguishes them from pastoral systems where the private benefits leading to over-grazing could conflict with the social needs for control.

i. Pastoral systems

In these systems there is a conflict of economic interest between the private ownership of cattle and the collective ownership of grazing land. Collective ownership does not necessarily imply that a tribal group has equal access to all areas of it since there are usually complicated rules governing the use of traditional water supplies, which effectively can limit access to certain groups. In principle, this conflict of interests *could* result in an excessive build-up of cattle numbers, over-grazing, and the degradation of the range.

In practice, the issue is more complicated. There are some observers who deny that **over-grazing** can exist. They would argue that the build-up of herds during years of good rainfall matches the reappearance of good grasses in the range which is sufficient to support the greater number of animals, while in drought years the poor, thin grass cover leads to a natural diminution of the herd. In both cases, the size of the herd adjusts to the carrying capacity of the range.

What can be said with some certainty is that local over-grazing does happen, where badly sited water points can encourage excessive cattle concentration. Also, stocking rates recommended for commercial ranches should not be applied indiscriminately to pastoralists (even if they could be enforced) because the objectives of the two systems are rather different. While ranchers try to cut their financial losses in bad years by not stocking up to full capacity in good years, pastoralists aim to maximise the number of breeding females in their herds in order to maintain their capacity to rebuild herds after a drought.

Many attempts have nevertheless been made to control the number of cattle. However, the very nature of the social system often inhibits control of numbers or access to water holes, and while attempts at control have been made none of them have been blessed with permanent success. The vast areas to be covered are difficult to police and require social control if they are to be voluntary. In any case, the droughts which occur may make it sensible for individuals to build up livestock as a form of insurance.

Attempts have been made to achieve a balance between cattle and pastures through the delimitation of areas, the appointment of cattle guards, compulsory destocking, and the formation of co-operative group ranches. None of these has so far succeeded, either because the ecological necessity for nomadism is not recognised or because the social structure could not cope with the need to control numbers or manage farms.

By and large, pastoral systems in marginal areas are an efficient way of using these fragile resources, although from time to time there is a rapid build-up of cattle which droughts serve to reduce. It is not always appreciated that cattle serve as the only means of investment in nomadic communities and that reluctance to improve quality by reducing numbers can be quite rational.

An efficient marketing system is useful in enabling pastoralists to dispose of their surplus cattle in a normal year. It also permits them to off-load cattle during drought periods, thus avoiding mortality on such a large scale. (In some countries the capacity of the government's abattoir is set at the level needed to take cattle off the range in bad years, rather than with an eye to the normal throughput. This does not of course improve the financial profitability of the abattoir!)

The easiest investment to justify is the provision of water supplies and protection against epidemics. Where additional water supplies open up hitherto inaccessible land there is clearly a benefit in extending grazing facilities. If there is a danger of local over-grazing, some system of control ought to be considered. One system could be the closure of the well during certain seasons or the building of shallow wells which, while retaining water for a slightly longer period, eventually dry up themselves. The social and administrative problems of water control do ultimately depend on local politics and there have been too many failures in this area for one to be confident of success. Pilot schemes are an essential first step.

Historically, pastoral systems change in favour of individual land usage when land becomes valuable (e.g. as a result of a cash crop being grown) or where ample unoccupied land remains available. The emergence of individual systems of ownership normally only occurs where the political and social system encourages the trend and where economic and technical circumstances facilitate it. To an increasing extent the frontier of crop production is being stretched into marginal areas unsuitable in the longer run for sustained crop output.

The most promising avenues of assistance to pastoral farmers are: health measures to bring major epidemics under control, the improvement of (well sited) water points, improved marketing arrangements, better prices and research.

The control of **epidemics** is perhaps the most important technical measure which can be taken to assist pastoral societies – provided there is a reasonable prospect of sales when animal numbers increase. But campaigns to control these diseases can only be successful if there is a good administrative system and sound technical support. In too many countries internal problems have seriously weakened administration and technical support, the foundation of successful health control programmes.

ii. Individual ranching systems
The logical sequence of improvement to ranches starts with nutrition, which is a principal cause of mortality among cattle and which also affects their rate of growth. Nutritional improvement is, however, costly and because of the slow natural growth of the cattle population it should proceed gradually.

Improved nutrition starts with good management of the cattle ranches, with cattle being moved as necessary to take advantage of the best grazing. The next stage is to concentrate on the improved nutrition of cows that are in-calf, cows in heat (to improve conception rates) and calves on weaning. This can be done through supplementary feeding, by improving pastures purely for this group of animals, or by transferring them to areas with better pastures. Since calf mortality rates (to one year) account for massive losses in dry areas (up to 50%) it is here that the biggest improvements can be made. In efficiently run commercial ranches 80%–95% calf survival rates are common.

The next logical step is supplementary feeding with conserved feed in the dry season. But suitable feed is often expensive and difficult to get to cattle on large farms. Where natural and economic conditions permit the growing of fodder on the farm, there are reasonable economic prospects that it could be used to stimulate the growth of cattle.

Herd improvement can be achieved by the selection of improved local breeds. Cross breeding is the most obvious next step. As the herd becomes more valuable through breed improvement it becomes justifiable to invest in reducing some of the endemic diseases.

Fencing is an effective way to ensure control of pastures but the cost per kilometre is high. It is doubtful whether in the more traditional systems of cattle ranching it would be justified other than to define property boundaries.

The transferring of younger stock to more fertile areas occurs in many parts of the world and this combines elements of all the above methods. A precondition is an efficient marketing system which obtains livestock at the right time in the right place for the favoured areas, and has the flexibility to sell when conditions are favourable.

Investments in improving beef output which require the improvement of pastures must be matched by an increase in cattle numbers to take advantage of these capital inputs. The rate of natural increase of a cattle population is so slow that it will probably take ten to fifteen years before the investment begins to pay off. It therefore needs a fairly sophisticated planning system for determining the rate at which to intensify beef production. The standard approach is to build up a herd model which stimulates the growth of the herd. In many cases ambitious technical improvements and high levels of investment per hectare require the purchase of cattle to increase the stocking rate and achieve the requisite economic rates of return. This not only requires a high degree of managerial competence but also a transfer of cattle from other areas. The consequent decline in production elsewhere needs to be fed into the economic model since from a national point of view this means transferring an asset from one farm to another.

Intensive systems

Intensive systems of livestock production – whether beef or dairy cattle, pigs or poultry – have a number of similar characteristics. Success depends on attention to the following:

i. Feed costs will account for 75%–90% of the unit cost of meat or milk in intensive feeding systems. Animal feed must therefore be cheap in relation to the price of meat, and available on a regular basis. Sometimes import tariffs and import controls artificially increase domestic meat and milk prices and make these intensive systems profitable for the entrepreneur, but not necessarily for the economy as a whole. The domestic production of feed is usually necessary to justify such systems. Small (particularly island) economies which need to import feed are unlikely to be able to economically justify an intensive form of livestock production

ii. A high standard of management is vital to ensure that food is purchased and consumed as efficiently as possible, and that health controls over stock are rigorously maintained

iii. Credit organisations will be called upon to give financial assistance to enable farmers to make purchases of livestock and other inputs

iv. The market for these products is restricted to major towns and could rapidly be saturated by an increase in supply (other than for beef). This is particularly true of pigs and poultry, where there are seldom any price controls and where it is possible to rapidly increase production. With dairy production surplus milk can be converted into cheese. The urban market is a limited one and in order to minimise transport costs these activities should be located as close to consumers as possible. Developing countries are unlikely to become exporters of these products since transport costs will act as a serious constraint and they are likely to face efficient international producers who can operate on a much larger scale.

Marketing

An efficient marketing system is essential to the success of livestock projects. It has frequently been claimed that middlemen make excessive profits and that only state or semi-public organisations can protect the producer. But it is far from proven that public systems are more efficient, and they may take advantage of the producer to an even greater extent than the private trader. There can be little doubt that the private trader will show more initiative in developing new markets and will be less bureaucratic in achieving and carrying out his tasks.

Public institutions should in theory be able to preserve a balance of interest between producer and consumer interests and minimise marketing margins (normally about 100%). But in practice this seldom seems to be the case – in many countries they have exploited the producer even more than the private trader and provided a less efficient service. Where practicable the existence of both systems, competitive with each other, is likely to be the most satisfactory system for the producer. However, if the private trader is allowed to sell to the most lucrative market and leave marginal or unprofitable areas to a semi-public organisation the latter will incur heavy losses. A monopolistic marketing organisation is thus often set up, but it is then necessary to combine efficient management with a system ensuring that producers and consumers get a fair deal.

Abattoirs and canning factories

These facilities have been set up in large numbers in developing countries but many of them fail. The principal reason, apart from poor management, has been failure to secure an adequate supply of animals throughout the year. An inadequate throughput increases the unit cost of production and makes the process uneconomic. Where abattoirs are competing in domestic markets they will face rivalry from butchers who do not have high overhead costs or such stringent health regulations.

Canning factories designed to export will have to compete with large cattle-producing countries that process vast numbers of stock and sell in consuming centres which usually have stringent disease control regulations.

Important practical points

The major problems met in the development of livestock include:

1 Attempts to develop systems of beef production too quickly. Investment in fencing, pastures, and bore holes can only be justified by increasing the stocking rate and this can entail buying more cattle than would be available from natural increase. If cattle purchases mean transferring assets from other

areas they do not add to the national herd. The management problems attendant on so many changes limit the prospects of success.

2 The use of technical coefficients not grounded in the facts of the situation and which engender a technical optimism that is not borne out by the results.

3 In pastoral areas attempts to intensify production without acknowledging, or finding, solutions to the social and political problems of controlling animal numbers.

4 Embarking on intensive systems of production which are uneconomic and managerially complex.

5 The over-optimistic assessment of effective demand for output, and inadequate assessment of the number of livestock available for processing.

6 Starting intensive schemes using imported feed supplies – which account for most of the unit costs of production.

7 An essential first step to considering any project is to analyse the production system for the area in question. This is particularly true in pastoral areas. The observer should discover what the motives and objectives of pastoralists are, without which estimates of 'surplus' cattle likely to go through the marketing chain are liable to be wide of the mark. Evaluation has shown that many marketing projects are based on incorrect assumptions about why cattle are held and, by extension, why cattle are disposed of.

Checklist of main questions

1 Effective demand
What is the effective demand for the output?
Is it international or domestic?
To what extent has an assessment been made of the effective demand for differing qualities of product?
How have prices varied over the last few years?
Who controls marketing?
Are prices to producers adequate?
How efficient is the system in transporting and processing livestock?

2 Supply
Is there likely to be a continued supply of stock for processing of the right quality, at the right time and of the right type?
Will the other inputs – feeds, equipment, veterinary supplies – come from local sources or be imported? Will quantities and quality be adequate?

3 Technical considerations
How realistic are the technical coefficients (e.g. survival rates, mortality, weight gains)?
What supporting evidence is there?
Are the technologies proposed already in practice? If not is it a pilot scheme?
What evidence is there that equipment will be maintained and that there are adequately trained staff to implement the proposals?
Are the foodstuffs proposed of proven nutritional value? Will they entail preparation? Will the livestock be responsive to feed?
What evidence is there that new breeds are adaptable, manageable and economic?

Are the health improvements proposed likely to lead to sufficient increase in output to justify the expense?

4 Social considerations

Is the community prepared to accept new technologies, or new management systems?

Who contributes most to change – and who benefits most?

How do proposals affect the family and the community?

Will religious or cultural factors inhibit new proposals?

How does land and livestock ownership affect the proposals?

5 Economic considerations

Is additional labour required? Where does it come from?

How profitable is the proposal to the owner or farmer?

Is it likely to be worth the effort, cost or risk to him?

Will the economy of the country benefit?

Would imports be more economic?

If recurrent costs are incurred how will they be met?

6 Management

How dependent is the proposal on a high level of management? Is it likely to be achieved?

Will salaries or wages attract adequate numbers of staff?

Further reading

Morag Simpson, *Sector Appraisal Manual – Beef*, ODA, June 1980. (A valuable introduction to appraising diverse types of beef production. Annexes contain useful technical data.)

Gudrun Dahl and A. Hjort, *Having Herds*, Stockholm Studies in Social Anthropology, 1976. (A good account of socio-economic problems of cattle-raising societies.)

FAO, *The Ecological Management of Arid and Semi-Arid Range Lands of Africa and the Near East*, Rome, 1974. (An excellent assessment of the inter-play between semi-desert areas and livestock production.)

W. J. A. Payne, *Systems of Beef Production in Developing Countries*, ed. A. J. Smith, Centre for Tropical and Veterinary Medicine, Edinburgh, 1976. (Important technical introduction.)

B. Halpin, *Patterns of Animal Disease*, Baillière Tindall, London, 1975. (Account of animal health problems of livestock.)

17
Tourism

'Tourism' is a service that can be supplied to either residents or non-residents. If other things are equal, it makes little difference to hoteliers, restaurateurs or taxi drivers whether their clients are locals or foreigners. However, governments are not indifferent between the two types; the effects on the balance of payments and the budget differ, and so does the socio-cultural impact. This chapter concentrates on foreign tourism, where the people spending on tourism services are not resident in the host country. Some elements of the approach apply equally to planning domestic tourism.

In the tourism sector, an 'export' means the arrival of a foreign tourist, and an 'import' means the departure of a resident on holiday abroad. As R. H. Green observes: 'Tourism is a peculiar product, a luxury export consumed by non-citizens in the exporting (not the importing) country. Many of the social, cultural, and political consequences of tourism flow from its being an internally consumed export.' (See section on further reading, page 195.)

Tourism is an internationally-traded service, and as a world-wide foreign exchange earner it is probably second only to crude petroleum. For many countries it is the chief export, and for many island states the only plausible way of significantly raising national income. For most countries tourism is a two-way traffic, with residents departing on holiday crossing with foreigners coming in. There is no particular economic significance in the 'balance of trade' in tourism, though this is often harped on by national tourist boards. Note that a government may carry out 'import substitution' in tourism by encouraging its residents to holiday within the country rather than abroad.

Types of investment

The 'tourist industry' is variegated and comprises many public and private sector activities of all sizes. However, three elements are essential in the planning or promotion of this sector: accommodation, transport, and attractions.

Accommodation may consist of hotels, holiday villages, private boarding houses or individual houses or apartments let off as holiday space. Much of the provision of accommodation can be left to private enterprise. Hotels are sometimes built and operated by the government, but it is more common for the state not to become involved, or to take a back seat in the development. There are many possibilities of joint ventures, the most frequent being state equity participation (e.g. through a national development bank) and state ownership with a private management contract. New investment is not always required to mobilise extra accommodation; a good tourist board can organise a network of private landlords so as to provide holiday villas.

In the **transport** area the prime requirement is a satisfactory means of access to the main destination. Since many tourists arrive by road, a good international road link is essential. Railways now carry a small and declining proportion of tourist arrivals. The growth of bulk package tours relying on air transport has made the provision of an airport to international flight standards virtually essential for serious tourist development. For warm maritime countries, e.g. in the Mediterranean and Caribbean, one type of visitor arrives in cruise ships or private yachts and in these cases investment in passenger berths or marinas is necessary. The latter are well suited to private investment. Transport within the country is normally left to private initiatives; taxis and minibuses are favourite forms of investment by small businessmen and outlets for investing remittance incomes.

Some **attractions** need little promotion or investment, such as that popular trinity of sun, sand and sea. However, many tourist 'draws' are contrived, such as cultural events, festivals, sporting occasions, casinos, and night clubs. Some events may be planned not primarily for their touristic value, but with a close eye on the likelihood of such benefits helping to defray the cost (e.g. the Olympic Games, the Organisation of African Unity Conference). While the larger of these attractions normally call for some state investment, sponsorship or organisation, many of the subsidiary services, like food, entertainment, etc., can be entrusted to private initiative.

Demand for tourism

The demand for tourism is fickle, competitive and price-elastic. Although well-established resorts can count on a regular clientèle, especially if they are located near the main markets, the newer or more remote resorts are much more at the whim of potential travellers and travel agents. Even large and well-established tourist destinations, like Spain and Greece, are subject to annual fluctuations in demand that are heavily influenced by fashion.

Vicissitudes of demand may stem from fears of political or social disturbance. A change of government may be perfectly peaceful, but if it produces photographs of tanks in foreign newspapers ill-informed travellers may take fright. The same is true of highly-publicised cases of epidemics of diseases, or of crimes against foreign visitors. Often the potential traveller remains unaware of these problems, but the travel operators become worried, especially if there is a change of regime ushering in a government that is hostile to tourism.

In any event, the industry is very competitive, and this is linked to the point about price-elasticity. In recent years a large number of new resorts have been developed, each competing for the tourist's dollar, pound and franc. The tourism 'product', namely the holiday, is highly visible, and news about good or bad experiences passes around very quickly, by word, broadcasting, or newspaper. Studies have shown that the demand for tourism is very sensitive to movements in foreign exchange rates, which affect both the initial price of a holiday and the amount of local goods and services the traveller can buy with his or her currency. In practice tour operators are even more sensitive to exchange rate movements (and expectations) since they carry future obligations expressed in a certain currency and work on margins – thus exchange rates influence the amount of marketing they will do for a particular destination.

Most tourist projects require a view to be taken of trends in the number of visitors at least five to ten years ahead. This is not easy, since the major component of most holidays – travel costs – is the outcome of the tug of war between a rising real cost of fuel and trends in the civil aviation sector producing marked economies of scale in carrying passengers. It does not look as though the trend towards economies of scale, and cheaper seats, is exhausted. The 1980s are unlikely to see anything like the real increases in the price of oil that occurred in the 1970s. Meanwhile, many major airlines are carrying surplus capacity and are losing money on the more competitive routes. It would be a brave person who predicted the outcome of these trends for the cost of travel in, say, 1990.

Judging the market

A calculation of the market for tourism must obviously start from an assessment of the country's touristic assets. The tourist area must contain some enduring feature, such as climate, beaches, sea, mountains, ruins, animals, shopping or night-life, within access of the tourists' destination. Most countries that are seriously contemplating tourism development engage specialised consultants who can advise on the existence and promotion of touristic assets. There is a feedback here with the identification of the target group, since clearly some types of tourist regard certain features as essential assets to a holiday, while other groups have their eye on other things. It is therefore helpful to engage consultants and planners with a knowledge of the countries from which the tourists are expected to come. American, German and French travellers, to take three at random, have different expectations of a holiday.

Once the assets are identified, and the cost of getting tourists into the country is estimated, a start can be made to identify the target group of visitors. Where the country concerned is easily accessible to a large number of potential visitors at relatively low cost, e.g. France, there is no need for this approach. However, where the country is remote, and the most feasible form of access is by charter flights and/or air-borne package tours, the target group needs to be carefully specified. Once identified, promotional effort and expense can then concentrate on this market, and preparations made to negotiate improved air services with the countries concerned. An important decision is whether to plump for mass tourism or to concentrate on a more selective kind, e.g. 'up market', yachtsmen, skiers, etc. The type of tourist vitally determines the social and cultural impact of tourism on local society. It is essential to make early contact with one or more tourism operators in order to obtain practical advice and to check that there is an organisation prepared to market tourism services. It is hard to overstate the importance of assessing the material and social idiosyncrasies of potential tourists.

Since the tourist market is so competitive, any assessment of demand has to identify the competition. Tourism is normally seasonal. Even where the climate of a country may not vary very much, the determinant of tourist movements is often the difference between the climate in the country of residence and that of the tourist destination, and the gap is normally greatest in the Northern winter. The seasonality factor can be mitigated by charging lower transport and hotel rates in the off-season, attracting a different type of tourist, offering special rates for business conventions and sporting occasions, etc.

The number of visitors, and their expected average length of stay, need to be tested against the likely average daily spending in relation to the cost of holiday facilities. The end product of these calculations should be expected occupancy rates for local hotels, who can then compare these expected rates with their break-even figures. It is difficult to stipulate general break-even occupancy rates, which obviously vary according to the type of facility and its capital and recurrent costs. However, 60% can normally be regarded as the minimum, and hoteliers commonly aim at 75%.

Organisation of the industry

The fact that holidays are normally arranged and sold in the tourist's own country, delivered in the country of destination, and usually involve a sizeable and expensive journey, means that the organisation of the industry can be quite complex. The question of who controls the different sides of the operation is central to the division of the benefits from tourism, as well as the risks involved. In the majority of cases tourism calls on the services of tour operators, travel agents, airlines, and hoteliers, while state tourist boards may also be involved in one or more of these stages.

Tour operators assemble package tours and orchestrate the way the other parties are involved. This is the classic entrepreneurial function, and as such can be very profitable, but it also carries large risks. Tour operators often make use of **travel agents** to retail the holidays, and indeed the two functions are often combined. Travel agents pure and simple work on commission, and have little risk.

The tour operator will buy space on airlines for his tourists. This can either be on specially arranged charter flights, or by obtaining favourable discounts on scheduled services. For the average package tour the cost of transport is the largest single element. Many airlines have expanded into hotel ownership and tour operation in an attempt to improve the utilisation rates of their aircraft.

At the destination end, the tour operator will buy hotel accommodation. Where the airline owns the hotel as well, the movement into tour operation is a means of increasing occupancy. Independent hotels will agree to reserve accommodation for package tourists as a way of covering their overheads, though the profit margins on accommodation are often very finely calculated.

Who owns and controls these various components of the holiday makes a lot of difference to the distribution of benefits. Where, say, a foreign airline acts as tour operator, carrier, and hotelier, the return to the host country cannot be very large. At the other extreme, where, say, owners of holiday properties in France market their accommodation through the various French tourist offices, the lion's share of the benefit goes directly to the property owners with very little intermediation. Countries with a weak bargaining position and little experience in tourism may be forced to conclude deals with international operators that leave little of the value-added remaining in the host country. Over time, the terms of such deals can be re-negotiated and improved, e.g. by the state reducing fiscal incentives, buying into the local hotel trade, setting up its own overseas travel marketing network, etc.

A frequent device is for foreign **airlines** to offer to set up and manage hotels which are owned by the local government. The airline, normally working through its tourism subsidiary, takes a management fee, and commonly a variable fee related to turnover. This is not an ideal arrangement from the point of view of the host government, since it guarantees that it bears the major share of risk, and that the largest profits accrue to the airline on its travel operations. (The offsetting advantages are the provision of managerial expertise and a knowledge of the tourism market.) Even a weak government should take steps to recover some budgetary revenue from the arrangement, e.g. by hotel taxes, customs revenue, etc., while insisting on a realistic programme for training staff and the gradual naturalisation of seminar management. Where the host country has its own airline, there is scope for negotiating reciprocal flying rights and a share in the carriage of tourists.

Benefits

As with other projects, the primary benefit is to local **incomes**, namely the extra value-added in the local currency. Thus, the standard tools of cost–benefit analysis (IRR, NPV, BCR, etc.) can be applied to individual projects. However, the form in which income arises is important, and tourism projects are often judged according to their impact on wage employment, foreign exchange, and the budget. There may also be other indirect benefits arising from the wider repercussions of tourism on the local economy.

In principle, value-added from tourism should be estimated for each component of the industry, such as hotels, restaurants, night clubs, airlines, etc. The snag with this approach is that most of these firms will not depend entirely upon tourism for their income. Put differently, 'tourism' is not a clearly defined sector in national accounts and does not feature in input–output tables. Thus, short-cut methods may have to be substituted for estimating the impact of tourism on local incomes. One common method is to estimate gross tourist spending from sample questionnaires or, where they exist, exchange control declarations by arriving visitors. A breakdown of tourists' spending can then be carried out, tracing where each dollar is eventually spent. 'Leakages' on imported goods, profits remitted abroad, etc. may then be deducted to arrive at rough estimates of national value-added. This will give a rough idea of the benefits which accrue locally rather than to foreigners, but to arrive at value-added in the strict national accounting sense the cost of locally pur-chased materials and services should also be deducted. (Such purchases, as well as wages, are often regarded as benefits rather than costs, an approach which is justified if the factors providing them are unemployed.)

In the case of foreign hotel companies and tour operators confronting small inexperienced administrations, the local value-added in a tourism project can be very low indeed, at least initially. In one such recent case in the Caribbean, virtually the only identifiable local value-added was in the form of wages to locally engaged employees and customs duty on the consumer items bought by the tourists. Most construction materials were imported, the senior management of the project were expatriates, little or no food was available locally, and generous fiscal incentives excused the foreign investor from income and profits taxes.

In case this seems too sceptical a view to take of benefits, we could refer to an actual example where tourism has brought undisputed and sizeable benefits. In a small and impoverished town in one of the Greek islands, where the impressive ancient Acropolis attracted large numbers of visitors, conser-vation measures prohibited hotel building and all tourists had to stay in locally owned villas. As a consequence the 700 or so inhabitants, who some fifteen years ago lived off remittances, are now enjoying net earnings of about $5 million per year.

Not all the income from tourism is a net addition. Many countries have seen a decline in other sectors of the economy as resources have been drawn into an expanding tourism sector. Agriculture is a common victim, as workers abandon hard, poorly paid farm work in favour of the ostensibly easier and better paid work in hotels, restaurants, taxis, etc. In a small country there is a real danger that an expanding tourism sector will monopolise the small pool of professional and skilled labour, and even unskilled labour, at the direct expense of existing activities. Public services find it especially hard to attract labour.

In estimating the impact on **employment**, tourism planners commonly use a rule of thumb that one job is created for every hotel bed, plus another job created indirectly in ancillary or supporting trades. Employment benefits need to be interpreted with caution. As we noted above, the creation of jobs in tourism may be at the expense of jobs in other sectors. In any event, tourism jobs are usually highly seasonal. This might cause idleness during the rest of the year, or, to view it more positively, it might release workers to find employment in other sectors, e.g. on their own farm plots. A high proportion of jobs in tourism fall to women, hence it is possible for the demand for labour and the supply of unemployed workers to be seriously mismatched. It is common to find the paradoxical co-existence of apparent idleness among the local population with imported labour performing the construction work or the menial hotel jobs. The type of work available may fail to meet the expectations of the local inhabitants, who continue to rely on remittances from their relatives working abroad. The creation of a cadre of skilled workers is also commonly frustrated by trained workers leaving to seek better work and higher rewards in other countries – a common complaint of hotels in the Mediterranean, for example.

Foreign exchange benefits might appear to be firmly based, since after all the tourists arrive with foreign currency in their pockets. The first point to make is that a large part of the spending on a holiday, namely the travel, has already occurred and this may or may not find its way back to the country of destination (it clearly will not if the means of transport are run by foreign companies with little provisioning at local ports and airports). In addition part of the tourist spending is on goods and services that are directly imported. A further portion leaks indirectly abroad out of the spending of factor incomes by hoteliers, workers, restaurant owners, etc. Where any of these local operations are owned by foreign companies, one should also expect a remittance of profits out of the country. If the holiday is organised by a tour operator based abroad, further income is forfeited on overheads and fees.

Local ownership is no automatic guarantee that foreign exchange profits will be retained. If a foreign group carries out hotel management, in return for a fee (often 'front-end loaded'), this is a further source of foreign exchange leakage. (To be fair to tourism, many of these 'leaks' would occur whatever type of project was being undertaken in a small economy open to international trade and reliant on foreign capital and expertise. In judging the specific foreign exchange benefits from tourism, it is only reasonable to compare it with feasible alternative sectors and projects. Given that tourism income originates in foreign exchange, this sector should normally compare favourably with other possible activities.)

The project should normally yield some net **fiscal gains**. The tourism sector can be taxed by such means as international airport taxes, hotel taxes, levies on hotels and restaurant bills, in addition to the usual panoply of direct taxes and customs and excise duties. Investors, and especially foreign investors, normally enjoy privileged tax status, such as exemption from income and profits taxes for a certain period, and exemption from customs duties on materials and equipment in setting up the facility. Apart from such forgone income, the government will normally incur extra spending arising from the presence of tourism, such as the administration of a tourism office, extra amenities, additional services (such as street cleaning), plus any services such as roads or water supply which are necessary as part of the initial deal with the investor. Thus the net fiscal benefit from tourism can be quite low.

Advocates and promoters of tourism often make extravagant claims for the **indirect benefits** from this sector, through its repercussions on the rest of the economy. The concepts of the multiplier and linkages are deployed with abandon. (See chapter 2 on project appraisal.) As with any other project, the multiplier impact of an initial bout of spending leaks away through savings and imports, and is lost to inflation when it runs up against bottlenecks. Under-developed countries, especially small open ones, are more prone than most to such leakages and bottlenecks, and therefore one would not expect the multiplier to be very high. In any case, tourism has to be compared with any other plausible project from this point of view.

Linkages are more likely where the project is located in an under-developed region, but one that nevertheless has potential. One of the linkages hoped for most strongly and frequently is the encouragement of local food production. In practice, this hope is cruelly deceived, since in many of the smaller developing countries dependent on tourism local agriculture is diminished rather than stimulated by tourist development. It may seem economically irrational, even criminal, for Caribbean islands to import fresh vegetables and even bread from Florida, but until local suppliers can undertake to supply these goods regularly and at the right quality such imports will continue.

Tourist visits by foreign businessmen have sometimes led to their setting up local operations. This has happened in, for example, West Africa and the East Caribbean islands. This most commonly benefits light industry, assembly, and service activities. Where an activity or operation is reasonably 'footloose' business executives sometimes prefer to locate it in a pleasant spot which gives them an excuse to travel!

Planning for tourism

A sensible first step is to commission an experienced consultant to identify the country's **tourism assets**. An important part of this study is to point to features which are absent but which would be required if tourism were to take off. Local attitudes towards foreign visitors are important data at this stage. A tourism survey should also provide information on the scale and type of tourist influx that would be appropriate to local capacity. Some consultants use the concept of 'saturation level' of tourists. This is an inflexible concept, but may be appropriate where tourism assets (e.g. beaches) are few and incapable of expansion.

The next step is to define the **potential market**. Large countries, where service skills are widely dispersed in the population, may opt for mass tourism, while countries that are more remote, with assets that are more likely to appeal to specialised groups or to wealthier tourists, may choose to tap selective markets. The cost of transport is an important consideration here, since people who have spent a large sum on the journey are unlikely to want cheap accommodation, so it is logical for remote countries to opt for 'up-market' tourism.

The host country's **organisational capability** is vital. For a country new to tourism, the important functions of tour packaging, marketing the holidays, and transport to the destination will probably call for foreign involvement.

Where a national airline exists, or where there are national tourism offices abroad, a country's bargaining position vis-à-vis potential developers is improved. There is then the question of what stake the local government or local investor takes in the planned accommodation. As already suggested, it may not be the best solution for local government to own the hotel with foreign partners managing it. An equity stake, even if small, is a spur to performance. Another possibility is for the government to accept a minority equity share, and to make the management fee subject to performance conditions. A condition of the investment ought to be a training programme for local workers, while the gradual replacement of expatriates by locals can be achieved through the gradual withdrawal of work permits.

The most important planning task that remains is to tailor the size and shape of the project to **local attitudes** and resources. Depending on the attitude of the local populace to tourism (and it is normal for the running to be made by local parties with financial interests in the scheme, while the majority of people directly affected by it have no voice), development can be either dispersed throughout the country or confined to an enclave. If contact with foreigners is considered to be 'disruptive' (people on holiday are not always on their best behaviour) confining the development to a particular enclave could be attractive. On the other hand, dispersing tourists throughout the population is one way of overcoming suspicion and ignorance on both sides, and guarantees that the benefits of tourism are more widely distributed. The dispersed pattern also makes fewer demands on scarce land, does not monopolise beaches, can involve private local people (such as small hoteliers), and can involve more appropriate techniques of construction and management. Against this is the preference of many high-income tourists for a high standard of services and a predictable package of attractions, which are best provided centrally in enclave developments.

Foreign groups may find they can save money by adapting their designs and construction methods to locally available materials, where the alternative is to mobilise expensive imported materials and equipment. The receptivity of foreign visitors to attractive local goods, styles and methods is often underrated. Labour requirements can be roughly estimated using the one-plus-one rule of thumb adumbrated above. The effect on the local labour market and on other labour-intensive sectors like agriculture needs to be carefully weighed.

In the last resort, workers seem to prefer work in hotels and restaurants to cutting sugar cane or tending cattle under the hot sun. It is their life and value judgement, not that of the concerned social scientist in a Western university.

One crucial determinant of the kind of tourist that is attracted is the availability of a casino. Governments concerned to keep out 'undesirables' should think twice before granting gambling licences.

Important practical points

1 The demand for tourism is unusually prone to fluctuate. This can be for reasons of fashion, boom and recession in countries of origin, political disturbances or public health hazards in the receiving country, or anything else that gives rise to unfavourable publicity. This is true even of well situated and long-established resorts; it applies with greater force to the newer or more remote destinations.

2 Forecasting tourism demand five to ten years ahead is especially difficult. A crucial variable is the cost of air travel, which is difficult to predict since it is the result of the trend in economies of scale in aircraft size and the rise in fuel costs. It is also hard to predict future fashion and changes in competing tourism destinations.

3 Successful promotion requires a strong presence in the countries of origin. The involvement of an established tour operator can make all the difference, at least while trade is being built up.

4 The division of benefits rests crucially on who owns and controls the various layers of the industry, and where the value-added sticks. Poor countries lacking managerial expertise and in a weak bargaining position may have little choice but to accept some involvement by foreign operators, airlines and hotels. A sensible strategy would be to come to terms with this and to gradually improve the terms of the deal, while not conceding too many fiscal benefits.

5 As an 'internally-consumed export' tourism can have a drastic social and cultural impact on the host country. The definition of the target group of tourists for promotional purposes is therefore a crucial political decision and the choice between promoting mass tourism or more select groups needs to be carefully weighed.

6 The 'tourism multiplier', often used as a measure of benefits, is frequently abused by interested parties to exaggerate the likely benefits. Few of the putative benefits may appear where there are large imports and other foreign exchange outflows, or where there are local bottlenecks that arrest the spread of tourist dollars. In the long run it is common experience for tourism to arrest the growth of other sectors of the economy. Thus the *net* effect on growth is the important measure.

7 Tourism can be a major stimulus to employment, but it is important to identify who will get the jobs. It is usually seasonal, and could either dovetail or compete with other activities. It may create a bigger demand for female labour than for men, with obvious social implications. Or the jobs may be filled by immigrants. Some jobs are more equal than others.

Checklist of main questions

i. What type of **investment** is proposed? (Accommodation, economic infrastructure, improvement in tourist attractions, construction of services for events, etc.)
Where did these proposals originate?

Is a proper objective study available of the proposal?
Do any local groups or individuals stand to benefit disproportionately, e.g. by the ownership of land?

ii. How is the industry to be **organised and managed**?
Has a national Tourist Board been formed?
What will be the role of the private sector?
Will a foreign travel agency be mainly involved in organising the trade?
Will the accommodation be owned or managed by an airline?
Will the local airline, where it exists, have the chance of carrying some of the tourist trade?
Has the possibility of the state being involved in joint ventures been explored?

iii. What powers does the government now possess for **planning and control**?
Is there a land-use plan, or zoning regulations for the use of land?
Is there a national tourism strategy?
Has there been an analysis of the amount of tourism that the country can physically sustain?
Is there an inventory of tourism assets?

iv. What is the **market** for tourism?
What is the size of the present flow of tourists, both in and out?
Has there been a market survey?
What is the likely area of origin of tourists, and what means of transport will they use?
What kinds of tourists are being catered for, selective or mass?
Where is the most likely competition?
What is the seasonal pattern of the proposed tourism, and what are its implications for hotel occupancy rates?
What are the likely trends in air routes and fares that will affect this proposal?

v. What are the **costs** of the project?
Capital costs, broken down into the major categories, e.g. land, building, furnishings and fittings, fees, etc.
Operating costs, by major items.
Breakdown between local and imported elements.
(For accommodation projects) Figures of cost per bed, compared with those in similar projects elsewhere.
Analysis of proposed local purchases. How far they can be increased.

vi. What **benefits** are claimed for the project?
Net effect on national income.
Net gain to employment.
Net effect on budget.
Net impact on balance of payments.
Repercussions elsewhere in the economy, e.g. in inducing other firms and services to locate there.

vii. What are the results of the **economic appraisal**?

viii. What does the **financial analysis** imply for cash flow and net profit to the various parties?

Have realistic assumptions been made about such key elements as rate of build-up of traffic, occupancy rates, operating costs, revenues, etc.?

ix. Has the **wider impact** of the project been considered?
Have there been studies of the social and environmental impact of the scheme?
What are the attitudes of the local population towards the increased number of tourists?
Have all measures been taken to ensure the maximum local participation in the scheme, e.g. by requirements for training of junior staff and a programme for the naturalisation of senior managerial posts?

x. What arrangements are being made for **implementation**?
Has the land been acquired, or are there plans to buy or lease it?
Has the contractor experience of projects on this scale in this area?
Does the contract contain financial penalties or inducements concerning completion on time?
Is there enough skilled and unskilled labour for the job?
Will immigrant labour be required?

Further reading

Emanuel de Kadt (ed.), *Tourism, Passport to Development?*, Oxford University Press for the World Bank and UNESCO, 1979. (Discusses the social and cultural impact of tourism on selected countries, with contributions from a number of writers. Especially valuable is the chapter by R. H. Green, 'Toward Planning Tourism in African Countries', which contains a perceptive discussion of the organisation of the tourism industry and the limits to national action.)

John M. Bryden, *Tourism and Development: A Case Study of the Commonwealth Caribbean*, Cambridge University Press, 1973. (A thorough debunking of the inappropriate use of the multiplier in tourism appraisal. Also a careful and realistic assessment of the impact of tourism on some East Caribbean countries.)

Michael Peters, *International Tourism*, Hutchinson, London, 1969. (An introduction to the subject by a well-known consultant.)

Anne Forbes, 'The Trinidad Hilton: A Cost–Benefit Study of a Luxury Hotel', chapter in *Using Shadow Prices*, eds. I. M. D. Little and M. Scott, Heinemann, London, 1976. (A rigorous application of a methodology for appraising tourism projects.)

J. T. Winpenny, *Some issues in the identification and appraisal of tourism projects in developing countries*. A paper produced for the Surrey International Conference, 'Trends in tourism planning and development', organised by the Department of Hotel, Catering and Tourism Management at the University of Surrey, Guildford, England, September 1982. The collection of papers is published in *Tourism Management* (Butterworth, December 1982).

A. J. Burkart and S. Medlik, *Tourism: Past, Present and Future*, Heinemann, 2nd edition, 1981. (A standard text.)

DEVELOPMENT BANKS

18
Development banks

The need to supplement the functions of commercial banks by setting up financial intermediaries to encourage 'development' is not confined to developing countries. There are very few countries, from the richest to the poorest, that do not have special funds of various kinds to promote investment in certain sectors, regions or types of firm. Such funds typically offer rather more favourable terms, or more sympathetic consideration, than commercial banks do, and temper the full rigour of commercial practice in the interest of national development objectives, In many countries development banks are the only banks offering medium- and long-term loans, and in some cases equity finance. Although the discussion in this chapter is addressed mainly to institutions in developing countries (hence the title 'development banks', or sometimes 'development finance companies') similar considerations apply to funds set up in developed countries too.

The basic purpose of most development banks is to combine reasonably strict financial lending practices with the promotion of economic development, frequently with particular sectors in view. The bank's capital structure may be wholly or partly state owned, or completely private. However, an essential ingredient is funds on concessional terms, either from the government or from foreign aid agencies.

A development bank acts as a wholesaler of credit and capital. It can use its financial strengths and know-how, based on its contacts, its reputation, and the guarantees of the government, to raise large sums on good terms, while the latitude in its borrowing terms allows it to break its funds up into smaller packages for its small, risky, or less credit-worthy clients. It is a convenient way of funnelling public money into the private sector, and a popular means of attracting foreign aid for the benefit of private and, frequently, small-scale industry.

When contemplating setting up a development bank or putting money into it, we are appraising not so much a project as an institution. The convenience of channelling money through such a bank is that it spares the lender or investor the job of checking the soundness of each and every project that is financed, although some aid agencies require the banks to submit details of sub-projects so that they can test the soundness and character of lending programmes. It is sufficient to judge the banks as a cog in the lending process, gearing down large sums in order to turn the wheels of many individual projects. The main questions to ask are about its objectives, the economic context in which it works, its structure, management, finances, and lending policy.

Objectives

Objectives should be clear, meaningful, few, and not mutually contradictory. The 'promotion of national economic development' is harmless but meaningless. To 'increase national economic self-sufficiency' is still rather vague, but if taken seriously could militate against 'lending to sound projects'. More generally, objectives concerned with 'promotion' and 'development' could impede the achievement of 'adequate financial rates of return', or 'covering costs'. There should be a clear statement of the main sectors that the bank will operate in, e.g. industry, commerce, tourism, or agriculture. This is necessary so that the bank can build up expertise in certain fields, and also to head off would-be borrowers in other lines.

There will often be a reference to 'equity' or 'balance' in lending to different geographical regions, or groups of the population. While the concept of 'equity' is an elusive one, most development banks have to accept some responsibility in achieving a wide social and geographical portfolio, provided this does not do undue harm to their finances.

If there are too many objectives, and they are vague and/or contradictory, this will weaken the position of management – who will be open to pressure from all quarters on the grounds that they are 'not fulfilling objectives'. It will also make it difficult to evaluate the performance of the bank – which is easier when there are a few clearly-defined objectives.

Context

A development bank is meant to provide a financial incentive to the development of target sectors, or at least to help relax a financial constraint on their growth. It operates within a larger financial sector, which in turn works in the framework of national economic policy. One's expectations of the bank should take account of its role in this larger context.

For instance, the bank may overlap other credit agencies, such as commercial banks, or other semi-official agencies, and one needs to ask what is the bank's distinctive contribution, and whether its terms are appropriate in relation to these other sources. One large development bank was unable to use a large foreign aid loan because the stipulated terms to the final borrowers were tougher than those on ordinary bank loans (requiring the borrower to carry the foreign exchange risk). There is no strong economic reason why a development bank should charge less interest than commercial lenders, but it ought to be lending for purposes, and over periods, which could not attract loans elsewhere.

Some countries follow financial policies which make it difficult for development banks to operate in a commercial manner, or else call forth peculiar operational techniques. An example would be government restrictions on the maximum rate of interest that can be charged, or even (as in some Islamic countries) a ban on the use of interest rates (which necessitates equity holdings or charging 'management' fees).

More generally, a development bank's performance will depend on the economic climate within which development occurs, and the policies of the government. Where governments are determined to industrialise at almost any cost, and give industry extravagant protection or monopoly powers, loans and investments by the development bank are likely to be financially secure, if economically unsound. On the other hand this would be a bad climate for the bank to set conditions making for efficiency in its borrowers, or to provide advice to them. The opposite circumstance is where the economy is deteriorating, investment and output declining, and firms are short of foreign exchange, petrol, transport, raw materials, etc. Here, with the best will in the world, it would be hard for borrowers to stay on target with their repayments.

There is a more intangible factor to allow for. Many governments, in their enthusiasm for 'development', possibly abetted by generous amounts of foreign aid, may bring about a climate where 'anything goes', where enterprise is spoiled by a welter of incentives and official agencies become all too ready to write off doubtful debts. These are impossible circumstances for a sound development bank. The manager of one such bank, just set up in a small country, was approached by a well-known pop singer wanting funds to build a recording studio. He was unenthusiastic about completing forms, or providing security or other assurance about his business prospects, arguing that the bank, set up to encourage 'national development', had a duty to lend to any national who was short of money!

Structure

No two development banks are exactly alike. Some are wholly in the public sector, with the capital owned by the government and the board of directors public appointees. Even in this case, though, the bank would normally be constituted as a semi-autonomous undertaking, with separate accounts and some requirement to cover its costs. Adventurous banking and a civil service bureaucracy do not often go together.

Some development banks, at the other extreme, are wholly private. There are even commercial banks, taking deposits from the public, but with an identifiable part of the business reserved for development banking functions. More common is a special bank set up with shareholdings and directors provided by a number of private banks and individuals.

A common structure is a bank comprising private and public interests. Whether we call it 'private' or 'public' depends on which parties hold more than 50% of the capital. Shareholders can be foreign. In the sphere of aid stocks may be held by such agencies as the International Finance Corporation, the European Investment Bank and the Commonwealth Development Corporation. The questions of the choice of directors and the length of their appointment are worth investigating.

A specialised development bank may arise as an off-shoot of an established institution. This is especially true of banks aimed at small operators, whether industrialists or farmers. Thus an agricultural credit bank, the bulk of whose lending is to large commercial farmers, may set up a 'soft window' (an odd term) aimed at smaller producers. The same applies for an industrial finance corporation creating a special fund for helping small industry. The two functions are normally kept rigorously apart for accounting purposes, and this permits the funds to attract aid from abroad or from government. At the same time, the special funds should benefit from the experience of the parent institution, and its ability to raise finance on attractive terms.

In principle the precise structure of the bank should not affect its ability to raise money from various sources. That will depend on its performance, the confidence it inspires and, in the last resort, the sort of guarantees it enjoys from government.

Most banks should be able to raise funds from their shareholders, borrow in the local capital market or from government, and tap selective foreign sources (especially aid agencies).

Management

The orthodox division of labour is for the board of directors to set overall policy within the objectives laid down for the bank, and for the professional full-time management to implement it. The implication of this is that management should have professional integrity and a free hand in implementing policies within guidelines passed down from above. Further, it implies that managers and senior staff should be selected for their professional qualifications and experience, instead of for their personal and party loyalties.

Although it is tempting for government to impose salary levels for managers similar to those of civil servants, this policy is short-sighted and will eventually drain the bank of any real talent (except in those few countries where civil service salaries are competitive with those in private industry). High salaries paid to attract good managers are a sound investment, especially for key personnel like the general manager, treasurer and secretary. The size of departments and the qualifications of staff are correlated with salaries.

The level of administration costs in relation to outstanding loans is of some interest in judging the efficiency of management. A high ratio may indicate high start-up costs in a young growing bank. It may indicate a high proportion of small, problematic loans requiring a lot of administration, and if this is one of the bank's objectives this should be treated as an inevitable cost. But in the last resort, if administrative costs are high (e.g. in relation to those of other banks with similar objectives and of comparable size) this is one possible sign of excessive overheads and weak administration.

Since a development bank is created partly to satisfy social objectives, it will be inevitable that its managers will come under some pressure to do things against their professional judgement and perhaps even inimical to the long-term health of the bank. This will be especially likely over appointments to the staff, and dubious loan applications from well-placed persons. The managers' position will be compromised unless there is a procedure for delegating decisions with provision for referring problem cases up to the board. If decisions are taken, in the interest of political or social goodwill, which impinge on the bank's financial health, any self-respecting manager will like to have the board take explicit responsibility for them.

Finances

The main points to look for in assessing the financial health of a development bank will be familiar to financial analysts. The most important questions concern the balance between liabilities and assets. Are the bank's sources of finance commensurate with the scale of its lending and are the respective terms of borrowing and lending such as to ensure the bank's liquidity and profitability?

As with any company, the bank's **equity base** should be large enough in relation to its total liabilities to give it security and freedom of manoeuvre in the capital markets. An equity base that is too small will make it hard to borrow on good terms and means a high 'gearing' ratio of debt to equity. This creates fluctuations in the incomes of shareholders and renders the bank vulnerable to illiquidity as a result of any arrears in interest and repayments by its clients. Not all the equity needs to be called up, but it should always be there for emergencies.

Borrowed capital should be on **maturities** long enough to match those of loans. It is reassuring to managers to have long maturities from which to make their medium- and long-term loans. In an economy starved of foreign exchange it is useful for a development bank to be able to raise its own loans in foreign exchange, but the question of who bears the foreign exchange risk needs close attention. The foreign loan may be to the government, which then on-lends in local currency to the bank. In this case the government would be responsible for making repayments in foreign currency, and could be liable for increased payments (in local currency terms) if there was a devaluation relative to the currency in which the loan was denominated. However, it is common for the bank to carry the **foreign exchange risk**, and may pass it on to its borrowers. This would make loans very expensive in the event of a devaluation.

It is normally desirable that the bank has some **borrowing capacity** independent of the government. If it obtains most of its capital from the government it becomes vulnerable to periods of budgetary stringency, and could be kept on a tight rein. However, unless the bank is private, it will usually need a government guarantee for its borrowing.

Managers walk a tightrope between **liquidity**/security and **profitability**. Liquid assets need to be adequate to cover contingencies and unexpected problems of cash flow. On the other hand, to lock up too many funds in this way is to miss the point of being a development bank – which is to help businesses develop – and can forfeit profits.

The bank should certainly aim to return positive profits to its shareholders, whether they are public or private. If it fails to make profits this could be a sign of inefficiency or the wrong choice of clients. Alternatively, the margin between its borrowing and lending terms could be too low for the kind of business it is going in for.

One measure of a bank's performance is the ratio of **bad debts** or **arrears** of payment to total loans outstanding. There are degrees of 'loan delinquency'. A payment may be one month in arrears, or twelve months. Or the debt may be wholly written off, e.g. when a borrower goes bankrupt or absconds. Every bank must expect a small percentage of its loans to become 'delinquent', which partly reflects on the choice of borrower but may also result from a deteriorating economic climate. A good bank can minimise this problem, e.g. by tailoring the period of repayment to the borrower's expected cash flow.

In approaching financiers, the bank will present a projection of its financial requirements over the next three to five years, and base its case for more funds on the resulting financing gap. Potential lenders need to judge whether the rate of expansion in the lending programme is realistic in the light of previous experience. The relevant datum is the rate of spending (disbursements), not loans commitments, i.e. the actual rate at which loan accounts are drawn down. (The proportion of disbursements to commitments is also a good pointer to past performance.)

Finally, every reputable bank should have an independent **auditor** to certify the veracity of its annual accounts. Financial information should be up-to-date and clearly presented.

Policies

A development bank should have definite criteria for lending, encompassing types of borrower, procedures and terms. Since the demand for loans will usually exceed the bank's available capital it is desirable to have explicit criteria for accepting or rejecting loan applications. Some banks give weights to each of their criteria and score applicants accordingly.

Since the purpose of development banks is to further national development, it will not be sufficient simply to look at the financial aspects of the project. Some allowance should be made for such factors as employment creation, foreign exchange impact, the geographical spread of activity, etc. Some banks perform a simple cost–benefit analysis on each project, using shadow prices to adjust for the economic cost of labour and foreign exchange. One or two, located in countries with a serious foreign exchange constraint, employ the **exchange cost criterion** to choose those projects which earn or save a unit of foreign exchange at least cost in terms of domestic outlays (the 'Bruno Method', named after the Israeli economist).

The bank will need a policy towards the kind of people and firms who receive its loans. Loans could be used for increasing productivity at a similar level of output, or for expanding output and employment. Which is to be preferred will be influenced by national policies. It would also be useful to know whether the bank's credit is being taken as a substitute for credit from other sources by people and firms who are perfectly capable of borrowing elsewhere.

The bank has then to decide on its interest spread, i.e. the margin between its cost of borrowing and the terms of its loans. Development banks are often put under pressure to provide loans at below the market rate of interest, such as rates charged by commercial banks, in the belief that cheap credit is necessary to promote development. This is a dangerous illusion. Cheap credit can stimulate unsound projects, can lead to excessive capital-intensity, and can burden businesses with excessive debt. Cheap credit can certainly be useful, as 'seed capital', to help small businesses to get started, but established firms should be able to pay the going rate of interest from commercial banks for sound ventures.

Development banks can improve on commercial banks by supporting riskier ventures in the national interest, by accepting novel forms of security (e.g. the collective guarantee of a group of small firms), by lending on longer maturities, and by adjusting repayments to fit the cash flow of the project. A development bank may also provide equity, or loans with an option to convert into equity if the venture proves very profitable.

In keeping with its promotional role, the bank may have a section concerned with advisory work (what in agriculture would be 'extension' work) among its clients. This might be concerned with advice on keeping accounts, suitable technology, compliance with official regulations, etc.

In the case of lending to small industry this side of a bank's work could assume great importance, and could make a big difference to its success (not to mention its loan recovery rate).

The bank may also have special funds to do feasibility studies of projects, which may in due course be financed from its lending programme.

Some practical points

1 In setting up a development bank, its objectives should be clear and few in number. It is tempting to saddle it with a lot of desirable, but irreconcilable, functions which complicate the lives of its managers and frustrate any evaluation of its performance.

2 Management should have a free hand in implementing policies within the guidelines passed down from the directors.

3 The bank should have its own salary structure. Paying its staff on civil service rates is unlikely to attract suitable talent.

4 Among the most useful, and revealing, indicators of a bank's performance are:

   i. the ratio of administrative costs to outstanding loans, due allowance being made for special factors

   ii. the ratio of bad debts and payment arrears to total outstanding loans

   iii. the ratio of disbursements to commitments, indicating the rate at which existing loans are drawn down.

5 A development bank might find it appropriate to set up an advisory service for its clients, especially the smaller firms. Apart from its potential value in stimulating development, this could well assist the bank's own loan recovery. This could be a better use of subsidised funds than keeping interest rates down to artificially low levels.

Checklist of main questions

   i. What are the bank's objectives? Are they clearly set out in its constitution, and are they consistent?

   ii. Does the bank enjoy operational autonomy? Can it raise its own funds? Can the board, or management, hire or fire staff? Does it have an adequate equity base?

   iii. Does the bank have responsibilities for lending to particular sectors, or particular purposes? Does this require a wide range of expertise?

   iv. What is the structure of the bank? Are there clear lines of responsibility and levels of delegation? How many staff are there in each department, and are they trained in relevant skills? How do bank salaries compare with those in similar occupations?

   v. How much has the bank committed and disbursed over the last few years?

vi. What are its interest rates, administrative charges, and maturity periods? Is interest adjusted for inflation?

vii. What is the bank's loan repayment record from its borrowers? Has it improved or worsened recently? What powers does it have to enforce loan repayments? Does it use them?

viii. What are its loan procedures? How are loan requests appraised, and by whom? What technique of appraisal is used? Does the bank help potential borrowers to analyse and submit proposals?

ix. Have any significant changes occurred in items in the balance sheet over the last few years?

x. Who are the main recipients of loans or equity investments? Would they have had access to credit from other sources? Are loans being used to increase productivity or to extend operations?

xi. Are the accounts properly audited and up-to-date?

xii. What proportion do the bank's administrative overheads bear to the value of outstanding loans?

Further reading

World Bank, *Development Finance Companies: Sector Policy Paper*, Washington DC, April 1976. (A useful short review of the main issues, with brief data on DFCs in developing countries, and a short account of how the Bank's policy towards the DFCs has evolved.)

W. Diamond and V. S. Raghavan (eds.), *Aspects of Development Bank Management* (EDI series in Economic Development), Johns Hopkins University Press, 1982.

POSTSCRIPT ON PROJECTS

Much of the focus of this book has been on projects, and especially new public investment projects justified on development grounds. This should not be interpreted to mean that we regard devising such projects as the most important endeavour of people anxious to foster development. But the fact is that much capital formation, especially in developing countries, is in new projects by or on behalf of government.

We do not wish to have given the impression that this is the best contribution that governments can make to development. In the urge to produce development projects, many governments have neglected their old-fashioned responsibilities for law and order, the payment of teachers and the upkeep of roads, and 'development' in its widest sense has suffered. We would certainly not advocate the search for new projects if there was any implication that the vital traditional tasks of government would thereby be shirked, or deprived of essential funds.

The other crucial role of governments is in setting the policies within which private economic agents can function. This book repeatedly harps on cases where the purpose of projects is frustrated by the policy context in which they operate. It follows that a change of policies in a desirable direction could reduce or remove the need for projects (of which the best example is a policy to devote more resources to road maintenance, which would reduce the need for major periodic reconstructions). Thus many projects substitute for reforms in policies, and are second best to such reforms, difficult though these might be.

Again, from the viewpoint of the donor of foreign aid, the focus on projects here does not convey a preference for project aid over other forms like programme (balance of payments) support, manpower assistance, or sectoral aid. Analysis of the problems may suggest that the aid donor should offer financial and/or manpower help in a non-project form, e.g. to provide a range of imports, or to strengthen the whole of a particular sector. We would not wish to discourage such attempts where they seemed appropriate.

Finally, readers should not take too exalted a view of the power of project appraisal. The principle of **fungibility** holds that the project being put forward for appraisal and detailed scrutiny is not necessarily the one that will go ahead if finance is provided. An individual may approach his bank manager for a loan, ostensibly for home improvement. If he intended to go ahead with such improvements anyway, using his own funds, the bank loan will really be financing something else, e.g. a holiday. Likewise, appraisers of top priority projects should be aware that the projects may go ahead anyway with or without their finance, and that the grant of funds would in that case be financing something else, in theory the marginal project.

Contemplation of such possibilities could induce fatalism and despair among project appraisers. This would be a sour note on which to leave readers of a book dedicated to promoting these skills. The real answer to the fungibility argument is that project appraisal should leave the investment proposal better than before. The real case for appraisal in these circumstances is in its potential effect on project design and on the choice of future projects.

GLOSSARY
Specialised terms used in the book

Despite their attempts at lucidity, the authors are aware of occasions where specialised terms have slipped into their prose. Some of these terms are peculiar to certain sectors, and are explained in the respective chapters. Others are part of the vocabulary of economics and the authors are uneasily aware that J. K. Galbraith once wrote: '... there is no idea associated with economics that cannot, with sufficient effort, be stated in clear English ...'.

The following short list contains the main terms that might cause non-specialists to pause in their stride.

Appraisal: the process of examining the attractiveness of a project, from economic, technical, social and other viewpoints, before the investment is made.

Benefit–cost ratio: the ratio of total discounted benefits over a project's life to total discounted costs.

Border price: the value of a good if it were to enter international trade. An exportable good would be measured f.o.b. (free on board, but would deduct domestic transport to the point of departure). An importable good would be measured c.i.f. (cost, insurance, freight, including domestic transport from the point of entry to the point of use).

Comparative advantage: an economic principle whereby countries specialise in the production of goods and services for which they are relatively better endowed.

Consumers' surplus: the benefits a consumer gets when he/she is provided with a good or service at a lower price than he/she would be willing to pay.

Cost–benefit analysis: a method of appraising projects that consists of quantifying costs and benefits, expressing them in annual streams over the life of the project, and discounting the resulting net annual flows to obtain a present value.

Cost-effectiveness analysis: an appraisal method that consists of defining the objectives of the project and choosing that solution which minimises total discounted capital and recurrent costs.

Cost recovery: the attempt to earn revenue from a project or programme, whether from fees, tariffs or other prices, sufficient to defray all or part of the cost of that project.

Cross-subsidisation: the application of the proceeds from a public service, deriving from its profitable parts, to keep providing that service to users where it would otherwise be unprofitable (e.g. because of their remoteness from the rest or their inability to afford the full economic charge).

Discounting: the procedure whereby future values of costs and benefits are reduced to reflect the lower value that society, firms and individuals place on future costs and benefits compared to those arising now. The **discount rate** is the rate, analogous to a negative rate of interest, at which future streams of costs and benefits are written down. **Discounted cash flow** is a common method of financial appraisal in which net annual cash flows from a project are discounted using the appropriate annual discount factor and summed to produce a **net present value** (q.v.).

Economic rate of return: a measure of the return on funds invested in the project, but – unlike the **financial rate of return** – the ERR looks at it from the point of view of the economy as a whole. This necessitates adjustments to the costs and benefits to correct for any distortions caused by, for example, monopoly or price controls, and the elimination from prices of taxes and subsidies since these are transfer payments rather than **resource costs** (q.v.).

Elasticity (of demand or supply): responsiveness of demand or supply to changes in the price of a good (price elasticity) or to changes in the incomes of consumers and producers (income elasticity).

Evaluation: investigation of how a project turned out in comparison with what was expected of it (see **Appraisal**).

Extension: attempts to induce producers to adopt new or improved techniques or practices by providing direct advice and demonstration. Usually applied to agricultural services, but also applicable to the promotion of small-scale industry.

Externalities: those costs and benefits of a project which do not accrue directly to the agency undertaking it and which cannot be directly attributed to the project.

Feasibility study: examination of all the important aspects of designing, constructing and operating a project. Sometimes used interchangeably with **appraisal**, but an FS is usually longer, more detailed and more technical. An appraisal is often done by the client or financier for their own decision purposes, using material contained in the FS.

Financial rate of return: a measure of the financial profitability of a project from the viewpoint of the enterprise undertaking it. It is the **discount rate** at which the present value of the costs would equal that of the benefits. Put differently, it is the maximum interest rate that the enterprise could pay on the capital invested in the project and still break even.

First-year rate of return: a decision rule for determining the best time to undertake a project. The benefits in the first year of the project's life are expressed as a percentage of the project's cost. If the result is below the discount rate being used this would suggest that the project is premature, and would benefit from a later start.

Fungibility: a principle whereby another project is substituted for the one that is ostensibly being appraised and financed. More generally, the substitutability of resources and projects for each other.

Import substitution: a process of industrialisation consisting of the domestic production of items formerly imported. It is normally done with various forms of protection against foreign competition, such as tariffs, exchange controls, discriminating public procurement, etc.

Infrastructure (economic or social): basic public services. Economic infrastructure is normally of a physical nature, covering such items as roads, railways, ports, airports and power systems. The main items of social infrastructure are education and health services, though housing, water and sewerage can also come into this category.

Internal rate of return: see **Economic rate of return**.

Linkage effect: the effect of a project on investment, prices and output in related industries and trades. **Backward linkages** (sometimes known as upstream effects) occur in sectors that supply goods and services to the project, while **forward linkages** (downstream effects) arise in industries that use the output of the project.

Multiplier effect: the effect of a project on other parts of the economy produced when income generated by the project works its way through the economy, reactivating idle capacity, and creating new income and employment to a multiple of the original stimulus.

Net present value: a common decision rule in project appraisal, resulting from summing the discounted difference between costs and benefits for each year of the project's life.

Opportunity cost: the value of a resource in its best alternative use. In the case of capital, the OC is the rate of return that funds committed to an investment could have earned in the most attractive alternative use.

Real values: normally refer to costs and prices which are not adjusted for expected inflation (constant prices as compared to expected cash prices). But may sometimes refer to economic values rather than financial costs and prices (**resource costs** rather than financial values).

Resource cost: the true economic cost of a good or service. It differs from a 'cost', such as a tax or customs duty, which is not a cost to the economy as a whole, merely a transfer payment from one group to another. The RC is equivalent to the **opportunity cost** of an item (q.v.).

Sensitivity analysis: an integral part of **cost–benefit analysis** (q.v.) which tests the effect on the rate of return or **net present value** (q.v.) of possible changes in outcomes, on both optimistic and pessimistic assumptions.

Shadow price: the **opportunity cost** (q.v.) of a good or service.

Target group: a group of people who are intended to benefit from a particular public action. The group may be defined according to their social, sexual, economic or geographical status.

Tradables: goods and services that can be bought and sold internationally.

Turnkey project: one for which a single firm (contractor) takes complete responsibility, to the point where it is handed over to the client in a fully operational state.

Urban bias: the tendency of governments to favour the interests of their urban constituents, e.g. by keeping farm prices low, by directing public investment disproportionately to urban or industrial targets, etc.

Value-added: the value of production that can be attributed to the activities of a firm or individual. Normally calculated by deducting the value of bought-in materials from gross output or sales. What is left is equivalent to wages, salaries, profits and rents.

Without case: the imaginary scenario in which the project in question is not undertaken. This exercise is undertaken in order to identify the net effects of implementing a project.